Hannes Erler
The Innovation Tribe

Hannes Erler

The Innovation Tribe

Looking Behind the Dynamics of Change and Adaption

DE GRUYTER

ISBN 978-3-11-144764-3
e-ISBN (PDF) 978-3-11-144832-9
e-ISBN (EPUB) 978-3-11-144881-7

Library of Congress Control Number: 2025944919

Bibliographic information published by the Deutsche Nationalbibliothek
The Deutsche Nationalbibliothek lists this publication in the Deutsche Nationalbibliografie;
detailed bibliographic data are available on the Internet at http://dnb.dnb.de.

© 2026 Walter de Gruyter GmbH, Berlin/Boston, Genthiner Straße 13, 10785 Berlin
Cover image: Barbara Gizzi, Berlin
Typesetting: Integra Software Services Pvt. Ltd.

www.degruyterbrill.com
Questions about General Product Safety Regulation:
productsafety@degruyterbrill.com

Dedicated to all those quietly working and innovating for what is right.
Who see where our natural ecosystems are suffering. Who see where injustice and the violation of human rights continue despite our knowledge and warnings.

May this book give you both inspiration and strength.
May it remind you that you are not alone—and that even small acts, grounded in clarity and courage, can start powerful movements.
That is my deepest hope.

The Innovation tribe is a living testament to our culture of innovation at Swarovski. It shows how attitude, trust and curiosity lead to concrete change – not once, but permanently.

With this work, Hannes Erler has not only documented experiences but also drawn a picture of the future that is encouraging. For our company, for managers – and for all those who understand innovation as human, cultural and strategic issue.

I am proud that such a groundbreaking work has its origins in our house.

Markus Langes-Swarovski, Majority Shareholder, Swarovski

Contents

Introduction —— XIII

A Philosopher's Preface —— XVII

Part I: **A Change Agent's Learning Stories**
Learning on the Live Stage of a Culturally Rooted Organization —— 3

Chapter 1
The One More Thing: The Power of Promoters —— 5

Chapter 2
Standing on the Shoulders of Giants: A Traveler's Log to the Innovation Journey —— 9
Robert G. Cooper's Stage-Gate Logics —— 10
Clayton Christensen's Disruptions and Dilemmas —— 21
Henry Chesbrough's "Open Innovation Model" —— 26
Harrison Owen's Open Spaces —— 32
A Galore of More Players and Theories —— 37

Chapter 3
Industrial Challenges and Academic Theories Start Dancing a Tango —— 44
From Open Innovation to Adaptive Innovation Ecosystems —— 44
The i-LAB experience —— 45
An Innovation Network That's Guided by Soft Leadership? —— 48
Next Level of Open Innovation – "The Königsdisziplin" of Innovation Practices —— 52
Innovation Ecosystems—The Answer? —— 53

Chapter 4
The New Importance of Collaborating in Dedicated Innovation Ecosystems —— 56
Innovation Ecosystems vs Natural Ecosystems —— 56
Trying to Find the Balance: Ecosystems of Business and Science —— 58
Adaptive Leadership and Right Time Messaging —— 60

Chapter 5
Ambidexterity —— 62
Establishing Planet Centricity —— 63
The Horizon Framework —— 64

The Role of Power Teams —— **66**
Escaping the Ambidexterity Trap —— **70**
Changing Mindsets vs "Setting Minds for Change" —— **74**

Part II: **The Philosopher of Reflective Practice**
Striving for Psychological Safety and Resilience Through the Understanding of
Human Nature —— **79**

Chapter 6
Findings from Sociocultural Ecosystems—The Human Side of Innovation —— 81
Embracing Innovation Without Fear —— **82**

Chapter 7
The Spiritual Dimension of Innovation —— **85**
Spirituality as "The Inner Driver" Beyond Religion and Secularity —— **85**
Why We Can't Act Alone—Goodbye, Old World —— **87**

Chapter 8
From Rigid Systems to Inclusive Tribal Leadership—Eye-Opening
Moments —— 91
The Gift from African Culture —— **93**
Ubuntu, Open Space, and the Rediscovery of Tribal Wisdom in Modern
Leadership —— **96**
Modern Leadership and the Spiritual Foundation of Learning
Organizations —— **97**

Chapter 9
Imagining the Future: Possibility Thinking, Prophecy, and the Power of Inner
Images —— 99
Imaginations We Hold of the Future —— **100**
Findings from Mayan Culture —— **102**
The Tribal Power Source —— **106**

Chapter 10
The New Role of Futuring and Foresighting —— 108
At the Crossroads of Sustainability and Progress —— **110**

Chapter 11
Multilevel Value Creation and AI—Potential Antagonists —— 113
The Pivotal Role of Values as Guiding Principles —— 113
Value Creation —— 116
Why Values Make the Difference —— 118
The 4-Level Value Model in Transformational Innovation —— 120

Chapter 12
The Importance of Systemic Thinking —— 125
Cracking the Code of Systemic Inertia: How to Lead Through Reciprocity —— 126
Bias, Survival Instinct, and Global Thinking —— 128
Strategy, Openness, and the Pitfalls of Top-Down Planning —— 131
Role Models and the Human Element —— 132
Balancing Chaos and Order: The Birthplace of the Unexpected —— 134

Chapter 13
Navigating the AI Epoch: Balancing Disruption with Human Dignity —— 137
THIS IS NOW AN ALARMING POINT!! —— 140
A Navigation Tool for Our Modern Era —— 146

Part III: **The Advocate**
A Changing Activist in a VUCA World —— 151

Chapter 14
The Quintessence of Deep Learning —— 153
Entering the New Era of "Integration of Everything" —— 153
Of Human Growth and Serendipity —— 161

Chapter 15
Homo Innovaticus: A New Release of Homo Sapiens —— 163
Cultivation of a New Way of Coexistence —— 163
Breaking Free from the Shadow of the Past —— 165
Holistic Human Nature —— 167
Can Daydreaming Collaborate with AI? —— 169
Homo Innovaticus Can Do Things Better —— 172

Chapter 16
The Innovation Approach of the *Homo Innovaticus* —— 175
The Process —— 175
Mode d'Emploi: How to Use —— 177

Chapter 17
HOMO INNOVATICUS for Beginners —— **189**
　The Island of "Intuition and Serendipity" —— **193**
　The Island of "Vision and Alliance" —— **195**
　The Island of "Open Space Actuation" —— **197**
　The Island of "Orchestrated Change" —— **199**

Chapter 18
The Basic Core Tools of the *Homo Innovaticus* —— **202**
　Tit for Tat, the Mindset Game Changer —— **203**
　AI as a Source of Inspiration, Knowledge, and Networking —— **205**
　Homo Innovaticus and the Role of Intuition —— **206**

Chapter 19
The Ultimate Destination: The Feeling of Connection and Safety —— **209**
　The Rise of the Innovation Steward: A New Role for a New Era —— **209**
　We Can Feel Safe in the Age of AI When Rooted in Human Innovation —— **210**

Words of Thanks —— **213**

Bibliography —— **215**

Index —— **219**

Introduction

When I look back on my professional and personal journey, I see a life deeply inter-twined with the pursuit of innovation, purpose-driven transformation, and meaning-ful human connection. Writing *The Innovation Tribe* is, for me, the culmination of more than four decades of immersive learning, experimentation, and reflection. It is both a personal story and a professional framework—not a biography, not a manual, but rather a lived experience made tangible for others to benefit from.

I was fortunate to grow up in a small village where one of the most unique global industrial companies—Swarovski—is home-based. It was there that I first saw what it meant for tradition and innovation to live side by side. What started as a summer job became a lifelong path into mechanical engineering, product development, and later, systemic innovation.

Over time, I moved from engineering roles into innovation leadership and even-tually into a space where cultural transformation, deep learning, and ethical responsi-bility became my primary focus. In my various leadership roles, most notably as Vice President of Innovation and later Director of Innovation Ecosystems at Swarovski, I had the privilege of building and shaping transformative innovation cultures and systems.

I learned that innovation is never just about technology or tools. It is about peo-ple—their fears, hopes, values, and the systems they inhabit. It is about recognizing the invisible patterns that hold things back and finding the courage to break them. My work has always focused on bridging academic theories with industrial practice and on translating complex concepts into actionable strategies. But more than that, it has been about creating spaces where individuals and organizations can thrive by aligning with their deeper sense of purpose.

In The Innovation Tribe, I share the arc of this evolution. I try to weave together learning stories, systemic models, cultural insights, and spiritual reflections. It is writ-ten in an accessible, story-driven style, reflecting my belief that storytelling is one of the most powerful tools for learning and transformation. I have worked closely with brilliant minds across disciplines, from renowned professors like Clayton Christensen and Bob Cooper to grassroots innovators and next-generation changemakers. Their influence is embedded throughout these pages.

I believe that in our era of AI, climate urgency, and massive social shifts, we must move beyond processes alone. We need new mindsets—what I've come to call the spirit of the "*Homo Innovaticus*."

This new mindset is not just about adapting faster. It's about learning to lead with values. It's about crafting innovation ecosystems where people feel safe to try, fail, grow, and try again. It's about remembering that daydreaming and intuition can be just as important as spreadsheets and strategy decks. It's about integrating indigenous wisdom, neuroscience, and technology without losing our human dignity in the process.

https://doi.org/10.1515/9783111448329-203

The book is organized into three parts, each reflecting a dimension of what innovation means in today's world:

Part I: The Change Agent's Learning Stories

In these chapters, I share real experiences from my time in industry, including my transformative years at Swarovski. You'll read about the impact of early innovation models, how we adapted global theories to our local culture, and what we learned from both success and failure. There are also reflections on mentors, partnerships, and the powerful role of promoters—those people who believe in something before it becomes obvious to others.

Part II: The Philosopher of Reflective Practice

Here we shift from the organizational to the deeply personal and cultural. This section reflects on the human side of innovation—how values, mindsets, and even spirituality shape our capacity to change. We explore African concepts like Ubuntu, the rediscovery of tribal wisdom, Mayan culture, and how psychological safety and meaning-making matter more than ever. In this space, I invite you to consider some of the more complex questions: What motivates us to make changes? What are the obstacles that prevent us from achieving our goals?

Part III: The Advocate for New Change Processes

In this final part, I present a practical framework for navigating transformation: the *Homo Innovaticus* model. It blends structured process with intuitive insight and lays out tools, stories, and patterns that I've seen work across teams, countries, and contexts. This is also where we touch on the challenges and potential of artificial intelligence, system change, and the urgent need for planetary alignment. You will find principles, metaphors, and frameworks designed to help you navigate change. Most importantly, you'll find an invitation to reflect, act, and connect. It seems that, regardless of how much progress we make in our tools and systems, innovation will always be a deeply human endeavor.

One of my deepest learnings is this: real change doesn't happen through top-down strategies alone. It happens when people feel they belong. When they are part of something greater than themselves. When their story matters in the larger arc of progress. That's what The Innovation Tribe stands for—a movement of people who innovate not just for profit, but for purpose. People who understand that transformation begins within but doesn't end there. It ripples outward. It connects. It heals.

This work is dedicated to those who have the courage to dream, to question, and to co-create new possibilities. No matter what your role is—whether you're leading large-scale innovation efforts within organizations or aiming to make small, positive changes in your own life, the basics of transformation remain pretty much the same everywhere. And they are showcased in a chapter for experts and another chapter for beginners. As Antoine de Saint-Exupéry once said: It seems that techniques tend to evolve from the simple to the complex, and finally to the useful. I wanted to streamline this process for the reader, offering a more direct path to the "useful" information.

I find myself particularly inspired by the younger generation, whose pursuit of purpose and authenticity is a source of motivation for me. You all have the potential to be the future architects of the Innovation Tribe.

To all readers: Welcome to this journey. It is my hope that this book will serve as a guide, a compass, and, on occasion, a mirror. The path of innovation is not always easy, but it is always worth walking, especially when we walk it together.

Hannes Erler

Wattenberg, May 13th, 2025

A Philosopher's Preface

It is an honor and a pleasure to pen these observations upon some hidden aspects of Hannes Erler's superb study of the genesis and dynamics of innovation.

Serendipity plays a decided role in the development of Hannes Erler's account of the genesis of successful innovation. And it was pure serendipity that we discovered each other as partners in conversation about his work. Having been casual private friends for over twenty years and frequently involved in free-ranging "Stammtisch" discussions, we had never really had a deep discussion about his work. One evening, roughly three months before I wrote this, we found ourselves sitting next to one another as he effusively explained what the book he was writing about, summing up a lifetime of experience centered on innovation in theory and practice. I had known bits and pieces about his work for Swarovski for some time but had never really heard much detail about the central preoccupations that had fired the innumerable discussions he had been involved in worldwide for over thirty years. So, I was more than surprised on that evening not so long ago when I found myself curiously familiar with aspects of his study and even in a position to comment upon them. Hannes, for his part, was no less surprised than I was to discover we were on a common wavelength.

By way of explanation, I declared that in another of my nine lives than that of professor of philosophy and cultural history in Innsbruck and Vienna, I had been involved in establishing the study of professional knowledge as a field of study in Sweden for nearly a quarter of a century before my retirement in 2013. Moreover, my work there, like his, involved action research, i.e., research aimed at furthering the practice in question rather than mere theoretical documentation. Starting at the Swedish Center for Working Life where I had been invited as a visiting professor, supporting a small but dynamic motley crew of researchers, including economic historians, linguists, mathematicians, etc., studying work, not from the standard points of view of economics or sociology, but as knowledge.

However, their perspective was under attack from mainstream sociologists and a few analytic philosophers, largely because my colleagues considered the sort of knowledge involved in working to be what the Anglo-Hungarian polymath philosopher Michael Polanyi, with contributions to physical chemistry, economics, and philosophy to his credit, termed "tacit knowing." In a controversial book called *Personal Knowledge* in 1958, he characterized tacit knowing as skill in doing something, a phenomenon that exists in the doing itself and cannot be captured by theoretical science. He was reminding scientists and philosophers that a considerable part of science was done in laboratories and never found its way into the standard accounts of what scientific knowledge is. My colleagues took this as the key to work as knowledge as well. Nevertheless, to our critics the idea of discussing tacit knowledge was simply a contradiction: if it's tacit, you can't talk about it, and that's all! My job was to help articulate why that was not the case.

https://doi.org/10.1515/9783111448329-204

To begin with, Polanyi discussed *knowing* and not *knowledge*, a fine distinction whereupon hangs a tale. My approach was to complement Polanyi by referring to the central idea in Ludwig Wittgenstein's mature philosophy, the idea of following a rule where there is no explicit rule but only an example to be imitated. Thus, Wittgenstein characterized the most rudimentary forms of knowing upon which theory-building and speculation generally rest. In short, Wittgenstein was reminding us that before we become scientists, we have to be normally functioning human beings. The point being that we get to be normally functioning by following rules, which are examples of action, and not by learning definitions. This implied that the most basic forms of human knowing could only be articulated in terms *of examples of how to do things*. Those examples are frequently accompanied by characteristic anecdotes that outstanding practitioners told about their work. Problems involved in implementing computer technology in the workplace (which in fact had led to a real-time crisis in the Swedish public health system in the late 70s) had made investigation into practical knowledge relevant to social discussion in the first place.

Over the years our research came to be resettled in the Department of Industrial Economics at the Royal Institute of Technology, where it became intertwined with discussions of creativity, and the perennial struggle between designers and engineers was a source of deep concern. Moreover, the perspective of business economics linked discussions of professional knowledge to the question of how to prepare budding engineers for assuming leadership roles in technological development. The step from creativity and leadership to innovation was not far away, even if we scarcely had a clue about its importance 25 years ago. We were aware that such discourse was highly complex (see Hannes Erler's schematic representation), but we were still struggling to move in what seemed to be an intellectual morass, seeking room to maneuver there, as it were. To reiterate, looking back from Hannes Erler's perspective today, what we were up to was primitive but, in a sense, part of the same discourse. In fact, it is a pleasure to see that questions over which we wracked our brains about a matter like creativity are now integrated into a comprehensive, intelligible framework within the discussion of innovation, as Hannes Erler presents here. Beyond my Swedish connection I worked for some fifteen years with the chaplaincy, where we were endeavoring to develop new methods of spirituality befitting the challenges that modern technology presents to young engineering students.

One particularly interesting point of intersection of Hannes's discussion of innovation with ideas developed within the philosophy of science comes at a point where Hannes will have astonished many a reader by emphasizing the centrality of *daydreaming* to innovation in technology. Here serendipity with respect to my own career in philosophy enters into the picture dramatically once again, for the idea of daydreaming is not at all foreign to discussion of the growth of knowledge as we might think. It is not widely known outside of France that daydreaming enters into the philosophy of science as a central notion in the thought of Gaston Bachelard, one of the most colorful figures in twentieth-century French philosophy. On Bachelard's view, logical positivists were right in their emphasis upon employing strict logical criteria with respect to the justification of new discoveries. The problem was the positivists entirely neglected the other side of science, the role that *discovery* plays in scientific development. Discovery is a matter of intuition and imagination, something poetic in the end, that we sort of systemize, each for him/herself, in daydreaming. Bachelard, adapting central ideas from Freud, emphasized the role of free association in innovative thinking in beautifully crafted poetical accounts of his flights of fantasy when meditating upon, say, the flame of a candle.

Further examples of the points of contact in Hannes Erler's work with discourse within the philosophy of science could be multiplied, but the three I have discussed make the point satisfactorily. However, there is one thinker who can never be neglected in any discussion of the philosophy of practice. I refer to Aristotle. He is far from being the Old Fart that we often encounter in discussion with the Philosophically Unwashed. In any case, Aristotle's discussion of ethics and politics, where we find his account of the primacy of practice in human knowing, emphasizes the priority of what we do over what we say in practical matters because it is what we do that determines who we become, not what we say about it. Moreover, he insists that the point of practical studies is to make us better, adding the positively astonishing caveat that any abstract or theoretical study would simply be useless (and perhaps even perverse). Like Hannes Erler, Aristotle insists that practical knowledge has both a scientific and an artistic side. That there is a lesson for modern social science here goes without saying. Hannes Erler's *The Innovation Tribe* easily passes muster here.

In conclusion, let me return to the point I made earlier concerning having been present in the infancy of studies similar to his work gives me an extremely acute sense to the enormous strides that have been made in the last twenty years in the study of technological development organized around the notion of innovation, strides made possible on the basis of lively open international dialogue (our forum for discussion in Stockholm was called The Dialogue Seminar, which entailed a cooperation between the Royal Institute of Technology and the Royal Dramatic Theater). The diagram, which traces the development of product innovation back to vague ideas floating around in someone's fantasy, finally embeds the discussion of creativity in a complex but concrete context that we could scarcely imagine.

These are some of the most important philosopher's considerations about the hugely wide-ranging scope and implications of Hannes Erler's work. They are by no means exhaustive with respect to the wide-ranging implications of his work. His view of the spiritual dimension of innovation in high tech and in human affairs, for example, deserves wide-spread discussion in an ethically impoverished society like ours. But that is another matter. All in all, it is scarcely possible to overestimate the significance of what he presents and for which he merits heartiest congratulations.

Allan Janik

Innsbruck, April 2025

Part I: **A Change Agent's Learning Stories**

Learning on the Live Stage of a Culturally Rooted Organization

It was a really formative experience for me to grow up in a village where a globally renowned and unique industrial company is headquartered. I had already decided to become a mechanical engineer, and I needed to get some hands-on experience during my summer breaks from school. At the time, it seemed like the obvious choice to approach the company. What resulted was a long-term professional relationship that opened a lot of doors for growth and personal development.

The first part of this book describes how the development of an innovative industrial culture, deeply rooted in the foundation of Swarovski, swept me away. This industrial culture laid the groundwork for many growth stories. The Swarovski family's leadership, along with the company's natural innovation, known as the "Swarovski Spirit," which was strongly influenced by the founder's personality, Daniel Swarovski, who started the company in 1895, and the collaboration with many colleagues, made it a lucky stroke for me to enter a period of significant growth and prosperity.

The plot of this part of the story aligns with the fifth industrial innovation wave, which we will explore in detail, spanning from 1980 to 2020. The transformation of innovation culture and philosophy into a new era of knowledge, information technology, and conflicting values has forced us to adapt and be aware of changing environments.

This first part of the book is intended to safeguard our organizational findings from the mentioned period. It is part of our self-understanding and our heritage. It is my hope that innovation managers currently facing new challenges will draw inspiration and learn how to address them. We have a strong innovation heritage. We can be proud of that.

https://doi.org/10.1515/9783111448329-001

Chapter 1
The One More Thing: The Power of Promoters

I would like to start our journey with the "one more thing" I had originally intended to include at the conclusion of this first part of the book. However, as I reflected on my personal learning journey, I arrived at the conviction that the systemic influence of the group of people, as described in Prof. Witte's Promoters model, is a fundamental aspect of every innovation or change project. Quite simply because innovations are always made by people, and people are always subject to the realities of systemic factors. Blood is always thicker than water! What does that mean? If we ignore the human nature of developers, we are doing a bad job! Professor Witte explains that promoters are not just administrators who follow the rules. Instead, promoters do more than what the rules say they should do.[1] This is exactly what we need in our time. It supports the important idea of psychological safety by focusing on integrating different influential areas.

Innovations are always made by people, and people are always subject to the realities of systemic factors.

As innovation and change always deal with different people in different roles, mindsets, and systemic biases, the promoters model's principles offer us beautiful guidelines to better compose the people to involve. This may sound a bit general and difficult, but trust me, I have seen the best innovators, the highest skilled people, and the most empowered project teams struggle to understand this sociocultural operating principle.

I am inviting you, as the reader, to use the described principle as a powerful checkpoint that is often underestimated in daily practice. Especially through the arrival of artificial intelligence, we must see the promoter model in a new light. A light that is even more important and redistributes the roles of promoters.

Promoters do more than what the rules and job descriptions say they should do!

Specifically in the form that the one who has the better knowledge also has better solutions and therefore may outperform those who might have the decision power or hierarchical position. What would be more obvious than directing our attention into a new direction and integrating the new powerful tools into our management practices?

---

[1] Jürgen Hauschildt and Hans Georg Gemünden, eds., *Promotoren: Champions der Innovation* (Wiesbaden: Gabler Verlag, 1998), see 11, 15.

https://doi.org/10.1515/9783111448329-002

In the chapter on artificial intelligence in this book, we will dig deeper into the implications of the fact that information, ideas, and innovations can flow more freely, breaking down many barriers that once separated us.

If we understand Wille's important demand to see promoters as people who actively and intensively support an innovation or transformation process with special commitment—beyond the usual commitment—then we see that the combination of power and professional promoters will help us overcome the lasting barriers of willingness and abilities. Willingness is about burning for it from the heart. Ability is about feeling empowered for change.

A lack of "Willingness" affects acceptance and resources heavily: This shows up not just in the refusal of single persons but also of resources (manpower, time, money, material resources) and in negative reactions towards all those who accept or even want to promote the innovation.

Barriers to "Ability" often appear when people want to contribute at their best but lack the necessary skills, are not accepted in their organization, or do not have the insights to understand what's important in terms of information, people, and knowledge of the whole project. Context is everything.

In day-to-day work, I always use a triangle to help me stay objective and avoid overestimating my freedom to operate or being arrogant. The triangle simply consists of 3 questions, one at each corner: Do I want to do it? Am I allowed to do it? Can I do it? And if the answer to the question of can I do it is no, whom could I ask for support and help?This approach always helped me to define my own position within every open question on why I should go the extra mile, beyond just doing my job. It helped me identify and overcome potential obstacles early on. It's always better to face a situation head-on than to downplay it by hiding the potential risks.

If I felt anxious or unsafe, the metaphor of the tiger that is hiding in the bushes helped me. If you look behind the bushes, you recognize its nature and real strength. It's always better to look the tiger in the eye than to run away from a threat you don't know about. You can always decide to run off, take the bull by the horns, or cry for help. You must be willing to face the tiger head-on.

Now let's look at the 4 types of promoters and restrictors (opponents) based on Wille's model that are useful in today's practice:

The **power promoter**: He has legitimized power with sanctioning possibilities due to his formal authority, and he knows how to use it.

– He accepts and sets goals and priorities, which must be respected by all contributors who are in his influenceable area.
– He influences idea generation, concept evaluation, and personnel decisions and has the power to block opposition and resistance.
– He provides resources or ensures that they are provided by using the hierarchical power play.
– He protects professional promoters from being weakened by others.

The **specialist promoter (innovation promoter)**: He has specific technical and/or methodological knowledge. He can come from a specific department or specialist group, or he can be external to the organization. The hierarchical position is irrelevant.

- He formulates or stimulates visions,
- is a teacher, guides, and supports in case of problems,
- develops solutions or provides support during development,
- supports or realizes concepts,
- knows critical details,
- supports the project with arguments and provides knowledge and context

The **process promoter** has organizational knowledge (knowledge of processes and structures), establishes the connection between power and specialist promoters and other participants, and controls the innovation process. Most importantly, he ensures targeted communication.

The **relationship promoter** has a proven track record of building and maintaining strong personal relationships with key individuals. He is adept at cultivating new connections and leveraging his network to achieve his goals. He knows how to talk to people and inspire them to support his cause.

Most importantly, he has the remarkable ability to connect people who can't seem to get along. This is the definitive text on the subject.

Particularly in the post-Covid era, I have observed that the role of the relationship promoter has been pushed more into the background and that quick project success is seen as the most efficient way, regardless of the sensitivities and importance of the individual contributors. Creative approaches and the courage to try things out are very often neglected.

Restrictors or **opponents** are persons who can delay or prevent an innovation or transformation process from so many angles in organizations that I strongly recommend thinking about them right from the beginning. Applying the promoter model is really easy when you practice it from time to time. And that is why I am giving the model a very prominent and important role in Part III, in my innovation development approach.

As the model is based on empirical studies in the context of innovation research, we can't say that it is a management tool, but it does raise awareness of the conditions for success and can help to find the appropriate governance action for each situation.

Regardless of the size of your innovation project, it is essential to consider your stakeholders and involve them in the change process. I met an innovation manager from a big multinational company at an international innovation get-together in Copenhagen in 2019. During a round table exercise on organizational change and reforming innovation settings, we shared ideas and experiences and helped each other find good solutions. He told me that he was nervous about a big presentation at work. After a few questions, it was clear that he hadn't spoken to the two key promoters before the big meeting. This meant he was at risk of the power promoter denying it and blaming him in front of the whole top management group. I told him to work with the promoter model and get them involved in the preparation. I recommended requesting a premeeting to provide them with the essential information before the large group meeting, and this has proven to be an important cornerstone for success. He did a great job at the meeting, and even the power promoters were happy because they could show that they support the project without having to field any ridiculous questions caused by misunderstandings. The evening of the presentation, he sent me an e-mail thanking me for this recommendation. Two years later, I met him, and he told me that he was using the model frequently.

I think it's important to note that people are often stuck in their roles and feel pressured to act and communicate in ways that don't align with the context of innovation. To get around this, it's a good idea to think about whether the roles are filled correctly. If the roles aren't defined or visible, I'll sometimes take on the missing role for a little while. In a lot of my recent work with young people and acting as a mentor for them, I've noticed that it's helpful to take on a role that's not yours to help a project go the right way or even survive. In many cases, they could raise their visibility throughout the organization and have been recognized for taking action that showed they could do that. Instead of pointing the finger at others or the organization for their shortcomings. As you might guess, the people have been officially appointed to their new role because they've shown they can be trusted, they're good at problem solving, and they're willing to contribute. It's just part of how organizations evolve that those who can think both broadly and in a focused way and connect the dots for others are really valuable when the boxes in their job descriptions are getting in the way of innovation. We can call this "gap-oriented behavior."

Those who can think both broadly and in a focused way and connect the dots for others are of the highest value in organizations.

Even if the promoter model has been widely accepted in research areas, we can find only small evidence that it is used nowadays in innovation projects.

It is now time to turn to the different innovation methods and procedures that I have experienced firsthand. I am sure that these are the basic skills that must be mastered in today's fast-changing world.

Chapter 2
Standing on the Shoulders of Giants: A Traveler's Log to the Innovation Journey

We're going to dive right into the methods, starting with the theories and organizational findings that have accompanied my professional life over the last 40 years. These insights are tied to my diverse positions within industrial structures, and I'm thrilled to share them with you! They are also the result of my lucky opportunity to execute roles that have always been related to international and inter-organizational networks. I have also prioritized lifelong learning and an irrepressible striving to understand the principles of innovation and change on a more overarching and global level. As a result, I am sure that the development and execution of innovation and change processes adhere to certain rules and behaviors. I will focus primarily on examining these aspects.

Innovation requires a personal and open mindset and a readiness to embrace new and unknown things. This evolution must occur on both a personal and an organizational level. These two aspects are inextricably linked.

Innovation methods are constantly emerging, and they're not easy to understand, especially when you're new to the field. The sheer number of them is overwhelming. At the same time, we are flooded with success stories that paint an idealized picture of heroic achievements. However, these stories conveniently overlook the numerous failures and pawns sacrificed along the way. This makes the situation more complex and makes it difficult for non-specialists to recognize whether a method is suitable for what it is promised. It's evident that navigating this landscape is becoming increasingly challenging for young and inexperienced individuals. The bottom line is, are the approved methods outdated, or are they still the basis? The boundaries of this question are fluid, but I can give you some insightful answers.

In part III, you will learn to apply a useful navigation tool to your personal innovation or change project.

My personal journey began in the 1980s when, as a young mechanical engineer, I read a comparison in an American Research and Development magazine. It said that developing new products was becoming more and more like a Red Queen's race. You know the story of Alice in Wonderland. The Red Queen's race is won by running twice as fast as the second-place finisher. I've held this metaphor in my mind for a long time, using it as a driving force to embrace best practices from other industries and management research. In hindsight, it's clear that we need to carefully examine this metaphor in our days. This suggests distorted competitive conditions and expectations that are no longer valid today. It captures the essence of the time, which was all about making national economies superior to their competitors in international competition through speed and technology integration. Today, it is more about the

https://doi.org/10.1515/9783111448329-003

new capabilities of global collaboration and sustainable development, not about out-smarting others to weaken them. This is the essence of this chapter.[2] The first experience I'll share is dealing with a method that I see today as one of the most influential and, on the other hand, often misunderstood principles in developing new things. It is about the Stage-Gate® Tool, as it is known by its creator and global proponent, Robert G. Cooper. To help you understand, I'll include some basic, common principles of innovation into the Stage-Gate process that our organization had to figure out and put together at the same time. This was during the pivotal years of the Stage-Gate evolution in our company, and I subsequently learned about industry practices on a global level.

Robert G. Cooper's Stage-Gate Logics

When I met Bob Cooper for the first time in Innsbruck during his European tour in 1997, I had no idea how much of an impact it would have. It was a total game-changer for my career and started a long friendship that's still going strong after more than 25 years. It also opened my eyes to new possibilities. This meeting was the first step in getting our company on the same page as the industry leaders in innovation management. After exchanging first emails, we invited Bob to visit the headquarters of Swarovski in Wattens, initiating a collaboration on how the Stage-Gate process could enhance our product development performance. This partnership ultimately led to the complete adoption of the Stage-Gate process, marking its first implementation within a German-speaking organization. Twenty years later, Bob reminded me of this milestone when he invited me to deliver a presentation at his Stage-Gate summit in Florida.

Hearing about Bob's experiences and insights from other companies helped us figure out our own status quo. Bob knew that to achieve broad acceptance and use of the Stage-Gate methods across different organizations, he had to visit locations and exchange ideas with other business leaders.

From today's perspective this as well is a wonderful example of how innovation, regardless of technologies, products, processes, or organizational practices, paves its way across organizations and industries. And this was the first time for me to be an active part of such a global distribution.

We started our collaboration with an anonymized benchmark study that was performed together with his partners in Denmark, and we have been incredibly surprised and, at the same time, not surprised.

---

2 *Author's* note: This text was written in October 2024. I believe its core arguments remain valid as of 2025, despite emerging trends that may suggest otherwise.

Bob asked us a lot of questions that had, at this stage, no direct correlation with the targets that we had focused on: Simply to enhance the product development process due to better definition of the single steps that have been defined by the responsible people in charge. In a well-organized and dedicated hierarchical structure. Successful and well embedded with a growth strategy and growing markets in terms of customers and regions. Bob sent us a bunch of interview questions that had nothing to do with my product development and design responsibilities. I had taken over those responsibilities only a few months before. Bob pushed us to invite as many people as possible to fill out the questionnaires from as many viewpoints as possible. It was crucial to include the owner family members who have been running the company.

After three months of collecting, discussing, and explaining the purpose of the exercise, we sent the anonymized questionnaires to Bob's partner institute in Denmark. Two months later, we received a report, and the findings were both encouraging and devastating.

We have been classified as a world-class in comparison regarding the commitment of the company owners to the support of innovation in terms of resources, structure, and guidance.

However, the substandard quality and execution of the development processes irritated us. Finding ourselves in the bottom quartile of companies very fast inspired us to act.

The insights coincided with issues like delayed product launches and global distribution challenges due to quality and capacity shortcomings. We knew right away that the next step was to restructure and stabilize the product development process. We invited Bob to present his latest findings on each of his European trips in the following years. We discussed possible changes and learned how to adapt fast and on a broad view throughout the company.

Our company was closed off in technology areas in the past, but it's changed since we started opening up. This change was made possible by the visionary view of my longtime boss and mentor, Helmut Swarovski, who we call Mr. Open Innovation. He was our technical leader. Whenever Bob visited, we had dinner at the renowned "Gasthaus Schwan" in Wattens. Bob shared insights from the various companies he had worked with. Each story brought us closer to applying Stage-Gate strategies to our field, meeting customer needs, and most importantly, improving our worldwide delivery times, availability, and product quality.

It is crucial to understand that the spread of new things in life always follows the basic principle of technology diffusion—but with different audiences, structural settings, and types of innovators.

It is crucial for anyone dealing with change and innovation to understand that such global diffusions always follow the basic principle of technology diffusion. However, there are important differences. These include different audiences, structural settings, and a different type of innovators. It is imperative to understand this principle more deeply.

The Hundredth Monkey and technology diffusion

From the start, Robert G. Cooper's Stage-Gate made me think of that study about how monkeys on different islands learn. It is believed that once a critical mass of 100 monkeys have adopted a new behavior, the knowledge spreads throughout the community and even reaches those on other islands. Back in the late 1970s, there was something mystical about this phenomenon. It was a simple explanation of how growth starts with a single action and then spreads to improve our lives. It is just another example of how science isn't the only way to explain the world. I've always been curious about such complexities of life, like biological processes, consciousness, and the human psyche—things that often defy scientific explanation. The desire to explore this powerful, enigmatic force that connects all life and manifests in ways that defy simple explanations felt quite mystical back then. In my job as an innovation manager, I had to focus on the science-based aspects of things because there was no way to talk about the supernatural stuff that kept happening and didn't have a logical explanation. In our days we have a much better understanding and scientific insights into how to mix creativity and art with practical economic frameworks. If we study the principles of innovation and change properly, we can use this combination to be successful.

To help you understand, let's take a closer look at the "Hundredth Monkey Phenomenon." It's a story that's been around in different versions, often used to explain how ideas and behaviors can spread quickly. The most well-known version of this story is about Japanese macaques (monkeys) on the island of Koshima in Japan. But it's important to remember that the story isn't exactly accurate. It's more like a metaphor or a parable, not a scientific fact.

The story goes that scientists were studying a troop of macaques on Koshima in the 1950s. They fed them peeled sweet potatoes, then threw them into the sand. So, the sand made the potatoes inedible. They observed that some of these monkeys learned to wash the potatoes in seawater to clean them and enhance their taste with salt. According to the tale, this new behavior spread slowly among the monkey population. The big moment, as the story goes, was when the hypothetical "hundredth monkey" learned to wash its sweet potatoes. This led to an immediate and widespread adoption of the behavior across all monkeys on the island and even to other monkey populations on separate islands and the mainland, without any physical contact.

Lyall Watson made the Hundredth Monkey Phenomenon famous in his 1979 book "Lifetide." He said that a new behavior can spread from one group of species to another once a critical number is reached. He explained this through a sort of collective consciousness or morphic resonance, a theory proposed by Rupert Sheldrake.

This story has been critiqued by scientists and skeptics alike. Researchers involved in the actual macaque studies did document the sweet potato washing behavior, but they didn't report a sudden, widespread change in behavior after a certain number of monkeys adopted it. The original observations showed a gradual spread of this learned behavior, primarily through younger monkeys learning from their mothers and peers, without the dramatics the Hundredth Monkey story suggests.

Today the Hundredth Monkey Phenomenon is a compelling story about the potential for rapid social and cultural change. It serves more as a metaphor for the spread of ideas and innovations rather than a documented scientific phenomenon. But thanks to more scientific research, we know nowadays that the diffusion of innovation always follows such sociocultural patterns and is many times approved by the work of different scientists. This process of adoption over time is usually shown as a normal distribution curve, also called a bell curve. The groups in this process are innovators, early adopters, early majority, late majority, laggards, and phobics. The names of these groups come from 20 years of watching how farmers in the US adopted new farming methods back in the 1930s. My best-known research comes from Dr. Everett M. Rogers and his book "Diffusion of Innovations."[3]

After taking a closer look at the research, it's clear that the early adopters' group is crucial in the early stages of innovation because they're more connected and respected in their communities. They're often seen as leaders in their field and trendsetters. When early adopters embrace an innovation, they influence the early majority to follow. When it comes to adapting to organizational interventions, or in our case to Bob Cooper' Stage-Gate logic, it's smart to follow the principles of diffusion, especially when most of an organization needs to adapt. While everyone doesn't need to know the nitty-gritty, those who can make the most of their contributions and make decentralized decisions need to be on board. In short, we need everyone to be on board when we follow the path from idea to implementation. We need the late majority and the laggards to contribute to the peripheral points of our innovations, and we have to carefully decide what type and level of information they are open to accepting. But we must get the whole organization on board. If we don't, we risk failing at the most important stages of launch and scaling.

It's important to understand how new ideas spread because, as innovators, we need to grow our impact and the number of people using our ideas.

As you can see in figure 1, the two groups of innovators and early adopters make up about 18% of the whole community. They are quickly enthusiastic about new technology and jump aboard quickly. Geoffrey Moore talks about the challenges that innovative high-tech products face when moving from early adopters to the early majority in the market. He came up with the term "Crossing the Chasm" for this. It's based on the idea that if the early majority, who are more practical and not as easily swayed by

---

3 Everett M. Rogers, *Diffusion of Innovations*, 5th ed. (New York: Free Press, 2003).

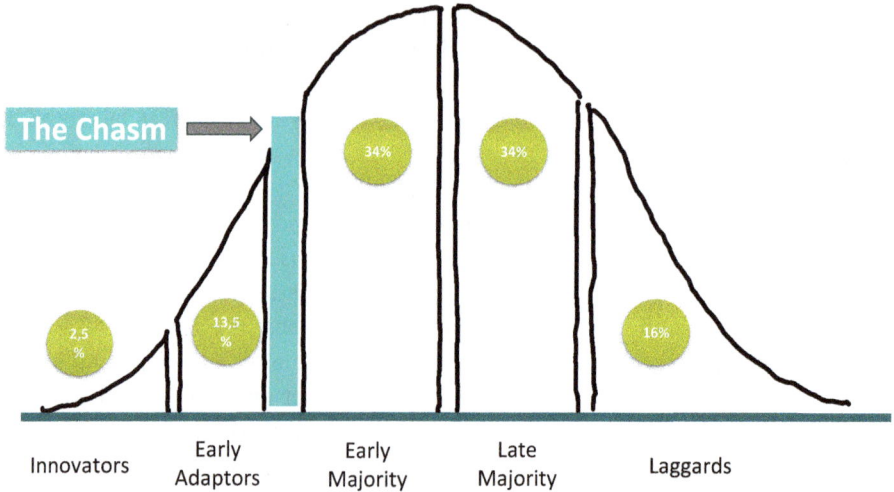

Figure 1: The technology diffusion curve by Geoffrey Moore: Showing the critical "chasm" point necessary to exceed for achieving broader diffusion.

new technology, are convinced, they'll be influential for the more skeptical adopters that need tangible arguments and examples of the benefits and value. Then, we'll reach a point where the early majority is big enough to pave the way for the next group, and the innovation will be successful and spread widely in the market. So, going back to our old monkey story, with the knowledge we have today, we could say the group of 100 monkeys was just the 18% group of the population that "crossed the chasm."

Let me be clear: Innovation without social diffusion on a broader level will have no impact and cannot be seen as an innovation. It can only be seen as an invention that serves a niche of beneficiaries with no hope of growth or a bigger impact.

There are many other stories teaching us that innovation requires us to embrace the unconscious, inherited capabilities of our species as a foundation for adaptation. This is how we find the right topics and ways. It's just how we've been shaped by thousands of years of evolution.

Innovation without social diffusion on a broader level will have no impact and cannot be seen as an innovation. It can only be seen as an invention that serves a niche of beneficiaries with no hope of growth or a bigger impact.

It's likely that this metaphor for the spread of ideas and innovations is a very underestimated effect of Robert G. Cooper's Stage-Gate logic. Why? It lets you split development processes into two types. The first type is all about getting key insights by being ready to "fail fast" and "learn fast." The second type is all about "failing forbidden" and being totally reliable. When an industry is all about unique production technologies but ends up competing in a world of fashion and accessories that is all about creativity and making people more attractive in their social environments, it can't just be about the technology—especially in the early phases of innovation. It has to appeal to people's instincts for what's attractive and in demand.

As we understand now that the adoption of innovation has different expectations of users and customers, we very much understand that these groups have to be picked up using different information and at different points of time.

Stage-Gate is a key enabler for surviving in a world full of complexity and interdependence.

To understand the essence of Stage-Gate thinking, we must delve into the foundation of Bob's work. I was skeptical that this straightforward concept could withstand the latest digital transformations and the advent of AI integration. My findings during the writing of this book made it clear to me that this is one of the key insights, if not key enablers, to surviving in a world full of complexity and interdependence.

From grown to formable structure

It is time now to explain a little how Stage-Gate works and, for those who are not familiar with the principle, to make a short and simple introduction. In the 5th edition of his book "Revolutionizing Product Development.",[4] published in 2017, Bob is reflecting on how the process was discovered. And it's important to understand not only the principle, but also that it is a wonderful story on the evolution of an innovation management discipline.

Bob is mentioning that Stage-Gate has become the most widely used method for conceiving, developing, and launching new products in industry today. Stage-Gate is much more than a business process, however. He explains that the model was originally conceived by observing successful product developers as they drove major innovations to the market. Those early observations led to the conclusion that there was a "better way"—that some innovation teams and project leaders had intuitively figured it out. Bob captured their secrets to success on paper and so was born the Stage-Gate system. He further describes that Stage-Gate is, from its nature, an idea-to-launch process, but one that encompasses a body of knowledge and a set of best practices—best practices based on studies of thousands of successful new-product developments and hundreds of companies that probed what the winners do differently from the rest.

---

4 Robert G. Cooper, *Winning at New Products: Creating Value Through Innovation*, 5th ed. (New York: Basic Books, 2017).

He did more research, including some that focused on these early adopters of Stage-Gate. More success factors were uncovered in benchmarking studies that followed, and more experiences were gained with the use of Stage-Gate methods (Bob first used the term "Stage-Gate" in an article that appeared in the Journal of Marketing Management in 1988). And so, the 2nd edition was published in 1993. It went on to become the bible for those businesses trying to overhaul their new product process and implement Stage-Gate. At Swarovski, we've been a part of this Stage-Gate evolution story, and it's been good for us. Looking back, we can say that together with Bob we delivered some significant cornerstones for the development of an innovative industrial culture. An industrial culture that laid the groundwork for many growth stories around the world until the age of the 5th wave of innovation that we are living in now. Due to the rapid advancements in artificial intelligence (AI), the Internet of Things (IoT), robots, drones, and clean tech, we are currently experiencing significant changes to our lives. We'll discuss this in more detail in part III of this book.

The Domestication of creativity

Meanwhile, I was appointed Vice President of Innovation, a role that was very uncommon in these days in the European industrial landscape. A significant challenge in my role was the lack of a decisive moment marking the transition from design to production, leading to inefficiencies. A learning expedition to Japan in April 1999, alongside McKinsey consultants, visiting companies like Toyota, Fuji, and Matsushita, made it clear that a definitive milestone was needed to signal the end of the design phase and the onset of full-scale production. We missed a clear decision point marking the exact point of time when no further change in design was allowed. The cost-intensive ramp-up phase was already deployed. Bob called this the Money Gate because after this gate, there was a heavy investment into tooling, production facilities, and global market communication. This pivotal moment, where we had to shift from an exploratory and experimental phase into a phase of realization, where failure was not an option, was challenging for everyone involved. It was a diagram from our Japanese benchmarking peers who practiced Total Quality Management (TQM) at this time that brought us nearer to solving our problem. They called this moment the "Freezing Point." My generation was profoundly shaped by the age of rocket science and the moon landing, so I used analogies that the high-class technicians at the company could understand. We decided to implement a freezing point in our process that we named "PONR—Point of No Return." We compared it to launching a rocket. This made everyone in the company understand that failing would have a significant negative impact. This approach empowered designers to be more innovative and willing to take risks at the beginning, while ensuring engineers could work efficiently and with motivation later, knowing that there wouldn't be any last-minute changes in design to disrupt their detailed plans for starting production around the world. Even in a highly adaptive and fast-fashion environment.

A freezing point signaling the change from 'failing welcome' to 'failing forbidden' that we called 'PONR—Point of No Return' helped to combine both designers' and engineers' requirements.

Today's view makes it clear that this was a crucial step in handling a topic we'll dive into repeatedly throughout this book. We'll discuss the shift between exploring new ideas and exploiting them. This is as well a fundamental aspect of corporate innovation and creative endeavors in our everyday lives.

We created a folder outlining the methodology we established to ensure our process was both repeatable and dependable. We engaged the entire organization to adopt this new mode of operation. Simultaneously, my colleague Gerhard and I devised a new quality framework, drawing inspiration from, again, a distinct rocket science analogy, in this case the FMEA (Failure Mode and Effect Analysis). All these important steps have been implemented into the folder. At the organizational level, the new method allowed us to bring people together and force them to find solutions for the most urgent requirements for the next level of design and technology evolution.

The basic idea behind a Stage-Gate process is simple, and figure 2 shows what it's all about. It shows an example that Bob used in the early days of product development. Over time, there have been more and more adaptations to many areas of innovation. We'll talk about these later.

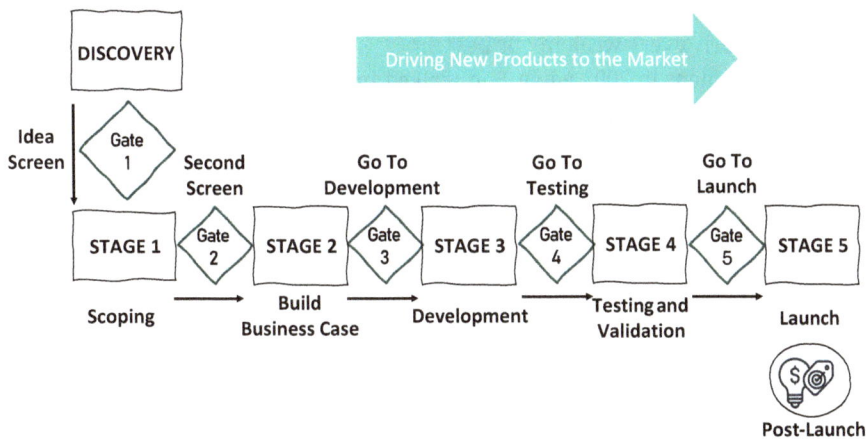

Figure 2: An early example of the initial Stage-Gate™ Process for developing new products from Robert G. Cooper in the 1990s.

The journey from conception to market introduction is broken down into key sequential stages. Each stage functions as an independent unit with its own set of resources, decision-makers, and leaders. At the conclusion of each stage, designated gatekeepers convene to allocate resources, provide guidelines, and green-light the progression to subsequent stages. Thus, the choice of gatekeepers—and their genuine interest and authority to offer the required backing—is of utmost importance.

In contemporary times, a more sophisticated framework known as the RASCI model has been adopted. This stands for Responsible, Accessible, Supporting, Creating, and Informed individuals. It's often humorously mentioned in the industry that the RASCI model thankfully took the place of the HIPPO model. For the uninitiated, particularly younger readers, the acronym HIPPO refers to the Highest Paid Person in the Organization!

The RASCI model can be used for nearly every change endeavor.

Balancing Creativity and mass production

So, the next step was to bring the new findings to paper, spread them, and implement them as a new process that was repeatable, strong, and encouraging to be creative take risks and that enabled a high degree of fast realization and availability on a global level in hundreds of stores.

The following years, until the arrival of the big crisis in 2009, have been the most rapid growth years of the companies, with 2-digit growth years over a time period of more than 10 years.

I remember the period as very exhausting and challenging. Our leadership capabilities were not used to such a growth rate, and I hired a new engineer for product development nearly every week in our best time.

I recall a moment in 2002 when Bob walked into my office and asked, "Hannes, are you a happy man? It was at that moment I realized that, despite outward appearances of success, I was overextending myself. Bob shared that he had noticed many such instances on a global level. As by that time there was neither a formal education for this role nor good descriptions from research on how to face the specific challenges of industrial organizational evolution. The main challenge I encountered was understanding that merely duplicating products within existing frameworks wasn't a sustainable strategy. This realization marked the beginning of the next significant phase in both my life and my thought process.

One of the undoubtedly most difficult decisions in my career was due. After five years of tirelessly investing in reorganizing, expanding, and adapting product development and design to the changing corporate landscape, I was at the pinnacle of my career. I had arrived in the role that I thought was the most desirable goal I could achieve at that age. Today, I must realize: It's more like a Super Mario game. Once you've mastered one discipline, it's time to move on to the next challenge. This is especially true during periods of rapid change. To stay competitive and maintain your edge, you must have unwavering inner conviction. Otherwise, you will inevitably lose ground and strength.

Once you've mastered one discipline, it's time to move on to the next challenge.

Despite outward success, I admitted to myself that I had begun to feel disconnected from my true passion for innovation and meaningful contributions. It was a difficult realization that I had strayed too far from my vision and purpose. I made the decision to focus on profound innovation by founding an agile team. This decision was nothing short of groundbreaking, as the i-Lab rapidly evolved into a leading incubator for innovation and a pivotal interface with the technology sector. Working with a highly cross-functional team of designers, technologists, and practitioners was an invaluable experience that accelerated my personal development.

IS the Stage-Gate™ process outdated today?

We've started the discussion on how and when to switch from exploring to exploiting behaviors. The question of how an ideal innovation process looks is becoming more and more important. The question that arises is whether Stage-Gate logic can fulfill this promise or must be replaced by something superior, or could be integrated into a more advanced one.

History clearly shows two initial strands in the emergence of the new when it comes to origin myths. These are the beliefs about the world and the forces that govern it, held by nearly all past societies. The first variation is a recombination of existing, familiar elements—a continuous evolution of what already exists, projected into the future on a timeline. The second variation is discontinuity, a sharp break that highlights the contrasts with the existing and emphasizes the distinctiveness of the new in thinking, seeing, doing, and living. The term for this is "breakthrough innovation," and we'll explore about the logic behind both during the course of the book. In most cases, we need to understand the interactive combinatorics of both.

Austrian researcher Helga Nowotny offers an interesting model of where we are today: *"Either the world and humanity are created (by whoever the creator is and however that creation happens) or the origin myth uses processes that create and regenerate themselves without a clear starting point. Today, we're in the process of creating a third origin myth: that of the scientific-technological civilization, which continuously produces innovations from within itself. These innovations come from unexpected scientific and technological breakthroughs or are created to solve problems in society. This scientific-technological origin myth says that each new beginning is similar to the last one but also different. It's all part of the innovation process, which relies on certain conditions but keeps creating new things thanks to our curiosity in science and technology.*"[5]

The Stage-Gate type of thinking helps us to understand these logics and enables us to repeat the experienced innovation procedures every time with more security. This pattern of continual self-generation is clear. Robert G. Cooper writes in his above-mentioned 5th edition of Winning at New Products about bold innovation and innovation in record time. He describes that he has watched that companies, a few industries excepted, have shifted their innovation efforts from true innovations and major projects to much smaller and less ambitious ones over the last few decades. For him it is somehow disheartening to see what these companies are calling "innovation" versus what it should be. In some firms, product development has been totally trivialized. Bob is hoping that his 5th edition sounds a wake-up call that true innovation and bold product development are within everyone's grasp. He emphasizes more here the role of speed specifically, agility, flexibility, acceleration, and adaptability, which are all linked. For him it seems that too many firms' innovation processes have become rigid and bureaucratic over the years—slow and cumbersome, unable to deal with today's pace of change. It's as though they're designed to hinder bold innovation and to stand in the way of doing anything worthwhile fast. He believes that some new techniques—some from the IT world—needed to get the innovation engine up to speed to where it should be agile, accelerated, adaptive, and flexible. And with today's view I want to add: Driven by the integration of the revolutionary help of artificial intelligence.

Regarding our experience and logical evolvement over the years, we have developed different Stage-Gate adaptions, especially to the challenges of fast-paced fashion industries that, on the one hand, need speed and trend adaptability but, on the other hand, high quality and global availability of physical products. One of these evolvements we called the fashion integration product innovation process, and another one was called the master process for all product developments that cross over different product categories. This basic process guarantees that we do not lose the basic stability of a company, both creative and at the same time, industrial-process driven.

It seems to be a common problem for organizations that, when the process is well defined, they rely on the process too much as the Bible. Bob Cooper

Bob further writes that a common problem for organizations is that, when the process is well defined, they rely on the process too much as the Bible. When people in a process stick around for too long, they often lose their creative vision and end up just copying and pasting.

5 Helga Nowotny, *Insatiable Curiosity: Innovation in a Fragile Future* (Cambridge, MA: MIT Press. 2008). (page 20–21 in German Edition, 2005).

And I must warn here: When the Stage-Gate principle is overstretched over time people often think the processes are uncreative, but that's not actually the case. From what I've seen, it's not the process itself that's uncreative. It's not the process itself, that's the problem. It's the organization and its people who simply forget to stay open to change and innovation. As Peter Drucker said, "Culture eats strategy for breakfast." So, we're back to the mindset and readiness for change debate. How we reacted to this fact is described in the chapter of the i-LAB experience where we defined how to improve our capabilities for idea solicitation.

Clayton Christensen's Disruptions and Dilemmas

Another big moment for me was meeting Clayton Christensen, the well-known academic, during my executive training class at Harvard Business School in 1996.

Clayton Christensen, best known for his theory of "Disruptive Innovation" and author of several influential books, including "The Innovator's Dilemma," was one of the professors in the course.[6]

Today, "The Innovator's Dilemma" is indisputably one of the most influential business books of all time and the definitive work on disruptive innovation.

In the book he shows how even the most outstanding companies can do everything right yet still lose market leadership. He explains why most companies miss out on new waves of innovation. No matter what the industry, a successful company with established products *will* get pushed aside unless managers know how and when to abandon traditional business practices.

We were among the first students to see his work in detail, and I feel fortunate to have had that opportunity. I distinctly recall the original handout that clearly outlined the main idea of this theory, and it was very straightforward. The foreword to the first edition of his book was written in April 1996, and our class was taken in July. The book had not yet been published.

In figure 3 you can see the original first simple drawing that was the basis of this theory that he used in his lecture for the next 20 years. It's so straightforward and self-explanatory that I still remember it nearly 30 years later.

Clayton confidently presented his mini mills business case, which disrupted the American steel industry with its smaller and more flexible steel production technology. The pattern is always the same. New technologies always improve product performance. He calls them "sustaining technologies." Some of these technologies are radical, while others are incremental. All sustaining technologies improve the performance of established products along the dimensions that mainstream customers in

---

6 Christensen, Clayton M. *The Innovator's Dilemma: When New Technologies Cause Great Firms to Fail.* Boston: Harvard Business Review Press, 1997.

Disruptive Technologies: A driver of leadership failure in a stunning range of industries

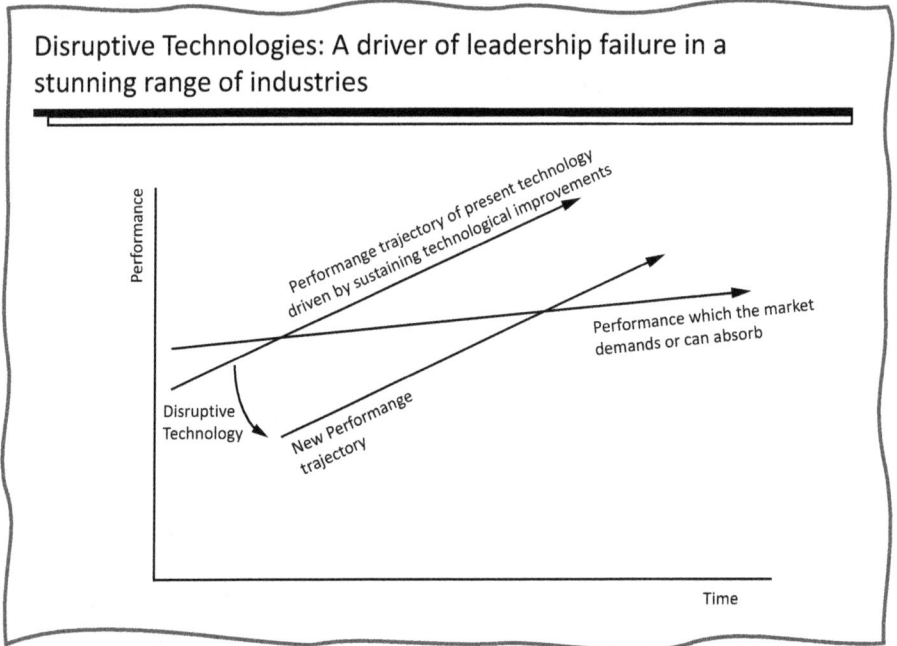

Performance

Performance trajectory of present technology driven by sustaining technological improvements

Performance which the market demands or can absorb

Disruptive Technology

New Performance trajectory

Time

Figure 3: The Impact of Sustaining and Disruptive Technological Change. Original from Clayton Christensen used in his classes in Harvard 1997.

major markets have historically valued. The majority of technological advances in any given industry are of a sustaining nature. Disruptive technologies are different. They emerge. They start small and seem to perform lower than other options, but they rapidly improve, eventually surpassing the flat performance curve of sustaining innovations. Big companies often fail to recognize the threat posed by emerging technologies. Underestimating the competition is a costly mistake. When you realize that you are going to get disrupted, it is often too late.

When you realize that you are going to get disrupted, it is often too late.

How this theory could impact our company was the trigger to ask many questions of him. One afternoon, he invited me into his cabinet to answer my questions. He wasn't the famous Clayton yet. He just finished his basketball training and is sitting in his sports clothes as the passionate professor in the industrial product development program.

Our discussion was later continued in the larger group and led to the conclusion that large companies must learn to disrupt themselves. Later, it was a common topic in management discussions on a global level, and it still is to this day. Disrupt yourself before your competitors do.

This question accompanied strategists and innovators over the last 30 years and fired my motivation as well to think about where and how the next disruption could already be on the way. And we all know what happened through the digital disruption periods in the last 30 years. How many companies disappeared? I want just mention here as one example digital photography and the Kodak case. Despite having invented digital photography in their research programs, Kodak struggled to adapt to digital photography. They couldn't see that people would soon prefer digital photography. Their film business was too successful. Their size and structure made it hard for managers to adapt.

This is not the end of the story. Only a few companies have been successful at disrupting themselves. Microsoft is one of them. Why? They excel at managing new ideas and innovations at the early stage and scaling them up to new or existing businesses.

Today the question of how to detect disruptive elements is, for instance, addressed by the "Nightmare Competitor Challenge" developed by Prof. Stephan Friedrich von den Eichen and the IMP counseling group.

In 2014, I was on the Advisory Board of the Front End of Innovation Conference. I brought Clayton Christensen to the conference in Munich, where he gave a great speech. I remember two highlights: Number one was that he emphasized the importance of the "job to be done" thinking.

The "Jobs to Be Done" theory helps companies understand why customers buy products or services. Clayton Christensen and colleagues developed this theory. Customers hire products to do specific tasks. Knowing what customers want and how they use products helps decide what to develop. Sometimes more of the same is unnecessary. This focus helps drive innovation by showing where there are gaps in the market. The method helped me later in my career to identify unmet and over-met customer needs. Focusing on the innovation portfolio by investigating statements from real users and listening to them on a diagram showing the degree of fulfillment over the importance for the customer. At the end of the process, you have a wonderful overview of relevant innovation areas.

His second focus in the speech was a surprise, given that we had discussed disruptive technologies in the conference preparations. He stated that, two decades on from our discussion at Harvard, his experience is that big companies are unable to disrupt themselves in most cases.

This question was still so important for me that in 2018, we invited eight colleagues from Swarovski to attend a dedicated Harvard Business online course on disruptive innovation led by Clayton. The course was excellent.

He said that when a company's main business is established, trying to grow by starting new things is difficult. Roughly one company in ten is able to sustain the kind of growth that translates into an above-average increase in shareholder returns over more than a few years. Too often the very attempt to grow causes the entire corporation to crash. Pursuing growth the wrong way can be worse than no growth at all.

At the end, he even showed examples of company bosses who had to reinvent their own company with a different focus and management style because they were unable to overcome the deeply rooted cultural, success-related, and systemic effects in management that were preventing them from doing so.

Pursuing growth the wrong way can be worse than no growth at all.

Finally, through the Harvard Business School program, I gained additional insights from Professors Wheelwright, Clark, and Iansiti and their research team. They introduced us to studies on the efficiency of Japanese car manufacturers in the late '80s and early '90s. Unlike their European counterparts, who took 5 to 7 years to develop a new model from scratch, Japanese car manufacturers managed to do it in just 3 to 5 years. That was at that time a little shocking, and everybody was asked to find ways to improve. One key factor behind this difference seemed to be rooted in the way Japanese managers organized their teams. Professors Wheelwright and Clark identified that managing different types of teams is crucial for responding to various types of innovation.[7] They described four types of product development teams: functional, lightweight, heavyweight, and autonomous.

Heavyweight teams are particularly well-suited for tackling complex, high-stakes projects because they bring together a diverse set of skills and resources. Lightweight teams are doing great when they're asked to work on parts of the company that are more familiar and have a lot of ongoing development.

These insights proved invaluable, and I applied them in my new role as Head of Product Development at Swarovski. As a first action I followed the recommendations of Prof. Marco Iansity and put together an overall project plan using something called the "Newness Matrix." This matrix has two axes: one shows "newness to the world" and the other shows "newness to the company." This gives a quick overview of the innovation topics, showing if the product or idea is a total game-changer that's never been seen before in the market, or if it's new for the company itself, even if it's out there elsewhere. This helped us not only figure out the risk and potential impact of different projects. I as well loved to use it as a tool to find the right engineers for the different innovation mindsets. For me, since I was new in my job, it helped me put together new teams and resources following the guidelines from Wheelwright and Clark's findings. Whenever I meet people who were around during that transformational time, they always talk to me about how it was one of the best experiences of

---

7 Steven C. Wheelwright and Kim B. Clark, *Leading Product Development: The Senior Manager's Guide to Creating and Shaping the Enterprise* (New York: Free Press, 1995).

their lives. They've been on highly motivated teams with clear processes and development goals.

Ideas of employees – how to hear them?

The democratization of knowledge and its increasing omnipresent availability have made it clear in the following years that colleagues' knowledge is crucial for innovation. We had implemented an idea system in 2001 to gain a competitive edge and to gather creative inputs across all levels in a changing work environment.

This was our next learning phase, and it was the same as before. We decided to implement an idea system and found Johann Fueller and his group in Munich from Hyve Company. We expanded our initial approach, which was manually created using Excel lists, into one of the first integrative idea development approaches, thanks to Hyve's IT expertise and software. It was clear that we needed to distinguish between idea development and the existing in-house suggestion scheme. I distinctly recall that, in the early days, this topic was not on many organizations' radars. In 2002, I attended a conference that focused on KIP (continuous improvement processes). I asked all the presenters how many of their improvement ideas had been relevant for innovation. The average answer was between 10 and 20%. We discovered that the issue with KIP Systems stemmed from the fact that the realization fell within the purview of the innovation division, and the decisions couldn't be made by the heads of departments directly. Our conclusion was clear: Go for a separate innovation idea development system. The split as well allowed them to overcome the critical know-how protection that was always an important factor. Our strategy was to solicit ideas from various fields that are relevant for new products and business, without talking about technologies in detail. We were early adopters and shared our progress. And we have been surprised at how strongly the use of information technology could support cultural change processes. With the open access to the ideas for everybody and the smart use of evaluators of them, we had a broad discussion of future opportunities for the company in a very short time. And this changed the openness and the willingness to contribute very strongly. It was very important for the organization to understand what was going on. If you don't know what you're doing, you won't know where you need to change.

The results were published in the book of Professors Zerfass and Moeslein in 2006.[8] Three years after the implementation, we had an idea generation machine that produced more than 2,000 ideas from 2006 to 2008, and we built a good idea database

---

8 Hannes Erler, Markus Rieger, and Johann Füller, "Ideenmanagement und Innovation mit Social Networks – Die Swarovski i-flash Community," in *Kommunikation als Erfolgsfaktor im Innovationsmanagement: Strategien im Zeitalter der Open InnovationOpen Innovation*, ed. Ansgar Zerfaß and Kathrin Möslein (Wiesbaden: Gabler, 2009), 159–176.

and interconnection in parallel with the development of the innovation network. The flood of ideas automatically created a need for better alignment, and we were forced to increase the bandwidth for evaluation, exchange, and realization. It was at this point that we realized that it was necessary to produce a lot of ideas to have good ones. And not surprisingly, with each feedback on the likelihood of realization and current strategic search areas, such as sustainability or "unexpected, surprising solutions for customers" in the fashion area, the quality and innovation level of the ideas evolved tremendously.

The greater the social exchange of ideas, the higher the quality and suitability of the ideas for the search fields.

One of the most valuable lessons learned from this experience was the need to expand our external idea base. Put another way, the ideas of employees require an environment in which their expertise and connectivity to their own networks can be discussed in a broader context and reshaped to align with the company's strategy or, in this case, search fields. The greater the social exchange of ideas, the higher the quality and suitability of the ideas for the search fields.

As you might expect, the help we received in preparing for this opening again came from academic research, specifically Henry Chesbrough's works on Open Innovation. And again, the finding established a new standard across the entire industry. This occurred in 2006.

Henry Chesbrough's "Open Innovation Model"

If we want to explain Henry's Theory in short words, the answer is that it's a model that encourages companies to use both internal and external ideas to drive innovation. The model has three main parts.

External Collaboration: Engaging with external entities such as universities, research institutions, and other companies to source new ideas and technologies.

Knowledge Sharing: Allowing internal knowledge to flow outwards to other organizations, which can lead to new market opportunities and revenue streams.

Flexible Business Models: Adopting business models that support the integration of external innovations and the commercialization of internal ideas through external channels.

These aspects are sound and logical. But the truth is, it's the organization's internal knowledge and expertise of its specialized and skilled workforce that truly sets it apart. The digital revolution has accelerated the exchange and availability of knowledge. In less than a decade, the model of Open Innovation has become the norm in most industries.

This has even happened in domains where knowledge is highly protected. Undoubtedly, Open Innovation accelerates, enhances, and invigorates the innovation process. At the same time, the mastery of this opening and the new flood of possible partners and networks creates new complexity that must be integrated into the internal innovation procedures. The evolution of information technology and the availability of data and platforms have enabled cross-border exchange between companies and industries.

In less than a decade, the model of Open Innovation has become the norm in most industries.

When I met Henry Chesbrough in Paris in 2016, we had a long discussion at the evening program of a network meeting in Paris. We discussed how our company has always worked collaboratively with customers, designers, and technology providers and our different approaches, which are a long-standing tradition within the company. He made it clear that he was aware of the existence of innovation collaborations, strategic alliances, and the transformation of technologies for a long time. That is the very nature of innovation. He told me he merely identified a name for it: Open Innovation was born. He based his theory on the industrial habits of the past.

The missing link to how the next step in evolution of an industry innovation culture that would enable us to adapt to the speed and multitude of upcoming opportunities was for us in adapting customer relation management (CSR) tools to the Open Innovation logics.

It's clear that all innovation is now considered Open Innovation. Innovation is a social process that only works with the diverse exchange of ideas. Closed innovation simply does not work in today's hyperconnected world. It didn't work then, either. Single, open-minded leaders in organizations drove it. In the old world, they had a knowledge advantage, which gave them a certain advantageous position. This is what we know as an effect like "the democratization of innovation" because innovation can be done by many more people and interlinked on a cross-organizational level. This shift led to a major change in our organizations. We fooled ourselves into believing that innovation could be delegated from the upper levels of organizations to the lower levels. The answer is "no." While it's true that the execution of transformation can be moved deeper into the organization, the responsibility for strategy, orientation, budgeting, and structural integration cannot be delegated to lower levels. It is and always will be a CEO's responsibility.

Because innovation can be done by many more people and interlinked on a cross-organizational level we can observe 'the democratization of innovation' taking place.

In my personal transformation and during the upcoming implementation of Open Innovation processes within a closed corporate environment, I stumbled over Prof. Gene Slowinski and his work in the fields of strategic alliances, joint ventures, and mergers and acquisitions. Prof. Slowinski is the Director of Strategic Alliance Research at Rutgers University. As well, he has experience in industry and held former management positions at AT&T Bell Laboratories and Novartis Corporation. He is known for his contributions to the field of Open Innovation, particularly through the development of the "Want, Find, Get, Manage" (WFGM) model, which helps to identify innovation needs, find external resources, acquire them, and manage them effectively.

The WFGM model helps orchestrate the critical opening process from closed to Open Innovation.

This model, which was developed at the same time as Henry Chesbrough wrote down his experiences, helped me to understand and orchestrate the critical opening process from closed to Open Innovation. From those experiences I say today that his theory is the basic mindset concept when reaching out for outside ideas. The model was first published in 2004, and it goes like that:

Want: What external resources do we need to succeed with our mission? We must determine whether our focus should be on new technologies, products, or another field where we want to make a move.

Find: Once the needs are identified, the next step is to search for potential partners, technologies, or ideas that can fulfill these needs.

Get: When the potential topics and/or partners are identified, the focus shifts to acquiring them. This could involve negotiations, forming partnerships, licensing agreements, or other forms of collaboration to bring the innovation into the company.

Manage: The final step is to effectively manage the acquired innovations and partnerships. This includes integrating the new technologies or ideas into the company, managing relationships with partners, and ensuring that the innovation process is aligned with the company's strategic objectives.

The WFGM model was instrumental in the second phase of our opening process. It helped us not only identify and acquire external innovations but also coordinate their integration and send them to realization.

As previously stated, the digital revolution and significant technological advancements have transformed the way we engage in Open Innovation, creating unprecedented opportunities for global collaboration. The improvement of virtual communication platforms, data sharing networks, and advanced analytics has made it possible to collaborate seamlessly across borders and to overcome logistical barriers inside and outside our organizations. Our cutting-edge tools for collaboration, project management, and knowledge sharing enable efficient and effective teamwork on a global level in nearly all areas of development.

And one final and important thing: Always remember that there are billions of potential access points to super smart people all over the world. They are the link to centuries of experiences. They are driven by creativity and passion. They are not part of our own organizations —and imagine if they were? At least virtually. Read more about our Open Innovation journey in chapter 3 and the next logical evolutionary step in global collaboration in chapter 4. We will learn together why the arrival of global innovation ecosystems and AI is the next revolutionary step in shaping innovation.

And in this moment as I am writing these words, my phone shows in the breaking news banner that the winner of the Nobel Prize in Physics going to the pioneers in machine learning with the committee's statement: "Machine learning based on artificial neural networks is currently revolutionizing science, engineering, and daily life." This underlines the significant relevance of artificial intelligence for future innovations and how we perform it. At this point I want to make a small insight into chapter 13 of this book: Surprisingly for me, artificial intelligence is completely turning our previous procedures to innovate on its head.

"Instead of surpassing humans in physical strength, AI will surpass humans in their mental abilities," says Geoffrey Hinton in his first statement, and at the same moment he warns, "We have no experience of what it's like when things are more intelligent than we are."

Hinton, who answered a few more questions, compared the increasing general availability of artificial intelligence to a historical event from the Industrial Revolution. This poses a challenge for humanity.

These first statements are a clear warning and a challenge to anyone who's going to make changes in society, companies, and politics. We must ensure that this new technology is a positive force in society. We will explore how AI is changing everything and how we can use it as a creative navigation tool.

Paths to Open Innovation under scrutiny

With the view of today and after 20 years of different OI experiences, I see that there are 5 main directions of approaches to OI, and they are of different natures:
- Corporate Lab
- Corporate incubator/accelerator
- Intrapreneurship Programs
- Challenges and Hackathons
- Partnership programs / Proof of Concept (PoC)

As I said before, you must decide what you want to achieve with Open Innovation and how you succeed in embedding scouting and collaboration into your core processes. Do you want to detect trends? Do you want to tell nice marketing stories about your collaborations? Do you want to detect new business opportunities? Or could some of the approaches even help you to implement new projects and to drive change with the help of outside experiences and knowledge?

From my personal experience with Open Innovation, I can say with confidence that partnership projects and intrapreneurship programs are the best way to implement projects, protect them from internal rivalries and "not invented here" effects, and boost your innovation portfolio. They are also an excellent way to start new projects automatically. Why? External negotiations ensure the organization keeps its promises and sticks to its budget. They also help you to motivate and inspire people from within. If they are in the right place in innovation environments, they will flourish. They thrive on challenges and are eager to embark on new endeavors. I think it's important to acknowledge that while partnership projects and other forms of Open Innovation can play a valuable role, they may not be a complete replacement for internal research and innovation structures, but they can provide a way to maintain a smaller, more agile structure that remains connected to external knowledge points. I would strongly advise against the idea that you can simply buy in innovation competences. I have seen firsthand how closed silos hinder innovation and create unnecessary roadblocks to adapting to changing market environments. I have also seen renowned companies stumble because they failed to invest sufficient resources and expertise in their major projects. These failures often stem from systemic shortcomings in their organizations and an underestimation of the complexities involved. Let me be clear: Adapting to a changing market environment requires investing sufficient brainpower and "change skills" into your big projects.

If we use Open Innovation more strategically to increase our dynamic capabilities by building up a wide range of partner networks for platform-based businesses and ecosystems, this will help us to stay competitive in the future. In that respect we should use digital technologies for our Open Innovation activities not only in the firm but also at the industry level and foster networks and platforms. As most old and new research in Open Innovation studies the individual and firm level, we need more research studying the effects of Open Innovation on the industry level.

But more about that later, when we dive into systemic organizational development and innovation ecosystems.

Open Innovation is not simply done with a campaign. It's an operating model for sensing, shaping, and scaling creative solutions.

Open Innovation is not simply done with a campaign. It's an operating model for sensing, shaping, and scaling creative solutions. And we always must keep an eye on the potential risks of Open Innovation.

Beware of Innovation Theater

On the way to open and to expect wonders from Open Innovation I must warn the reader about a trap that I have observed very often in the last years in many companies on a global level: I am speaking of innovation theater.

The term "innovation theater" is often used to describe organizational announcements that promise to generate more innovation but ultimately achieve nothing more than putting up a façade of innovation. It sounds good for the organization when leadership teams speak about their love of innovation and commitment to positive contributions. Set up an innovation lab, introduce revolutionary innovation software, organize a trip to Silicon Valley, set up an idea collection point, or hold a two-day innovation workshop for employees. These approaches signal to customers that your products are superior and valuable. These measures will make your company look like an innovator in the short term. I am not saying they are useless. They only work if they fall on fertile ground, and this ground must be developed through many investments in people, culture, and organizational trust. You can't simply buy fertile ground. Cultivating fertile soil takes time, intensive work, and a thorough examination of the topic of innovation. Innovation theater actions are downright dangerous. Once expensive actions prove ineffective, innovation quickly becomes a hated empty phrase, and employees lose enthusiasm for it.

In my time as Head of Innovation, Director of Open Innovation, and Director of Innovation Ecosystems, I encountered numerous instances of half-hearted, piecemeal approaches to innovation. At innovation conferences where I was invited to speak, I made sure to take full advantage of the opportunity to listen carefully to the presentations of colleagues from different areas. I have seen hundreds of presentations and spoken with many of the presenters in person. Many of them are partners in our innovation network. Let me be clear: the picture that can be drawn from those experiences is not good. The majority of them had a difficult time within their own organizations. It's clear that many organizations are unwilling to fully commit to risky projects. In the case of the money gate and the decision of whether to remain involved in such projects, many organizations could do more to support their teams. One might suggest that this is simply the nature of innovation. I feel it may be indicative of shortcomings in leadership, a lack of trust, and a failure to respect human values.

I put the different methods at the top of the book because I am convinced that to study the different methods, ideally attending a workshop on it makes sense. And once you have established it in your company or for your personal development, the desired eureka moments will occur. Unfortunately, there are no methods that meet all requirements. A change project and the knowledge of how it works in your own environment is like a fingerprint of your implicit capabilities to deal with change. These implicit capabilities have a history, a now, and an impact on the future. In this book I intended to show examples of what worked under what circumstances and mainly that the evolution of change skills is always driven by people, encouraged by teams that make the methods impactful, and leadership structures with strategic vision and high emotional IQ! I can say with confidence that our process for opening up has been a 20-year journey of transformation. It has been a journey of embracing the new age of openness, connectivity, and focus. And it is a journey that is still ongoing, with regular revisions. Those who have recognized this fact drive the creation of new versions of the world. And again, let me be clear: The most adaptable will survive.

Harrison Owen's Open Spaces

With the Open Space Technology we come nearer to the title of the book. The Innovation Tribe.

In the time when our organization grew over the years with different business fields but with centralized development, technology, and production structures, we were forced to enhance exchange between the growing number of potential contributors.

We were able to set up and run an experimental internal network that was governed by the business's needs and powered by the research and innovation actors at the same time, thanks to the help of AIT (the Austrian Institute of Technology) and two of their innovation researchers. This development and learning were so important for our organization and my personal growth that I want to describe the process of implementation in detail in Chapter 3.

Let's start by going over the basics of the method and how it's been developed over time.

In his book, *Open Space Technology*, Harrison Owen explains in detail how and why he developed this method. I can say with confidence that it has been an invaluable and indispensable aid and guide in my life.[9]

It allows for meetings where the participants create and manage the agenda themselves. The sessions can accommodate from five to 2,000 people—if you have a sufficiently large venue. This method is the ideal way to get participants to take ownership of a problem and find solutions.

I experienced Open Space Technology as "the" most fascinating method for facilitating large group meetings. It allows for self-organization, creativity, and collabora-

---

9 Harrison Owen, *Open Space Technology: A User's Guide* (San Francisco: Berrett-Koehler Publishers, 2008),13.

tion. Harrison Owen, an American consultant and author, developed Open Space Technology after observing how African tribal meetings work. Owen set out to create a new way of organizing conferences that would capture the energy, spontaneity, and learning he witnessed at the event. In his book he is mentioning his frustration when he organized global conferences with hundreds of global participants as part of his job, and after months of hard work, the participants said, "Harrison do you know what we best love at your conferences? These are the coffee breaks!"

I can say with confidence that Open Space Technology has been an invaluable and indispensable aid and guide in my life.

And that was why he started to think about this fact. He found out that people love to define the real topics that matter, the included participants, and the right time to discuss in a very relaxed manner. And when he, an educated ethnologist, observed the principals of the tribal meetings that worked with nearly no preparation time and only a few simple rules for behavior, he immediately started to transform these observations into his method.

I have participated in 3 professional Open Spaces in my life that have been conducted by outside consultants from AIT, the Austrian Institute of Technology, and I have conducted one Open Space with nearly 70 people on my own. And I must say the latter was one of the most energizing experiences in my life. It's fascinating what can be done with a diverse group of people without having an agenda for a 3-day get-together.

But now, how does it work? At the beginning, there is usually a big, unsolvable problem. In his book, Owen talks about a highway that was meant to go through an Indian reservation and a company that had to change their entire structure. And a lot of other complex challenges have been solved by listening to all voices and considering different points of view.

An open space starts with an invitation to all parties involved. The challenge is to say just enough to catch attention while leaving room for imagination. Words like "provocative," "imaginative," or "open-ended" set the tone in the invitation. Open questions let your imagination grow.

A typical Open Space project takes three days. In our company, we completed it in two days because the physical involvement of participants for three days in a large organization is impractical. We experienced that most people that are involved in innovation and change processes do not care about the process. Most of them want to go directly to solve the problems, fix them with small efforts, and proceed. But you can't invite people for big meetings and tell them nothing about it. Harrison recommends telling the participants the truth, and this is about:

1. Every issue of concern to anybody would have been raised, if they took responsibility for doing that.
2. All issues will have received full discussion, to the extent desired.

3. A full report on issues and discussions will be in the hands of all participants.
4. Priorities will be set, and action plans will be made. (The last two typically only occur in two- and three-day meetings with computer support.)

When I moderated my first Open Space, we discussed how to help a product group recover from the 2009 crisis. Top managers asked me for ideas that could help them get through the crisis. They trusted me and supported the open space proposal because they had been to our company-wide innovation meetings in our innovation network initiative. Everyone wanted to attend the two-day meeting. We used the physical presence of the global sales managers because of their annual sales meeting. This let us hear from markets and customers around the world.

At the starting point of an Open Space meeting all participants are sitting around in one circle. The big advantage of this setting is that everybody, regardless of it's hierarchical position feels involved and heard and receives the same insights into the often complex issues. Standing in the center of the circle can give a lot of pressure. But the method is exactly about capitalizing on this atmosphere of new beginnings. And at this moment the facilitator sets the scene, and it is time to go for action. Each participant is asked to write here or their issues that they want to have discussed and their name on a piece of paper and present it to the group. The participants are still sitting around in the big circle, and they observe when the provider of the issue walks with his issue to the prepared wall that shows the time slots and names of the breakout rooms where it will be discussed. The provider as well lists the name of the core participants that he would like to have in the group.

Now we have set our agenda with the help of the issues of the participants.

Often it is the case that some people wait until the end with their announcements, and sometimes they just say that exactly their topic is already on the wall. But that's exactly already one of the benefits of the exercise. The attendees already develop their plan for their contribution during this exercise, and they start automatically on the first process of prioritizing and balancing. And if someone does not find his favorite issue, only he is to blame.

Now that we have our agenda wall, which includes the topics and already has the rooms and time slots developed by the group, it is time for the important explanation of the rules.

The Rules
In Open Space, there are four principles that have been developed based on Harrison's observations of how tribal meetings work. Do you remember the frustration of Harrison that he felt when people offered the preference for the Coffee Break atmosphere? The rules are his answer:
–   Whoever comes are the right people —whether one or 25, and everyone is important and motivated.

- Whatever happens is the only thing that could happen —unplanned and unexpected is often creative and useful.
- It starts when the time is ripe —the important thing is the energy (not punctuality).
- Over is over. Not over is not over. When the energy ends, the time is up.

and one law:
- The Law of Two Feet—as an expression of freedom and self-responsibility: The participant remains in a group only as long as they find it meaningful, as long as they can learn and/or contribute.

The four principles used in Open Space Technology are based on Harrison's observations of how tribal meetings are working.

These rules are clearly stated and displayed for all to see. They create a relaxed atmosphere where you can move around freely, speak up when you have something to contribute, and draw inspiration from others' views. Or even to meet somebody in between the rooms when you float around.

Now people start to look for what they really care for and think about the right timing later. In every room, and thus for every topic, there is the provider of the topic, and one person will be announced to write down the basic content of the discussion and the recommendations along with the people who are willing to contribute to the next step in realization. This crucial information will be posted immediately on the wall, which we are now calling the "Bulletin Board." This will allow everyone to monitor the proposals and to see who is involved, enabling them to develop their own follow-up agenda or to claim themselves to be part of the realization after the conference.

Even if sessions in different rooms had the same general focus, the results are different but, in most cases, showed the important things that have to be taken into consideration for further handling by no means. And the other is that if you are the facilitator, you simply have to go out of the way because people are taking your process very seriously.

At the end of this first round of our Open Space breakout groups, a brief review of the discussions is done, standing around the bulletin board. The agenda for the next round or days is adjusted in agreement with the group and with the focus on new topics or merging similar ones.

The next round of breakout sessions follows the same rules, and it is very important that people still move between sessions, following the "Law of Two Feet," which means if they are not learning or contributing, they should move to another session.

Now the key insights, themes, and action items should be clearer, and the energy of the supporters at a high level. And now the last round of breakout groups is ready to start. And it is now much more about concrete action plans that are developed in smaller groups to outline steps, assign responsibilities, and set timelines.

The conference ends with a closing circle where participants share their experiences, insights, and commitments. This helps to reinforce the sense of community and shared purpose, and very important, the people come back now to their hierarchical reality and day-to-day working logics. I experienced that this is now exactly the point where the hierarchical leaders and power promoters of the topics should give their full commitment and encourage the defined teams and empower them for realization.

All notes, summaries, and action plans are now compiled into a comprehensive report. They are shared with all participants, and most importantly, they have to include a follow-up logic for the realization topics.

If you've never experienced such an open space, it might sound a little complicated at first. But it's true. I can say with confidence that this method works. There is no better way to develop a drive for change and believe in the power of your own organization and especially the involved people. At the heart of Open Space Technology is the belief that individuals own wisdom, insights, and ideas that, when unleashed, can drive change and innovation. Unlike traditional meeting formats with pre-set agendas, Open Space Technology will raise precisely these skills and bring them to the surface, or at least to the bulletin board. The rest is, like always, up to smart organizations and visionary leadership.

Open Space Technology has proven to be a catalyst for transformative change in organizations, communities, and societies many times since its introduction in the late 80's.

And there's one last thing I want to add. For me in person, the learning from the Open Space work had many other dimensions, and if I recap, it changed the way how I took decisions about my personal development and how I reached out for the future profoundly. And I strongly recommend thinking about integration into daily life. The four rules and the law of the two feet will transform the culture of interaction and your personal behavior—I guarantee it. Apply these rules not only during the conference, but every day. At home with your partner, your children, your friends, your colleagues at work, in your private surroundings. Try it. You'll like it. I guarantee you'll be surprised at what happens. I guarantee your life will turn out more positive, calmer, and more authentic.

Harrison writes in his book, *"Why does Open Space work anyhow? How could something simple do so much? Something that brings together so many people without having an agenda in hand in advance. The short answer is that self-organization works!"*

It is up to us to bring the profound knowledge on tribal principals into our new age that is driven by "AI and the integration of everything".

I am really saddened to find out that Harrison died at the age of 89 while I am writing this chapter. His ideas are going to be around forever. I never met him face-to-face, but he changed my world view and my life. He was called the "Father of Organizational Transformation" in the "Open Space World" news; now it is up to us to bring his profound knowledge on tribal principles into our new age that is driven by "AI and the integration of everything." And imagine a dream, where the world leaders would be locked up in a 3 day Open Space location and not released until they have found out solutions for more peace and humanity? I am sure they would like it and it would give all of us a better feeling about the future of the planet.

A Galore of More Players and Theories

The procedures described are my favorites, and they will return as key players in part III when we talk about the integration of everything. The better we understand the logic behind the development history and the relevance for today, the more impactfully we can shape the future.

As already mentioned, there are no recipes that fit all. The best management model for an innovative company can vary depending on the specific nature of the company and its goals.

A quick rundown of some other processes and experiences should not be missed to know what is around and may possibly hold value for your exact innovation topic. If you want to learn more, you'll find a lot of material in many publications and in the shared links. The appropriate model must be chosen based on several factors, including company culture, industry, team members, and company goals. In most cases, a combination of different approaches is the most effective approach. The best way to avoid confusion is to implement and communicate one change at a time, as the organization matures and is ready for it.

One of these models is "Design Thinking." This approach prioritizes human-centered innovation, where problem solutions are developed through a creative and iterative design process.

Design Thinking

The Gartner Hype Cycle Curve for innovative management practices shows that Design Thinking is already rated as a well-adapted and approved method. We are close to reaching the point where we can become enlightened and start being productive.

I know Design Thinking as the method that adapts the process that designers use to deep dive into behaviors and needs of users. After my first crash course in design thinking, I knew this method was a potential game-changer. This tool gives engineers and technology-oriented researchers the ability to think like designers. It provides a better understanding of the factors that drive the development of new services and products.

Design thinking helps engineers and technology researchers think like designers and understand users' needs better.

The basic principle is to go through the different mindsets iteratively and with different settings.

It's a very human-centered approach to problem-solving that emphasizes empathy, creativity, and experimentation. It involves understanding the needs of users, generating ideas, prototyping solutions, and testing them iteratively.

The five stages of Design Thinking are **empathize, define, ideate, prototype, and test.**

In every stage it's important to engage with users throughout the process to ensure solutions meet their needs.

In various smaller integration projects, I saw that the benefits are dependent on the project nature itself. In any case, Design Thinking improves the user experience, fosters a culture of experimentation, and motivates teams to collaborate.

Design Thinking as a formal methodology has evolved over time and has contributions from various individuals and organizations. However, several key figures and institutions are often associated with their development:

Herbert Simon (1969), a Nobel laureate in economics, introduced the concept in his book "The Sciences of the Artificial" (1969), emphasizing the importance of a systematic approach to design. David Kelley, the co-founder of IDEO, is the driving force behind the widespread adoption of design thinking in the business and design communities. IDEO's pioneering work in the 1990s on human-centered design practices laid the foundation for formalizing the methodology. Tim Brown, the CEO of IDEO, spread the principles of Design Thinking through various publications and talks, including his influential 2008 TED talk and the book "Change by Design" (2009). The Hasso Plattner Institute of Design at Stanford University, or the d.school, has been a leading force in teaching and promoting Design Thinking. Its curricula have successfully standardized the approach in educational settings.[10]

Design Thinking improves the user experience, fosters a culture of experimentation, and motivates teams to collaborate.

There are many other examples of further development. Overall, Design Thinking is a culmination of ideas, practices, and methodologies from diverse fields and individuals over decades.

---

[10] I recommend further reading on design thinking at *Stanford Online*. "Design Thinking," *Stanford Online*, accessed July 19, 2025, https://online.stanford.edu/courses/design-thinking.

With the arrival of start-up communities, the basic thinking has more and more shifted to speed, failing early and fast, and focusing on lean start-up approaches.

As well, there is some interesting new work out there that combines design thinking methods with systems thinking. There's some insightful and impactful work on LinkedIn from "Si Design Hub" that's definitely worth checking out.[11] Systems thinking is more about identifying where to design and how to find the right question and fields of activity based on systemic facts. Design thinking is more about how to create value. So, they're like two sides of the same coin.

Lean Startup

The Lean Startup methodology is designed for early-stage startups to validate their business ideas quickly and efficiently.

The method is best suited for uncertain contexts where the market and product needs are not yet understood or even defined.

It focuses on building so-called MVP (Minimum Viable Products) with simple and fast methods at the very beginning of the idea phase and was introduced by Stanford Professor Eric Ries. Measuring its performance and learning from user feedback to drive improvements and build the next simplest version of the product in order to learn about customers deeper needs. Based on the data collected, startups should either change direction or continue the current path. It's best suited for uncertain contexts where the market and product needs are not yet understood or defined.

Here's an overview of the steps:
- *Identify an Ideate*
- *Build a Minimum Viable Product (MVP)*
- *Measure*
- *Learn*
- *Pivot or Persevere*
- *Iterate*
- *Scale*

Together with industry partners and learning cases from various industries, Eric Ries adapted these principles of start-ups into the corporate environment to help large or-

---

11 LinkedIn, "SI Design Network," LinkedIn, accessed February 10, 2025, https://www.linkedin.com/company/si-design-network/posts?lipi=urn%3Ali%3Apage%3Ad_flagship3_company_posts%3Bl3j0Ry5nTm%2BZPrhQ0Ibiaw%3D%3D.

ganizations become more innovative and agile. And we used some of the findings in a transformation phase of our company in 2019.

Our experience was that the application of principles only works with dedicated teams that have the driving innovation question, a good budget, and end the right anchoring in the innovation portfolio of the company. Not to forget that the cultural embedding must be communicated by the leadership team. Without the latter protection, the teams will lose drive and motivation.

The startup way for large organizations

The book "The Startup Way" by Eric Ries builds on the principles from "The Lean Startup" and applies them to larger organizations.[12] It focuses on how established companies can adopt entrepreneurial management techniques to drive innovation and growth.

I was, and I am still skeptical if this can work. Can big companies really act like start-ups? It is a contradiction of itself. But with the view on Eric Ries's work and practical samples, I would say from today's point of view: It is difficult, but some of the principles can help to manage innovation zones that have different natures in terms of strategy, time horizon, and organizational ambidexterity. We all know that it is crucial to implement innovation projects that challenge the status quo and explore new avenues that may not align with traditional business strategies. They must have a separate home in the organization.

Exploring new avenues that do not align with traditional business strategies requires a separate home.

It is essential to provide sufficient protection from existing business paradigms while also ensuring that the leadership has the insights and control points to stand behind the budget financed by today's businesses. I'm going to talk more about what we did in 2019 in chapter 5. I'll show how we put a lot of effort into trying out and using our own version of "intrapreneurship" through something we called "Growth Boards." These were based on Professor Ries's publications.

Eric Ries is sharing many case studies from companies like GE, Toyota, and Amazon that are demonstrating how these principles can be implemented successfully. Here is a very helpful link to further readings: http://thestartupway.com. There is enough material to find your own decision if this route is of value for you.

The examples show that the theory works. GE needed to innovate and stay competitive in a rapidly changing market. GE adopted the Lean Startup methodology to

---

12 Eric Ries, *The Start-Up Way: How Modern Companies Use Entrepreneurial Management to Transform Culture and Drive Long-Term Growth* (New York: Crown Publishing Group, 2017).

create a more agile and innovative culture. They implemented the FastWorks program on a global level, which focused on rapid prototyping, customer feedback, and iterative development.

Examples show that the theory works.

Amazon uses Lean Startup methodologies to test new ideas quickly and efficiently. They emphasize small, cross-functional teams that can operate like startups within the larger organization.

Zone to Win by Geoffry Moore

"Zone to Win —Organizing to Compete in an Age of Disruption" is a book published in 2015 that focuses on how established companies can deal with disruptive innovations and stay competitive in fast-changing markets.[13]

It provided for the first time an understandable model of how the seemingly unsolvable ambidexterity trap could be handled. Moore introduces a framework consisting of four distinct zones within an organization, each with different focus areas.

Performance Zone: Describes the heart of the core business, focused on optimizing current products and delivering consistent revenue and profits.

Product Zone: Responsible for developing new products that can be launched successfully into the market.

Transformation Zone: Focuses on creating entirely new business models and offerings, often necessary for addressing disruptive changes.

Incubation Zone: Designed for exploring breakthrough ideas and innovations that may not fit into the current business model.

When we remember our findings from Clayton Christensen's sayings about disruptive technologies, it seems logical to organize differently but again to manage both, or in this case all four, zones differently. The book emphasizes the importance of being proactive in recognizing and addressing disruptions rather than reactive. Companies must create a structured way to innovate while maintaining their core business. Moore argues for reorganizing traditional corporate structures to align resources and talent according to the four zones. Each zone should operate with different metrics, team structures, and management styles.

---

13 Geoffry Moore, *Zone to Win: Organizing to Compete in the Age of Disruption* (New York: Diversion Books, 2015).

Each of the four zones operates using different metrics, team structures, and management styles—if they are understood and supported by the top management, they are key to managing innovation in turbulent times.

Microsoft is the most well-known example of a company that has successfully adapted to Geoffrey's model. Satya Nadella led Microsoft in adopting the zone management framework, which transformed the company's business model. The company made a decisive shift towards cloud computing and other innovative technologies while maintaining strong performance in its traditional software business.

The insights are invaluable for aligning organizational structures, resources, and strategies to achieve a culture of continuous innovation and maintain a competitive advantage. That's precisely why I'm including them in this book. Readers who want to learn more about "Zone to Win" must read the book. I must issue a warning, however. The prerequisites must be met—namely, a top management commitment and strategic adaptation through the provision of resources and metered budgets. Otherwise, there's a high risk that it will remain a nice reading exercise with no chance of realization in the practical work. The prerequisites must be met.

Strategic adaptation through the provision of resources and metered budgets is the key.

Agile Management

One widely used and successful model for innovative companies is "Agile Management." This model is based on flexible work methods, continuous adaptation to changes, and a strong focus on creativity and efficiency.

From my experience I must warn: Agile Management works in information technology areas, and I would say there it is a powerful tool to accelerate, plan, and distribute tasks and identify solutions.

In the early phases of innovation, it can have counterproductive effects if the process is not clear and needs to be iteratively revised. It is very difficult to apply the thinking to the early creative iterative landscape.

When I met Prof. Robert G. Cooper at the 2016 Stage Gate Summit in Marco Island (FL), he mentioned the transformation of agile methods, such as Scrum and Sprint—proven principles in software development—into the area of physical product innovation. He believes that this is one of the biggest opportunities to increase the speed and drive of physical product innovation and one of the biggest moves since the introduction of Stage-Gate logic in the 1990s. I agree with him: product development is a dedicated task oriented towards development and scaling. In the earlier phases of innovation, I am critical. A few months later, I met Prof. Henry Chesbrough, known for his work on Open Innovation, in Porto at the EU OI-Net conference. He zeroed in on the profound societal shifts we're witnessing and how to find purpose and meaning in innovating within new ecosystem environments. We'll delve deeper into this in the upcoming sections on ecosystem management. But one thing is clear: Agile methods have been outpaced in the last years by more intelligent, interactive, and collaborative innovation ecosystem settings. However, this does not negate their efficacy in conjunction with robust project management, particularly within the domain of information technology.

Acting agile where it makes sense!

Yet the best answer on how to work agile came from a very high-ranged manager of Tata Company, India: We are agile where we need to be agile!

Meaning that it only makes sense when we understand the benefit for the specific application.

Chapter 3
Industrial Challenges and Academic Theories Start Dancing a Tango

From Open Innovation to Adaptive Innovation Ecosystems

As an innovator, you've got to make sure you don't fail, change quickly when you have to, and get the right people involved in innovation and change.

After everything we have heard in the first two chapters, may it sound almost impossible?

In this chapter, we will talk about how dealing with an ever-changing environment can be addressed.

The main story is about our journey from a separated incubator in 2003 to the implementation of an Open Innovation Network from 2012 to 2018 and how we've evolved into the innovation ecosystems we see today.

After all our efforts to build a high-performance product development organization, I felt disconnected from my true passion for innovation and making a meaningful contribution. It just wasn't in line with my vision or purpose. The foundation of an incubator for new ideas and product innovation that we named i-LAB was our answer to connecting the outside world of technology with internal capabilities of creativity and development.

After learning how to ask for ideas from different parts of the company, as explained in chapter 2, we had to think about how to support this huge source of creativity. The company's founder believes that *if we support each other, we can take care of our company and our families in the future.* So, how can we take this culture and move it forward into the 21st century, where information technology is starting to change our working environment and knowledge is more available on a global level? And let's not forget the upcoming opportunities from virtual support through platforms and information technology. After extensive discussions with over 20 direct reports during my product development phase, it became clear that many of them and their teams were eager and capable of contributing their full potential and creativity to our ambitious goal of a successful and thriving company. We devised a method called the employee cultural dialogue. We tried it out, and it ended up becoming a regular part of our leadership culture.

The half-year employee cultural dialogue soon became a regular part of our leadership culture.

It always started with a chat about the highlights, and it always included feedback on the highs, the lows, and personal motivation. This built a personal connection be-

https://doi.org/10.1515/9783111448329-004

tween the leader and the team member, which laid the groundwork for good solutions for the next parts of the performance review, setting performance goals, and behavioral development. I'd say the idea to implement an incubator lab was a direct result of listening to the ideas of and wishful thinking for a future organization that could continue the success story of innovation and growth that came from those involved persons directly: The amazing team members from the design, product development, technology, and prototyping parts of the organization that I had the honor to lead into the next evolutionary step. I felt like the next step for me should be more creative work on new inventions instead of repeating the same ideas and hiring new staff. So, I started working on some plans for a new organizational move. After I came up with the concept, I showed it to my boss, Mr. Helmut Swarovski. We made a few changes based on his ideas and vision, and then we started the project in 2003.

The i-LAB experience

We started an incubator group with seven people from these areas, called it i-LAB, and started outside the company's existing boundaries, but not too far away. I think it was a good idea to move into a rented office space outside the company's premises but within a few minutes, walking distance so as not to lose contact with the existing organization. We defined our own process for the creative sourcing of ideas, their internal social exchange, and the integration of internal idea providers into an early incubator team.

At the same time, we have got all the company's departments involved in an innovation network.

Our approach was cited in Robert G. Coopers' 3rd edition of his famous book Winning at New Products.[14] Back in 2005. We quickly realized the potential of this creative approach, but we also had to improve our ability to find and focus on the big bets and abandon the nice, promising ideas. We started hearing a lot of criticism, and it was clear that we weren't connected directly to the product development team. We took on this challenge by creating and putting in place an innovation network based on self-organization and decentralized leadership. During this time, we connected a bunch of new product groups and product management teams, which was a big step up. It was clear that everyone had to support the network approach because the resources for product development were directly tied to the portfolio of the product line architecture. On the other hand, the technology and central research departments operated overarching. The fight for resources and prioritization wasn't ideal, but the network approach was useful right from the start.

---

14 Robert G. Cooper, *Winning at New Products: Creating Value Through Innovation* (New York: Basic Books, 2000), 160–161.

As a manager, the most important lessons for me were on one side learning to lead a group of very diverse people from very different areas like design, technology, prototyping, marketing, and research. And on the other side, a deep confirmation that the key to innovation and change is fostering better collaboration across different disciplines, cultures, and ways of thinking.

One story that is worth sharing in this book is how we have been inspired by Walt Disney.

The inspiring influence of Walt Disney

From my time leading the product development and design departments, I knew that when a new business takes off, there are always leaders behind it who made bold decisions. These leaders have a strong inner compass that guides them. They've got values that are set in stone, and they've used those values to get real results.

Walt Disney, the great storyteller and innovator, is my favorite role model for how creativity and business results can be combined.

Walt Disney was my role model. He was a great storyteller and innovator who combined creativity and business results. I was a fanatic reader of Disney's comics as a child, and I was an admirer of his idea of an experimental prototype community of tomorrow (EPCOT Center). I first read about this vision at nine years old. In 1983, I was part of the Swarovski music band. The band was started by the company's founder, Daniel Swarovski, who encouraged employees to play music after work already in 1901.

The Swarovski family initiated a trip to celebrate the 10-year anniversary of our Tokyo sales office. We also went to Disneyland Tokyo for two days. We were granted a day off and received a special card from Disney to use and learn about all the amazing installations. I was completely overwhelmed by this experience, and it was a very early turning point in my career in innovation. It combined creativity and engineering. This vision, 20 years later, fueled my ambition to delve deeper and draw inspiration from Walt Disney. That's why I read everything that I could get my hands on about the management aspects of his life. By fortune, at the same time, a family member of the Swarovski family, Markus Langes-Swarovski, gave me a book named "The Walt Disney Way," and we started conversations about the contents and their relevance to our company. Exactly amidst this discussion, the i-LAB was commissioned by our technology leader to visit the **California Institute of the Arts (CalArts)**. The private art school located in Valencia, California, was founded in 1961 by Walt Disney and his brother Roy Disney as a merger of the Los Angeles Conservatory of Music and the Chouinard Art Institute. The institute is known for its interdisciplinary approach, combining visual, performing, media, and literary arts under one roof. We collaborated for 2 years, provided internships for 2 students in Austria, and worked on small promotional "crystal figurines introduction animation movies" that have been shown in our shops. When I spent a week at the institute, I could feel the spirit of Walt Disney, especially during the evening sessions when experimental musicians, animators, and dancers met in the center of the institute to freely perform and create. It's a great example of emphasizing experimentation, individual mentorship, and creative collaboration, encouraging students to explore and push the boundaries of their artistic practices. Disney used the term "cross fertilization" for this kind of work. At the institute, there was a lot of information available on Walt's working methods, especially his color model. He used different colors to represent different feelings, like blue for calmness, trust, and stability; yellow for optimism, joy, and playfulness; red for passion, urgency, and courage; and green for growth and harmony.

In this time, we more and more ran into some major problems with our creative internal development when we tried to speed up the process of coming up with new ideas and quickly making prototypes with the whole i-LAB team. This was because of different ways of thinking among the engineers, designers, and prototypers. We realized we could improve by using the color scheme of Walt Disney, so we came up with our own way of assigning colors to different rooms and combining them with rules for communication and interaction. Otherwise, the team was at risk of breaking apart. At this point, we had already tried out Edward de Bono's Six Thinking Hats. It's a method that encourages looking at problems from different perspectives by "wearing" different colored hats, each one representing a different way of thinking. We just mixed both methods.

We worked as a team and quickly found a solution to our internal team tensions. It turned out that the designers and engineers had different approaches and thought processes when it came to problem-solving. When the designer is dreaming big, the engineer might come up with phrases like "that will never be possible" early on, and vice versa. The designers will love to stay in their creative dream phase as long as possible. So, we decided to dedicate four different rooms of our offices to specific colors and mindsets. We even set rules for how to communicate in each room. For example, the yellow room was all about creativity. Everything is possible in this room. No criticism, just support and encouragement to keep going. In the red room, everything was up for discussion. In the blue room, we talked about the detailed questions and tech issues. In the green room, everyone was on the same page and helped each other out to get the project done fast and in a new way. Any new project or question that came up from either the main business, the top management, or our wide-ranging idea development from the employees we sent through the rooms. Sometimes these ideas came from folks all over the organization, and we made sure to give them a chance to bounce ideas around.

As we got more familiar with the rooms, we started to see more and more how this respectful involvement of all mindsets helped create a creative and powerful culture that boosted team performance. After a year, the colors weren't needed anymore, and the color pictures could've been taken out because the team figured out how to work with different mindsets, no matter where they were. It was really inspiring to see how each team member's motivation evolved. The more we've all learned a lot about personal development, like how to improve our social skills and understand our thought patterns better. We've also learned how to be more open to new ideas and approaches, which is important for teamwork. In short, it helped us get into the mindset of adaptability and innovation.

My biggest learning on a personal level was that I could apply and evolve Disney thinking by living with a mindset open to diversity and continuous growth. This approach allowed me to identify my own natural leadership style. I could still improve by focusing more on team performance and being a supportive leader who encourages change, rather than a leader who makes all the decisions.

On the corporate level, Walt Disney also had another big learning in store for us. The intensive exchange on the book *"The Disney Way —Harnessing the Management Secrets of Walt Disney in your Company"*,[15] brought us closer to an interesting part of our innovation philosophy. There's a theory in management that a company's innovation DNA is shaped in the first years of its existence. But is this still true for a company that's been around for over 110 years?

In *The Disney Way* the authors describe the basic Disney's core philosophy as: "DREAM – BELIEVE – DARE – DO." They say that these principles serve as an inspiring guide for making dreams come true. Dream big, believe in yourself, be courageous, and take decisive action!

Thinking about the first days of the company, we immediately recognized that the basic DNA of Swarovski was held within the basic innovation principles of "Explore – Experiment – Deliver." In other words, be open for the new, experiment with it, and apply it to your own business field, in our case fashion and jewelry. What we learned from Walt Disney's approach about dreaming encouraged us to dare the bigger dream. During my first visit to the EPCOT center in Florida in 1995, I found a soap on my bed with Disney's quote: *"You can do it if you can dream it."* This was exactly the right "add-on" for the i-LAB incubator and the right time to implement it, directly reporting to the CTO.

An Innovation Network That's Guided by Soft Leadership?

The question of whether a diverse and decentralized organization can be powerful, fast, and manageable is still in our days a much-discussed topic. Today we know that

---

15 Bill Capodagly and Lynn Jackson, *The Disney Way – Harnessing the Management Secrets of Walt Disney in your Company* (New York: Mc Graw-Hill, 2007).

this is possible but hard to realize. What we do need and what we have to learn on a broader level will guide our thoughts in the next sections.

The Implementation of a Soft Governance Model based on networking principles

The global movement of goods, services, people, information, and knowledge enabled and accelerated by the digital revolution in the late '90s and early 2000s undeniably increased the complexity in businesses.

To manage this complexity, new capabilities were required to deal with change, risks, and uncertainties.

It was a challenge to facilitate knowledge sharing and collaboration within organizations while also capitalizing on external benefits from new technologies and industrial best practices. The existing structures and behavioral mindsets could not meet this challenge.

I was fortunate to meet Dr. Doris Wilhelmer, an innovation researcher at the Austrian Research Centers, who was working on her PhD thesis. She invited me to join her experimental group on complementary, systemic innovation methods. By experimenting with different settings, I gained a comprehensive understanding of the dynamics of innovation from an external perspective. My *insights grew with every meeting in the experimental group that met in Vienna.* I quickly recognized that the key to solving the complex challenge lies in the principles of how networks can be implemented, governed, and used to achieve specific, overarching goals in complex systems.

The ability to adapt to changing environments and improve overall performance by leveraging collective intelligence and fostering continuous learning was the ideal side effect. This proved to be the biggest win in the following years of intensive collaboration and systemic intervention into our organizational structure.

It was clear that this approach would require new organizational frameworks and continuous leadership learning. Making it work in an organization was undoubtedly one of the most challenging and rewarding experiences of my career.

A complete description of this development was published in 2010 in the book "Realizing Open Innovation" in German language.[16] An English version of this organizational intervention, that was designed and accompanied by the Austrian Institute of Technology (AIT) with Dr. Doris Wilhelmer as Innovation researcher and Dr. Klaus

---

16 Hannes Erler and Doris Wilhelmer, "Ein neues Paradigma – Mit Netzwerken Innovationsprozesse steuern," in *Open InnovationOpen Innovation umsetzen – Prozesse, Methoden, Systeme, Kultur,* ed. Serhan Ili (Düsseldorf: Verlag Symposion, 2010), 225–270.

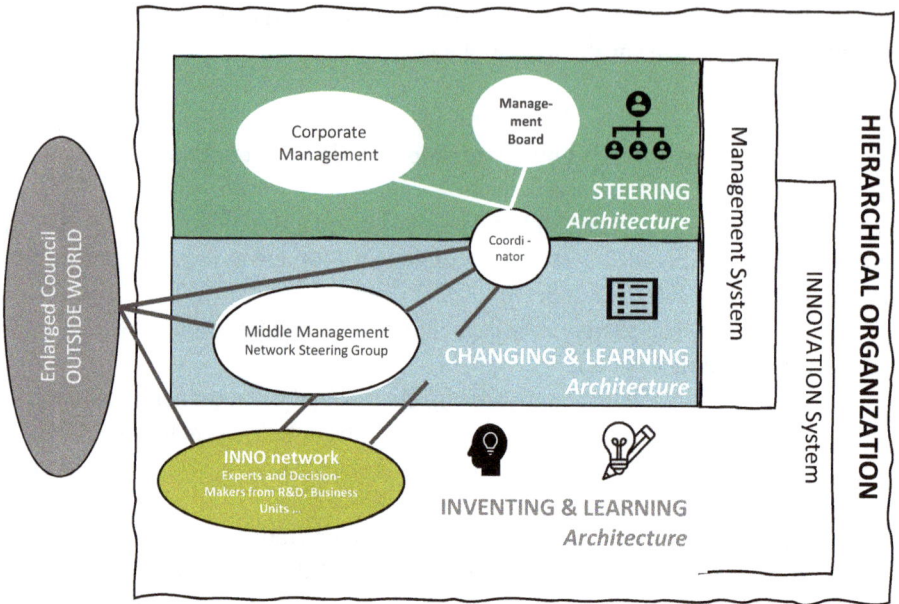

Figure 4: Interaction of Network Steering Modes and Hierarchical Organization.
Based on Dr. Doris Wilhelmer, The Swarovski INNO Network.

Schulte in his role as Organizational Psychologist was published in a conference paper later.[17]

Thanks to the visionary skills and highly professional special knowledge on innovation, networks and consultancy we built a governance framework that involved a few hundred different internal innovative minds that have been driven by the founders' spirit that was traditionally called intern the "Swarovski Spirit".

The development of the "Soft Governance" approach started with the identification of communication gaps as a critical issue. Subsequently, we recognized the necessity to intertwine the business functions, leading us to establish a steering group and appoint innovation managers within each business unit. This strategic move underlined the assumption that, despite having a centralized innovation group, innovation initiatives were to be predominantly driven within the business units themselves. A

---

17 Wilhelmer, Doris, Johannes Erler, and Jeff Zimmerman. "Innovation Network – An Integrated Organizational Structure for Organizational and Management Learning." In *Leadership Learning for the Future*, edited by Klaus Scala, Ralph Grossmann, Marlies Lenglacher, and Kurt Mayer, 2013.; Doris Wilhelmer, Hannes Erler, and D. Holste, "Innovation Network – An Integrated Organizational Setup for Management Learning," *paper presented at M/O/T 2010 – International Conference on Management Learning,* 2010.

steering group emerged as the pivotal entity and facilitated extensive communication across the organization, ensuring optimal but not excessive exchange.

At this phase of organizational development, these initiatives significantly enhanced our capacity to convey market insights and critical inquiries to the technology-oriented divisions such as research and development and technical development. The I-Lab was both an incubator and a facilitator, while the steering group functioned as a soft tool to enhance communication. The I-Lab incubator was instrumental in consolidating overarching technological advancements, maintaining unified budgetary oversight, and fostering external collaborations with Research and Development entities and internal and external contributors. It also provided strong support to idea originators, allowing them to work on their own visions.

This framework remained effective for seven years up to 2012, fostering double-digit growth until the global financial crisis of 2009. Despite the economic turmoil, the established network demonstrated resilience by emphasizing the enduring nature of networks rooted in a shared purpose, unaffected by shifts in management or hierarchical structures. This resilience was a significant takeaway from this period.

Especially during the mentioned period of global crisis, the "INNO network" approach not only remained stable in its strategic orientation but also enabled it to adapt very fast to the changes in market and customer requirements. And not to forget, it enabled us to bring brand-new technology integrations on a regular basis.

The enduring nature of networks rooted in a shared purpose can strengthen resilience because they stay unaffected by shifts in management or hierarchical structures.

The key success factors for this organizational intervention from today's perspective have been:
- The need for change to secure the company's future was clearly addressed.
- The solutions have been produced on the basis of the key principle of organizational systemic development: the affected people have been integrated into the development of solutions. The focus on continual innovation allowed Swarovski to adapt and succeed in a chaotic business environment. The concept of "zooming out" to see beyond immediate chaos helped to turn crises into opportunities.
- Empowerment of people to enable them to act as co-entrepreneurs, motivators, and shapers of organizational structures was negotiated with and allowed by the existing hierarchical leaders because they have always been informed and kept in the communication loop of the network activities.

The interdependencies of all innovation actors have been clearly addressed through the network activities and fostered organizational learning at high speed. Like shown in figure 4. Both at management and individual leadership levels. The role of the network coordinator, who was democratically elected by the innovation actors, was a critical point in the evolution. As I was this person, I had to learn how to balance personal interests, support of the key steering group, and selling the approach to the hierarchical leadership colleagues.

We made sure to set up the network to fit the company's needs, and that was key to getting the budget and support. We also benefited from the fact that networks are different from traditional hierarchical structures because they encourage long-term cooperation and communication based on trust.

Next Level of Open Innovation – "The Königsdisziplin" of Innovation Practices

The Open Innovation network period

In 2012, a significant restructuring took place, leading to the decision to reorganize for innovation and to discontinue the i-LAB and the integrated network setting. It's natural for such incubators to fade after a while as organizations evolve. We have shown a structure that works, but it has outlived itself. It has paved the way for a next-level, better, and focused approach to innovation. It was time to use new communication technologies to embrace the evolving world of Open Innovation and crossover company networks.

This was a very transformative phase because we had to open our technological insights to the public for the first time. After extensive discussions, we have devised a strategy that focuses on our needs rather than our methods. We defined five search fields and introduced them to the industrial and research communities. I discovered these fields overnight in my new role as Director of Innovation Networks. This was made possible by a group of conference producers who invited notable figures from various industries to participate in unique conferences held in exciting global locations. It's clear that these meetings have provided spaces for exchange and learning from best practices, and they've also evolved into spaces for experimentation and inter-organizational social development. At the beginning of this movement, cross-industry participants were cautious about openly discussing the new experiences with open settings. Over time, however, an unwritten rule evolved: It's beneficial to discuss how new processes are benefiting the bigger industry network, not just a single company.

My new colleague Graham Hench was the perfect strategic fit for this new approach. His tremendous experience establishing and managing networks for researching new technologies was a perfect fit for our new strategy. We spoke with over 150 companies and developed more than 80 Open Innovation business opportunities. Each business opportunity included a description of at least one or two external partners who had identified a technological competency that enabled a new innovative product solution when it was transferred to our world of fashion. We gave over 60 speeches at these conferences, and it's been incredible to see the types of companies, people, and tech fields we've connected with after introducing our innovation philosophy, our search areas, and how we work with our OI partners. We achieved this by strategically refining our customer relationship management (CRM) tool to align with the principles of Open Innovation. We replaced the customer with the OI partner, the product with the business opportunity, and the way to collaborate was based on a clustering of interest matches. The match was based on the nature of the opportunity and the different interests of the technology providers. Are they a start-up, a mature company, a technology broker, or an established business model based on technology licensing, sales, or implementation?

We gained more and more attention in industry expert areas. We were honored to receive the "Best Open Innovation Award 2017" in the "Best Open Innovation Network" category from Zeppelin University of Friedrichshafen, led by Prof. Ellen Enkel.

Now we have our connection to the internal networks and the external world of technology and organizational findings. But we knew that Open Innovation in the days of unlimited open access to knowledge and people could not only be done by a small group of hand-picked people working in the new open style. That insight led us directly to the next challenge. We dissolved the OI department in 2016. Why? "Those who are not ready to set out for new shores are at risk of paralyzing limpness," Hermann Hesse writes in one of my favorite poems, "Steps." Now my job title changed from "Director of Open Innovation Networks" to "Director of Innovation Ecosystems."

Innovation Ecosystems—The Answer?

This was exactly the next level of operation and enabled both internal and external development of networks for the subsequent eight years. The main takeaway was clear: you can't just talk about innovation and networks. You must take the lead and guide through the different development phases. You must use the ecosystem of people and technology opportunities to put together a dedicated ecosystem with shared goals and motivation. And you always must deliver results in the form of tangible innovation projects concurrently to the enabling processes and settings. This transitional period is described in another publication that we wrote with researchers Justyna Dabrowska, Henry Lopez-Vega and Paavo Ritala in 2019.[18]

You can't just talk about innovation and networks. You must take the lead and guide through the different evolutionary phases of innovation ecosystems.

With that, over time, the innovation network transitioned into a flexibly adjustable innovation ecosystem.

---

18 Justyna Dabrowska, Henry Lopez-Vega, and Paavo Ritala, "Waking the Sleeping Beauty: Swarovski's Open Innovation Journey," *R&D Management* 49, no. 5 (2019): 775–788, https://doi.org/10.1111/radm.12374.

The case study on waking up the sleeping beauty

The case study describes our move from a centralized Open Innovation approach to an organizational model that allows subcultural ambidexterity to overcome the "rigidity trap" on many levels. We saw that the ambidextrous organizing principles of exploitation and exploration are closely linked to Open Innovation. While we didn't know how to implement them, we were intrigued by the idea and knew it would help us evolve. Changing the focus between exploitation and exploration is a logical stream in all innovation processes. Those who have dealt with such processes know that every creative action requires a convergent opening-up-to-everything phase and a following divergent focusing phase. Every single one! Our network revealed numerous examples in companies, but there were no descriptions or identifiable patterns to guide us in aligning on an organizational level. In the context of organizational transformation, our collaboration with professors interested in examining how mature firms can overcome organizational rigidity by undergoing a transformation to Open Innovation using organizational ambidexterity mechanisms was a very valuable opportunity to better understand the logic behind it and to react accordingly.

Our strategy defined the challenge, but the question remained: how to encourage the broader organization to Open Innovation, tapping into the collective intelligence of diverse communities worldwide, amplifying creativity, and accelerating the pace of innovation? Continuous learning and close feedback loops among the meanwhile unified departments in a brand-new R and I (Research and Innovation) organization were still an open issue. Our initial findings from the preliminary processes were very encouraging. Transcending geographical boundaries and organizational silos empowered many of us to adapt to the new leadership and innovation model. Effective collaboration remained crucial, however, and demanded a disciplined portfolio approach that respected the different natures of early and Open Innovation models. Systemic and ambidexterity issues had to be addressed. The new ecosystem soon had to deliver by encouraging the free flow of ideas, promoting interdisciplinary collaboration, and facilitating networks of innovators.

Especially the fact that advancements in technology and digitalization provide so many unprecedented opportunities for global collaboration, the role of virtual communication platforms, data sharing networks, and advanced analytics was crucial for success. The empowerment of innovation drivers was critical and an organizational challenge, especially to enable them to collaborate seamlessly across borders, overcoming the natural logistical barriers to cooperation in a still hierarchical organization.

The most motivating factor during this period was the proximity to networks and the rapid pace of technological changes that we observed in real time. This clear vision of the future increasingly forced us to trigger and align the collective efforts of all innovation drivers. Only a spirit of cooperation, trust, and shared purpose can be the driver for such innovation approaches.

Only a spirit of cooperation, trust, and shared purpose, together with the strategic definition of the 'Problem to Solve' can be the driver for powerful innovation ecosystems.

Collaboration between governance and non-governance institutions, companies, and universities was the key to addressing global challenges and fostering positive change. But breaking down barriers, pooling resources, and leveraging technology to accelerate the pace of innovation is always an art and a science. The vision of a prosperous future on a broader scale was forcing us to constantly improve on both an organizational and management level.

Chapter 4
The New Importance of Collaborating in Dedicated Innovation Ecosystems

In the former chapter we have spoken about how to transform our cultural roots as living beings into the innovation ecosystems area. And as already explained earlier in the book, an innovation ecosystem always must know a common purpose that is supported by most of the ecosystem participants, and it brings together the possible contributors within a shared framework.

In order to understand the real value and tremendous potential of modern innovation ecosystem models, we have to take a look at the origins of the concept of ecosystems.

Innovation Ecosystems vs Natural Ecosystems

Ecosystems, whether natural or industrial, are intricate networks that thrive on interconnectedness, competition, and collaboration. In natural ecosystems, an array of plants, animals, and nonliving components like rocks and water coexist in a delicate balance. These living entities often compete fiercely for resources but also engage in remarkable cooperation—like bees pollinating flowers, a relationship that ensures mutual survival and benefits the broader ecosystem.

In the past decade, the concept of "innovation ecosystems" has surged in popularity, especially in industries like IT. Unlike their natural counterparts, innovation ecosystems are purpose-driven arenas where businesses, technologies, and stakeholders unite to tackle specific challenges. These ecosystems aim not for survival but for progress—driving economic growth, creating novel products, and achieving collective goals. They are strategic by design, with participants motivated by market leadership, profitability, and societal impact.

While natural ecosystems evolve gradually over millennia, adapting to environmental changes like a slow-moving river carving a canyon, innovation ecosystems are dynamic and ever-fluid. They respond rapidly to the swift currents of technological advancements, constantly reshaping strategies to stay ahead. Both systems, however, share a core principle: interdependence. In natural ecosystems, every species plays a vital role in maintaining stability, like a spider weaving its web to catch prey while contributing to the food chain. Similarly, in innovation ecosystems, each participant—from researchers to policymakers—brings unique expertise that strengthens the collective framework.

To harness the full potential of innovation ecosystems, it's crucial to understand the roles of their participants. They can be categorized into two groups: those who delve into exploring and creating knowledge, akin to adventurous trailblazers charting new territories, and those who focus on delivering results to customers and driving financial outcomes, much like skilled merchants bringing treasures to eager markets. Success in this realm requires a fine balance between fostering creativity and achieving economic objectives.

In conclusion, both natural and innovation ecosystems are fascinating constructs that thrive on interdependence, competition, and collaboration. While their purposes and mechanisms differ profoundly, they share an underlying rhythm that drives adaptation and success. Natural eco-

https://doi.org/10.1515/9783111448329-005

systems narrate a tale of survival and instinct, while innovation ecosystems offer a dynamic story of strategy, growth, and shared human endeavor.

The latest findings about how modern innovation ecosystems can be implemented successfully are in the publications of Dr. Bernd Lingens from the University of St. Gallen, together with Oliver Gassmann and Veronika Seeholzer. Their paper is excellent and encouraged us to find our own ways to organize for such innovation ecosystems.[19] Researching multiple projects in various industrial areas gave us plenty of examples, encouraging us to think bigger than we thought from an internal perspective. This is another great example of topics starting very primitively and then being developed into something useful.

We must tackle tough issues like climate change and social and economic inequalities. To do so, we must act globally and make the most of the data available to us, such as that from the UN Sustainable Development Goals. Some researchers are calling this a "poly-crisis." Innovation ecosystem thinking is a key part of the solution to this challenge. We must join hands and work together towards collective progress.

It's crucial to recognize that innovation doesn't guarantee positive change.

Improving cooperation among innovation drivers is the key to a brighter tomorrow and a more prosperous and sustainable global society. Researchers are speaking of a human crisis of disconnection. We must understand the implications of our actions to feel connected and reduce anxiety. We must delve deeper into understanding the sustainability challenges and simultaneously grasp the significance of the inner dimensions of our lives. We must offer a balanced mix of cognitive, emotional, and relational practices to nurture transformative capacities and foster a deep connection with self, others, and nature. This is the only way to solve the phenomenon of disconnection. Collaborative, action-oriented approaches are crucial elements of the course. They ensure that inner development work aligns with tangible impacts in everyday life and work contexts.

We must offer a balanced mix of cognitive, emotional, and relational practices . . . .

Innovation is the cornerstone of human progress. Its potential is amplified when different actors come together. However, it's crucial to recognize that innovation doesn't guarantee positive change. To understand the interdependencies, we must look at modern challenges through the lens of inner development factors and the necessity of

19 Bernhard Lingens, Veronika Seeholzer, and Oliver Gassmann, "The Architecture of Innovation: How Firms Configure Different Types of Complementarities in Emerging Ecosystems," *Industry and Innovation* 29, no. 9 (2022): 1108–1139, https://doi.org/10.1080/13662716.2022.2123307.

integrating personal development with collective and systemic change. I am convinced that we can and must take control of our destiny and shape the change we want to see in our reality. We must no longer let others dictate our fate; we must become the actors in our own lives. My personal answer to this challenge is a basic Open Innovation Model, which I developed over my Open Innovation network period and which I use in order to develop and drive positive changes.

Trying to Find the Balance: Ecosystems of Business and Science

Business and science must be integrated, and the best way to do this is by using our findings on how to drive Open Innovation—remember the WFGM model of Prof. Slowinski. This brings us back to the ambidexterity issue. To successfully navigate the worlds of business and research, we must embrace both open and closed thinking, or ambidexterity.

I laid out a clear plan for doing so in my letter to the industry, which was published in the Journal of Innovation Management in 2017.[20] I previously described this model and explained its efficacy in the current era of pervasive knowledge and opportunities.

Our network approach has brought us new findings about ecosystem dynamics and the transformation of design thinking and agile development methods. What most of these methods have in common is a divergent and a convergent phase that allows one to think boldly and broadly on the one hand and to recognize priorities and enable speed on the other hand. But industry logics are very different from theoretical settings, as there are complex organizational factors at play that encompass diverse cultural and subcultural behaviors. The challenge for our Open Innovation Networks approach was to find ways to manage diversified networks of connections that blur boundaries, collaboration, and interdependence, thus characterizing the real logics of modern innovation ecosystems.

We had excellent results using the WFGM model. We made the switch from one mindset to the other over time, and it was the right decision. It is essential to remember that we must speak the language of the corresponding representatives of the phase. The overall model shown in figure 5 is self-explanatory. It shows that we start in the business ecosystem environment (1), where we meet people who know how to bring innovation into the world and have a more exploitative mindset. With these insights, we transition to the science ecosystems realm, where we encounter individuals who are driving innovation and knowledge creation (2). With an explorative mindset,

---

20 Hannes Erler, "Why the New Logics of a Connected World Affect Traditional Innovation Structures from the Bottom Up – and the Role of Open InnovationOpen Innovation Networks & Ecosystems in Finding Proper Answers," *Journal of Innovation Management* 4, no. 3 (December 19, 2016): 7–11, https://doi.org/10.24840/2183-0606_004.003_0003.

THE NEW LOGICS OF INNOVATION ECOSYSTEMS

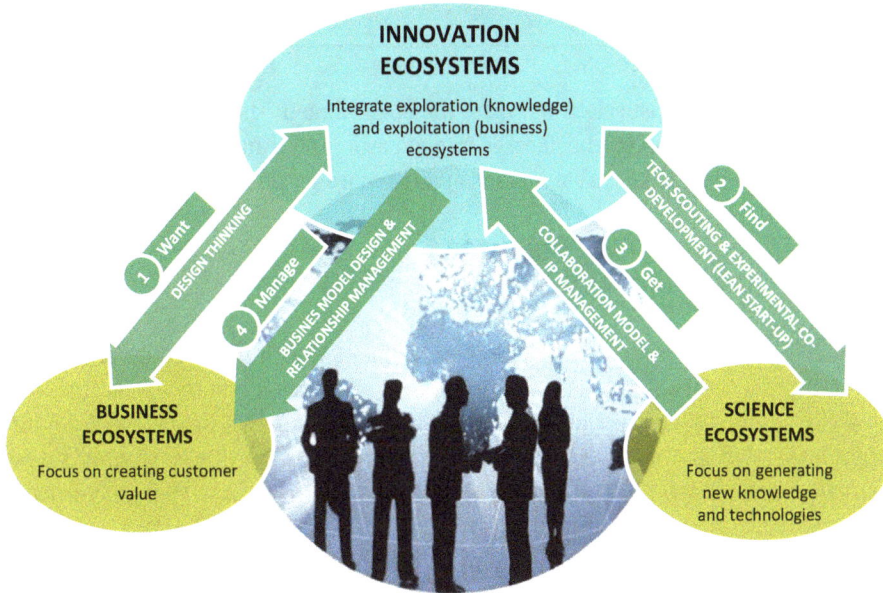

Figure 5: Connecting Business and Science Ecosystems within a model of dynamic iteration and feedback loops.

we start first experiments and discussions and try to fail smart with small experiments and learning loops. We also try to understand what collaborations could look like. Once we have sufficient insights to define the innovation and potential collaborative development pathways (3), we define our business model in an exploitative mindset (4) and transition to the scaling-up phase of our innovation.

It is clear that industrial experiences must provide data and management learning, and the circle of empirical and theoretical management learning is essential for developing new solutions and answers. The integration of Design Thinking, the Lean Start up Model from Eric Ries, the Business Model Canvas from Prof. Oliver Gassmann, and "Jobs to be Done" from Clayton Christensen demonstrates that industry logics are distinct from theoretical ideal settings because they encompass hundreds of people in different organizational settings, including diverse cultural and subcultural behaviors. These processes cannot simply be transferred 1:1 into an organization. However, the fundamentals of application models remain.

Closing the circle between empirical and theoretical management learning is essential for developing new solutions and answers.

As practitioners, we must select and train the optimal methods for each challenge. As we venture beyond our core businesses into adjacent and transformative innovation, we must strategically orchestrate methods with a more profound comprehension.

Adaptive Leadership and Right Time Messaging

After the different stages of creativity and experimentation, it is important to not miss this clear point where the general mindset must change from a more explorative to a more exploitative thinking. These phases of implementation and impact ask for a different leadership and management style. I described it as the PONR (point of no return) already in chapter 2. The appropriate Leadership Style has to change now from AKI (Aspirations and Key Insights) to OKR (Objectives and Key Results).[21]

In today's fast-paced world, traditional ways of doing things often get left behind as people look for ways to break free from restrictive structures. In the past, people used to leave because of their bosses not giving them enough free space for their creative path. Nowadays, people are more likely to leave because they don't have the chance to grow personally or to use their ideas, beliefs, and educational skills in new ways. This is probably one of the biggest challenges in innovation. We really need to tackle this head-on, and I'm confident we can find solutions. The thing is, when you're just starting out, you've got to encourage people to explore, fail, and learn quickly. Then, in the next phase, we have to tell them that failure isn't allowed because we're now transitioning from engaging with to serving customers. It's not always easy to know when a change is needed. But a good innovation process makes sure this happens and decides who's responsible for what.

The thing is, when you're just starting out, we've got to encourage people to explore, fail, and learn quickly. Then, in the next phase, we have to tell them that failure isn't allowed because we're already interacting with customers.

If an organization wants to be forward-thinking and adaptable, it needs to embrace the shift towards a new model of leadership. This new, adaptive leadership style

21 Alexander Osterwalder, "Rebells and Pirates will be hung up," *Die Presse*, February 28, 2023.

means adapting messages to different people at different stages of development. At the same time, it's important to mentor newcomers and support them as they grow. We should also empower more experienced team members to take on challenges on their own and find their own paths. If we don't understand this "Ambidexterity Trap," we can't come up with the right solutions.

Chapter 5
Ambidexterity

It is a given fact that we can't act in different mindset modes at the same time. In his book "Brain Research for Managers," the German brain researcher Ernst Pöppel writes that in an organizational context a company must realize both the principles of exploration and exploitation but manage them separately.

The German brain researcher Ernst Pöppel writes that in an organizational context a company must realize both the principles of exploration and exploitation but manage them separately.

So, when is it time to move from Explore to Exploit? "When you understand the customer's problem. When there is evidence that it might work."

This is also known as "organizational" or "contextual" ambidexterity. In production-related areas, which are geared to "exploit" mode from their outset, it makes sense to switch to "explore" mode from time to time. This allows us to get new ideas and developments on track and not miss out on changing customer and technology environments.

Building such an environment that encourages professional innovation is a big challenge for companies these days. Especially when we talk to young managers in different industries, it doesn't seem like they're feeling very optimistic.

No matter what your role is—whether you're a senior manager, have a hand in innovation, or are pushing for change at any level of the company—please think about your influence, your responsibility to encourage real, widespread innovation, and how you can speak up about your concerns, including the tools you have to voice your concerns about systemic issues.

I've always been of the mindset that you should love situations, change them, or leave them. If I wasn't sure what the right answer was, I found that drawing a simple triangle helped me by making me think about it in a different way. Do I really want to pursue this? Am I the right person to do this? And finally, do I have the right skills for the job, or do I need some help?

Especially in complex scenarios where coordination of the communication flow and transparency are important in order to overcome systemic biasing of the involved people, these questions help to find orientation.

We as well can take inspiration from Alexander the Great and the way it is told he solved the problem with the Gordian knot. He combined his passion for battle with strategic thinking to solve the Gordian knot by using a combination of partial destruction and division.

We can see destruction as more of a Joseph Schumpeter concept, where you take existing resources and capabilities and put them into a new and adapted setting.

https://doi.org/10.1515/9783111448329-006

This analogy really captures the situation many companies find themselves in, where they're investing a lot in short-term gains but losing out on long-term innovation and talent. Think of a greenhouse where future food crops are grown. Would you leave broken glass panes in a greenhouse? They're essential for maintaining a good environment for growing things. If you don't do this, it shows you're not committed to the future. These days, it might seem like a good idea to cut back on funding for the front end of innovation, but a responsible manager would never completely dismantle it.

Innovation is always about gathering different types of information from many different areas, including the humanities, the natural and engineering sciences, art, and everyday life. Thinking about the future means to think about what you think it will be like. The many forces, processes, institutions, and power relations that make up our world must be seen as a continuation of modernity.

This means that we have no other choice than to indispensably cooperate with the inevitable aspects of modernity—and in most of the cases these aspects are not determined by us.

But one aspect is very clear: Responsible companies nurture responsible mindsets. In our days that can't happen without respecting our planet.

Establishing Planet Centricity

I was profoundly influenced by TV scientific fiction series like Star Trek during my youth. The way the Starship Enterprise explored the galaxy was truly captivating. Exploring unknown places and different cultures to gain knowledge for the benefit of civilization—all made possible by amazing technologies like teleportation, faster-than-light travel, and materializing objects out of thin air—fueled my ideas about the future. This science fiction story made me think about how I could contribute to a future where intrepid explorers discover new worlds. Being like serendipitous pioneers, returning with new insights that enrich life on Earth for generations to come. Daydreaming about such a role in my own life opened my eyes and made me realize that relentless innovation and a consistent drive for research have driven human progress and will continue to do so in the future.

I was also really affected by the Club of Rome in the late 1960s and beyond when I was a young engineer at the engineering school in Austria. This experience showed me that engineers must do more than just crunch numbers. They need to become agents of change who can imagine, act, and innovate to create a better world—one that's multi-dimensional and puts humanity at its core.

In parallel to the insights gained from the Club of Rome's early publications, I found resonance in a quote by Ortega y Gasset that underscored the intertwined nature of technology and human progress. Although the exact wording eludes me now, the essence of his message emphasized the imperative for technological advancement to be paralleled by advancements in human development, suggesting that true progress cannot be achieved through technology alone but must be intricately linked to human advancement.

It would be harmful, especially considering the current state of our world, where numerous challenges demand our attention and action when we take the wrong turns and risk destruction and chaos.

This book aims as well to function as a channel for individuals to reconnect with their fundamental aspirations and personal narratives. It seeks to facilitate learning, encourage introspection, and guide readers towards embracing new perspectives, respecting others, and navigating obstacles with convincing courage. Planet-centricity thinking is a no-brainer of all future innovation approaches. Corresponding values must build the guardrails for finding the right decisions, and they are described in detail in part III of the book.

The Horizon Framework

We already took a look at Geoffrey Moore's "Zone to Win" approach, which suggests thinking in four different zones to handle both short-term wins and long-term, breakthrough innovation at the same time. This approach is only recommendable for mature organizations with a high level of innovation management knowledge, experience, and structure. And it needs the full commitment of all levels of management. In practice this very often is not the case. With the standard classification of short- and long-term innovation topics in the form of the "3 Horizons Framework," the integration of ideas into both existing and new business settings is much easier to understand and to communicate within organizations. And it is somehow a standard in communicating within a company over spanning networks.

What is it?

The Three Horizons Framework is a strategic planning model that divides growth strategies into three distinct clusters, each with its own focus and timeframe.

We used the model, like shown in figure 6 especially to protect long-term thinking for breakthrough innovation from short-time implementation pressure and dirty corner cutting.

The model is very simple and easy to understand:

- **Horizon 1** describes all ideas and developments that **support the existing core business** and can be implemented with existing resources, processes, and routes to the markets.
- **Timeframe: Typically, 1–3 years.**
- **Horizon 2** is about focusing on **identifying and nurturing new opportunities that complement the core business**. But in most cases, they ask for integration of new technologies, services, or development partners.

- **Timeframe: Usually 2–5 years.** Activities: Launching new product lines, expanding into new markets, or developing new services that build on the existing business.
- **Horizon 3 is the long-term goals focusing** on transformative opportunities and groundbreaking innovations.
- **Timeframe: Typically, 5–12 years**. Pursuing disruptive innovations, entering entirely new markets, or researching/developing new technologies that could shape the future of the business.

The Three Horizons Framework helps not only to balance short-term operational needs with long-term growth ambitions, but it also represents a professional standard in Open Innovation processes when companies share ideas. Especially when future-oriented workshops of two visionary-oriented parts of a company meet, it is important to label the discussed ideas with the expected time frame. For instance, when we met with a famous German car manufacturer that invited us to participate in a future-oriented workshop with a time horizon of 4–7 years, we have been happy to open our portfolio. As a result, we defined 3 visionary horizon 3 ideas that found their way into a collaborative path, starting in 2016 and building a good new business today.

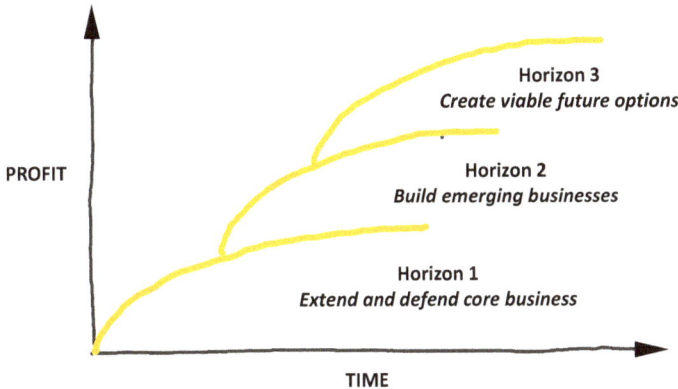

Figure 6: Thinking in 3 horizons for clustering short- term and long-term innovation.

It also ensures not to become too focused on immediate gains at the expense of future innovation. By categorizing goals across these horizons, defining resources, and embedding them into the portfolio structure, it is a very easy method to communicate and balance short-term and long-term innovation and development.

The model's implementation allowed our innovation network to dedicate Horizon 1 projects to direct business product development, Horizon 2 projects to shared budget allocation among different businesses, and Horizon 3 projects to the company's family board for long-term strategic thinking and innovation.

It is clear that making the logic visible to the different innovation actors in the entire company had another positive effect. People knew exactly what was already planted, how to nurture it, and what conditions were needed for it to flourish. Another effect is that the organization learns how ideas develop over time and how positive futures might be created. And one very important point that is rarely discussed openly in organizations: How to make space for the new, finding ways to degrade what is no longer fit for purpose and set resources free for the defined priorities.

Research on innovation shows that this capability is a cluster of behaviors that are deeply embedded in the processes and policies of the organization. Again, it's not like there's one right way to do it. The 3-horizon model will help to adapt dynamically.

Our evolution from the centralized model with the i-LAB incubator to the decentralized model with the Inno network always followed the necessary (gap-oriented) change to deal with given economic situations.

It was a difficult experience, but it again proved that things can change from simple to complex and from useful over time. In our case, it took more than 20 years.

The Role of Power Teams

I want to emphasize the role of teams, particularly the pioneering experience, during my time at Harvard Business School. I have always sought to achieve the "Power Teams" effect.

And over the last 25 years there was a book that never left the nearest place to my desk chair. As the study of the book "High-Performance Teams" written by Jon R. Katzenbach and Douglas A. Smith belonged to the preparation work for the mentioned training in Harvard.[22] I studied it very deeply, right at the time when I took over responsibility for several teams in the product development and design area.

Since I started working in product development, I've noticed that having the right team and investing in these principles are key to innovation and performance.

Let's take a closer look at these principles and my evolving understanding, because in today's world, where so many things are happening virtually or even in immersive ways, it's important to consider what we're at risk of losing when we lose the positive psychological and motivational measures of working in truly physical and humane teams.

---

22 Jon R. Katzenbach and Douglas A. Smith, *High Performance Teams* (Boston, MA: Harvard Business Review Press, 2016; originally published 1995).

Effective teams are usually between 5 and 12 members. This allows for effective communication and collaboration. Like experienced within the i-Lab team, high-performance teams, or let's call them better "power teams" comprise members with a variety of skills. As they are small, effective communication and collaboration are possible even because of their different skills and mindsets. Setting the right framework for listening to each other (remember the Walt Disney approach mentioned above) allows the members not only to perform on their original functional expertise but also to explore and to extend their competences to problem-solving and decision-making skills or interpersonal skills.

It is of the highest importance that the team members have a clear vision of their common goals and the purpose of their dedicated innovation target. In the best case they have been part of the forming of the team and the development of the shared purpose. This inspires their best work and helps them to stay focused and motivated. If the members are involved in decision-making processes, communication methods, and roles and responsibilities, they hold each other accountable for the team's performance. This creates a sense of ownership and commitment, even in critical phases of their projects.

In the world of literature, these types of teams are often described as "real teams" with these attitudes. I've found that sometimes these groups are just teams with a specific goal in mind and a shared commitment to achieving it. The main thing that sets high-performance teams apart is that they meet all the criteria for a great team, but they also bring a lot of energy, enthusiasm, and commitment to the table. That's what makes the difference when you need a high output in complex situations.

Katzenbach and Smith are describing the life cycle of such high-performance teams happening in five phases.
- Forming: The team comes together and starts to understand the goals and tasks.
- Storming: Conflicts and challenges arise as team members begin to work together.
- Norming: The team starts to develop norms and cohesive working relationships.
- Performing: The team reaches a stage where they can work efficiently towards their goals.
- Adjourning: The team disbands after achieving their goals.

This shows that such teams can't exist forever. As soon as their mission is somehow completed or over because of changing framework conditions, they fall apart or simply lose motivation. I remember the early days of forming our i-LAB team and setting it apart from the existing organization. Robert G. Cooper predicted that such incubators would not survive more than 5 years, and one high-class innovation executive stated that in his company he would give us not more than 3 months.

Our described integrative approach with the integrative innovation network as a "broker function" in the organization helped us adapt to changes and crises, survive over a period of 9 years, and pave the way for the opening up of our innovation eco-systems journey.

The main learning on the level of teams and their embedding into the organizational framework is undeniable in the area of agility and adaptability: Such teams can quickly adapt to changes and tackle new challenges efficiently, making them invaluable in dynamic environments.

I want to mention that from my experience power teams only work when their core participants are dedicated at a level of a minimum of two-thirds of their full working capacity. Otherwise, it is difficult for them to feel a full belonging to the team and be motivated enough to go the extra mile in innovation.

Finally, I want to come back to the work of Professors Wheelwright and Clark that I mentioned in chapter 2. From the four types of teams that are always to be defined according to the degree of innovation, power teams, in my experience, need autonomous team status. That means that they need to meet on a different home base at least 3 days a week. If they can't keep working in the same place, they need a dedicated team room so they can have their own way of doing things. That includes how they communicate and their own special ways of having fun, working together, and getting things done. In these situations, they tend to be the most self-directed, so they just need upper management to define an innovation question and allocate a budget. Wheelwright and Clark call these types of teams "autonomous teams."[23] They're the best when it comes to speed, innovation, complexity, and entrepreneurial spirit. The only problem is that it's not easy to get the team members who were temporarily working together to go back to their old jobs.

Remember: No matter if you go for functional, lightweight, heavyweight, or autonomous teams. You've got to balance the decision with how much change you expect. Either way, teams and people are always worth it. You should give them the best environment for development on both the project and their personal evolution levels.

It is not just about bringing different people together and creating a space where they can learn and adapt; there is other evidence for the role of teams in providing learning opportunities at the organizational level. So, let's now jump one level higher, from the team level of considerations up to what Peter Senge is calling the "Fifth Discipline." Senge strongly refers to the essential challenge of creating learning organizations and how to achieve it. Senge states that at the heart of learning organizations are great teams[24] built on trust, relationships, acceptance, synergy, and results:

> *It's great at learning, adapting, and changing in response to new realities. It can switch up functions and departments when needed, either because of changes in the work environment or because*

23 Lateral Works, "Fast Autonomous Teams," *Lateralworks.com*, January 17, 2019, accessed May 27, 2025, https://lateralworks.com/ideas/2019/1/17/fast-autonomous-teams.
24 Senge, Peter. *The TFD Field Book: How to Proceed to Build Learning Organizations.* Crown Currency, 1994.

of poor performance. A learning organization has a few key traits. It's got a culture of learning, a flexible and experimental spirit, a focus on its people, a commitment to continuous learning at the system level, a culture of knowledge generation and sharing, and a critical and systemic way of thinking. When we look more closely at the development of such teams, we see that people are changed, often profoundly. There is a deep learning cycle.

And now, with the arrival of the AI revolution, with the arrival of great methods to hold virtual meetings across the planet, and with people performing best when they are alone with their trustful connections to the digital world? Do we need to rethink how we learn to create learning organizations? Absolutely.

But, from what I've seen on our own learning journey, team members naturally pick up new skills and abilities that change what they can do and what they understand when they're part of a high-powered team. As new capabilities emerge, so do new ways of seeing things and new sensibilities. As time goes on, people start to see and experience the world in new ways, which leads to new beliefs and assumptions. This helps people develop their skills and abilities even more. And this, in my opinion, is the deep learning cycle that is endangered if we lose the personal interaction in virtual replacements. We must understand the principles and embrace new leadership styles. This is a lot of work. Senge was clear: development involves more than just cultivating new abilities. It also entails fundamental shifts in mindset, both individually and collectively. I know that the key to constantly re-initiating new learning cycles lies in our abilities and our success in providing culture, budget, open processes, and, most importantly, a new understanding of power teams built of responsible, connected entrepreneurs. I see weak signals getting stronger, and I know we are at the dawn of a new type of Homo sapiens. I've chosen to call this type of man *"Homo Innovaticus."* When this type of person gets started, the resulting innovations inevitably lead to changes that are significant and long-lasting. The idea that the world is made up of separate, unrelated forces must be replaced by a sense of shared purpose. We must collaborate. Our survival depends on it. We must give every human being a chance to live a meaningful life.

The i-Lab team was my best experience of a power team that I have experienced in person. We transformed it into a team that respected the diversity of its members and knew how to enable collaboration over its own and organizational restrictions. And at the same time, the more we spread this subculture of trust, openness, and mutual support across the organization, the more the people that have been involved in that network have found confidence and motivation to contribute to the bigger vision. As well, Peter Senge's description of such power team places is very clear on that point: it's a space where people expand their capacity to create the results they truly desire. Here, new and expansive patterns of thinking are nurtured. Collective aspiration are set free. People learn how to learn together. Are we in our days, 20 and 30 years after Senge first revealed his visionary but profound insight, nearer to such a vision? My answer is both yes and no. Yes, because I believe that our new tools and insights have increased our desire for a better world. No, because I see too many examples of leadership setbacks that are contradictory. These setbacks only focus on short-term achievements instead of investing in strong, lasting structures.

Let's keep it positive. Today, we're undeniably more connected, more complex, and more dynamic. Even new Harvard research emphasizes the critical role of leadership that fosters a sense of safety through inclusivity, transparency, and support. *"Psychological safety is essential for innovation, learning, and employee well-being."* Harvard Professor *Amy C. Edmundson* makes this clear in her new book, *The Fearless Organization.*

And not to forget, we've got AI, which gives us better knowledge at a faster rate and lets us "discover" and "disassemble" things that were never seen before. So we can go for new "experiencing and learning journeys." The alliances that will truly excel in the future will be the ecosystems of innovation and change that provide learning and "places of togetherness" at all levels of human interaction. We can truly collaborate, and this will keep improving because deep down, we're all part of the same tribe. Like the kid who's always curious and loves a good challenge, we're all natural learners and adapters. Infants don't need to be taught to try new things and learn. They're naturally curious and learn quickly, picking up how to walk, talk, and pretty much run their households on their own. We can learn and experiment because it's in our nature and we love to do it. That's exactly why I've come up with a new innovation process—to make sure we start with this belief and joy!

Escaping the Ambidexterity Trap

We hear a lot now about the "ambidexterity trap," the challenge organizations face in balancing exploitative and explorative activities. And it is always one of the biggest management tasks to optimize current operations and innovate for future growth.

In Chapter 2, we explored "Zone to Win" by Geoffrey Moore, which outlines the strategy of organizing businesses into four distinct zones. We also examined Eric Ries's "Startup Way," which emphasizes the crucial need for modern companies to adopt entrepreneurial innovation as a key part of their operations. We also recall Clayton Christensen's assertion regarding the challenges faced by large corporations in navigating the ambidexterity trap, or more precisely, their inability to effectively leverage it.

In the realm of innovation, adapting organizational structure according to a systematic approach inevitably creates new challenges. Our described systemic organizational development process presented opportunities for innovation mainly through our Open Innovation Networks approach, in addition to strategic changes in the company's future orientation. The primary challenge, therefore, was to enhance the strategic business's reorientation while concurrently sustaining the long-term strategic innovation projects with reduced resources and budgets. Fortunately, the new Company Campus in Wattens provided a communal space for employees from various departments, facilitating collaboration and innovation. The new campus facilitated "activity-based working" and provided an environment conducive to enhanced and expedited communication, collaboration with customers, innovation networks from within and outside the company, and rapid prototyping in the recently established manufacturing facility.

We gained significant insights from the "Lean Startup" experience. We followed the approved route that combines industrial experience with management research theories. Geoffrey Moore and Eric Ries have shown us the way.

Michaela, our former VP of Human Resources, took over responsibility for a transformation office in 2018 as part of a systemic intervention. This office temporarily controlled the innovation group within the company. It was not clear where to best anchor the innovation team, and there were multiple organizational adaptations to be executed. The innovation team's cross-functional and cross-hierarchical operations made this a natural move for them. It quickly proved that top management made the right decision to position the team at this higher level. The innovation team was now able to support long-term projects that haven't been dedicated to single product groups. It also allowed the business leaders to engage in strategic directions for the team. Today, it is clear that driving change from the human side of innovation was the right move. We implemented a "growth board logic" that helped us focus on a balanced portfolio of seven innovation projects, which we ran concurrently with business product development projects. We implemented a Growth Board according to the recommendations of "The Startup Way." This board included the SVP of Marketing, the SVP of Operations, the head of the Transformation Office, and appointed project leaders from different areas of the company. These leaders were supported by their functional leaders and shared budgets for growth. The portfolio included projects that represented the future strategic battlefields of the businesses, based on breakthrough visions and technologies. It also included the elected innovation programs of the innovation teams, provided by network collaborations and innovation networks. The portfolio kept a few empty spaces for fast-track interventions to address unforeseen threats to the businesses. My role was straightforward: I designed the framework, provided training, and fostered understanding of the process. I also coached the project leaders of the programs that we gave the role of entrepreneurs. We called them not only program owners but also "startup CEOs." As a senior manager, I was responsible for protecting project leaders from organizational barriers and threats of resource or budget cuts. I ensured they possessed the entrepreneurial culture and awareness necessary for success.

We held quarterly meetings with the SVP of Marketing, the SVP of Operations, and the Head of the Transformation Office, who was my functional leader. The agenda was defined by three questions.

1) What have we achieved (Status Report)?
2) Where does the team need support to speed up, and how is top management expected to take action?

3) What are the next steps and the next funding (metered funding) that we need from the organization?

We operated with metered funding for every program by keeping a basic budget line in the yearly planning but with the option to shift or adapt in the course of the progress of the program. The term "metered funding" was new to most of us. But we quickly got the value of this expression and really understood it. When you're just starting out and innovating, you can't really map out the exact steps ahead. Sometimes it works out. Sometimes you've got to make tough calls. If you set the budget too low, you risk failure and slow progress. But if you set the budget too high, you (and your managers) will probably run out of support from the financial side. No matter what, managers who handle budgets never quite understand why you're off the mark with your budget predictions, and they end up losing trust in your abilities. So, it's better to be straightforward and handle it with metered funding. Meaning that you negotiate the budget according to the new situation and findings. I distinctly recall one meeting where the SVP made a statement about the estimated market launch of a very important product feature that was highly requested by our customers: "Two years from now for implementation? That's unacceptable. That is far too long." The project leader, who had a deep understanding of the technology, the realities in the departments, and the best way to accelerate, returned with a plan to significantly reduce the time to one year.

The SVP immediately decided to put more resources and money into the project. On the other hand, this helped us to kill one other project with an argument everybody understood: We simply do not have more money available in the innovation budget basket. This is the best proof of concept that such settings work. As it was top management making the decision to shift more resources into this customer-oriented core project, this fact immediately elevated the project leader to a powerful role. The project leader returned to the project team with the critical questions, and the team fell in line with the push from top management. In traditional settings, such decisions risk being subjected to lengthy and exhausting debates that stifle the entrepreneurial spirit of the project drivers. It frequently results in the wrong projects.

This is the only real-world example I've encountered that proves the exploitation and exploration principles in one setting by providing:
- Sufficient protection of entrepreneurial programs from existing business paradigms
- Ensuring that the leadership has the insights and control points to stand behind the budget financed by today's businesses.
- Provide decisions to the entire organization by overcoming the seemingly unsolvable contradiction of letting people work on the explorative mindset and at the same time keeping the core business on track of exploitation and stable promises for the customer.

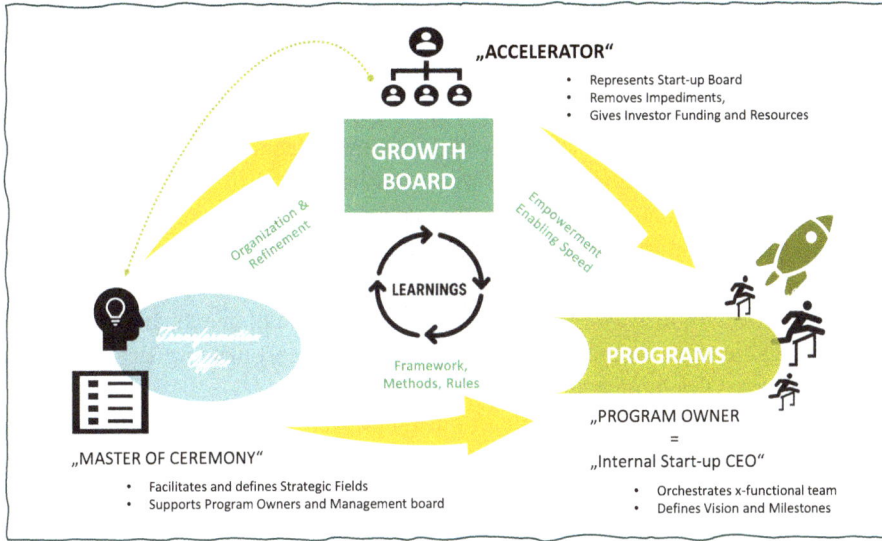

Figure 7: Interplay of Growth Board–Transformation Office–Hierarchical Organization.

Here is a simple overview of the system that was used and is shown in figure 7:

The most important findings from this managerial period were clearly in the addressed area of

- A unified vision of the leadership team that balancing short-term gains with long-term innovation is possible and needs to be communicated effectively throughout the organization.
- Fostering a culture that values both efficiency and innovation is possible and helps to encourage employees to embrace change and to see failure as a learning opportunity.
- Implementation of adaptive processes that allow for flexibility and include agile frameworks that can pivot quickly based on market feedback and internal discoveries.
- Promoting continuous learning and development within the organization.
- Developing balanced performance metrics and incentives that reward both exploitation and exploration efforts, or in other words, include innovation and operational efficiency.

The biggest advantage was that the first time we had found a manageable solution for breaking free from the ambidexterity trap and ensuring that through working with external start-ups, academic institutions, or any other partnership organizations, you can perform within your core fields and at the same time care for the future!

A rule of thumb that came originally from a private conversation with Henry Chesbrough and that I experienced as applicable in practice is about 80% of the budget and resources to be held in core field activities and about 10–20% in the future oriented activities. But as mentioned, this is always a decision to be made according to the actual strategy and circumstances.

The company faced some big challenges as the pandemic hit hard and forced them to make more changes, even though the money was tight. In the coming next phase, we needed to be quick on our feet and focus on growth. We had three main projects to work on, one of which was all about the digital glass process. It's worth mentioning that the three projects were based in different areas. One came from the earlier network and technology push initiatives; one came from top-prioritized marketing and customer insights—things like personalization and on-demand production—and one came from serendipity and from talking to start-ups and strategic allies during the recent Open Innovation network approach.

Our today's concept of "Dynamic Use of Innovation Ecosystems" can be seen as the logical answer to the necessary strategic adaptations in order to keep the brand relevant and attractive.

Changing Mindsets vs "Setting Minds for Change"

I will finish part one of this book by paving the way for the next part of our journey together. It is about a deeper understanding of the human aspects and things that rise above the everyday. The first part focused on perceptions as part of societal and organizational structures. It made it clear that we must commit to being more creative and smarter about how we define and use innovation ecosystems on a global and culturally diverse scale.

If we know that early human societies tried out different types of social organization and that inequality and hierarchy aren't unavoidable parts of civilization, then it makes sense to think about our time as a huge opportunity to overcome misguided developments. The findings from our organizational experiment with the soft governance of innovation networks fill my heart with faith in such a new leadership mindset that allows us to define innovation ecosystems that are based more on decentralized working mechanisms.

The more we try to understand how we ended up with the current world issues, the more we have to realize that we're more independent from our instinctive behaviors or mindsets than we realize on a conscious level. I think that to break out of these sometimes-harmful patterns, we need to be more aware of them and how they influence our thoughts and decisions in daily life. I'm especially interested in the systemic influences that were mentioned. Otherwise, we won't be able to achieve a new mindset, which I call a mindset of growth and change. The best way to apply the tribal principles we've brought with us from our evolution and that are deeply anchored in our inner minds is to learn how to gradually change different mindsets and learn how to switch into the thinking pattern that is most helpful for the situation. In short:

In a more adaptive and dynamic way. It's obvious that money isn't the only thing people think about when it comes to the future. We should also start thinking about whether the ideas of a Western capitalist society that are based on ownership and wealth should be reconsidered. We can mix them with other ways of thinking, like tribal experiences. We've got to figure out a way to make economic operations work for us without completely throwing out the rules of economic success.

Now it's time to come up with some new solutions.

Instead of seeing history as a straight line from hunter-gatherer societies to agriculture, then to complex states and civilizations, human history is way more diverse and creative than we thought. Let's be realistic. Change doesn't happen overnight. It happens through disruptive innovations, starting small and gradually impacting established domains. I'm convinced that research without any practical applications just ends up confusing us instead of moving us forward, socially or individually. Usually, only a few researchers get to use the insights gained. It's tough to get past 18% of early adopters and make the solutions useful to more people, in society or in a professional field. We should support the drivers of change in their daily lives.

My book is meant to support these folks in different areas who are tasked with coming up with practical solutions to the challenges of our time. We've got to understand where we went wrong and show how to do things right.

With the knowledge and practical examples from this part of the book, we can now create frameworks and dedicated ecosystems that allow us to shift into appropriate thought patterns within protected social structures, delineated by time and space, for specific periods. This helps us figure out the best way to develop and optimize performance for specific types of tasks and innovation phases.

We all know that the road to success often involves many hurdles along the way. As Antoine de Saint-Exupéry said, things evolve from the simple over the complex to the useful. But as speed and change continue to accelerate, many factors are at play. It's clear that traditional, centralized organizational models aren't suited to the early stages of genuine innovation. It's important that we understand and better integrate these phases. Otherwise, we might get stuck in these ways of thinking that we know from the past without realizing that the environment has changed and that the solutions from yesterday may be the preventers of a better tomorrow.

Things always evolve from the simple over the complex to the useful.
Antoine de Saint-Exupéry

The challenge with innovation is obvious. We look back to see our traces and learn, but we'll never follow the exact same path. The world around us is always changing. When I look back at my own journey, I realize I've learned a lot. But now, with a new perspective and framework, I see that today's priorities are different. If I could go back and make different decisions, I'd do it because the context has changed.

It's clear that we need a process that supports both learning from past stories and staying aware of current issues. It's key to bring these two aspects together to make the best choices for the situation we're in with the people around us.

It's time to take another look at Darwin's theory. The idea of "survival of the fittest" is pretty simple: The most adaptive survive. Those who can define the scenes in ecosystems and the rules of modern ecosystem theories will be the most adaptive ones in the future. In part III, we'll look at how this process can be done, even by people who aren't experts in innovation.

Part II: **The Philosopher of Reflective Practice**

Striving for Psychological Safety and Resilience Through the Understanding of Human Nature

It's great to hear: Psychological safety and resilience in all situations are what we must master in our modern world. Even renowned Harvard professors like Amy C. Edmundson are pointing out the importance of this topic in relation to innovation and growth. Is this even possible, or is it just an illusion that we need to nurture from time to time to survive psychologically?

Politicians and management are getting hit with some pretty serious accusations of weak leadership these days. This is creating an environment where extremist ideas and populist leaders are gaining traction. Laissez-faire and anti-authoritarianism are out. But what's the future of leadership going to look like?

If leadership is forced to act opportunistically and be short-term oriented, this leads to a loss of trust and uncertainty among people. The opposite of psychological safety.

When too much attention needs to be paid to political correctness, popular opinions, and maintaining power, the making of courageous and profound decisions gets nearly impossible.

Taking on leadership and being a driving force in our new world now needs a new and different approach. To succeed we need a way of thinking that is able, on the one hand, to cultivate the experience and our processual knowledge about cooperation of networks and ecosystems and, on the other hand, our firm belief that we can shape our own future. With courage and intelligence. With diversity and focus. With a strong belief in our personal strength and capabilities.

We must delve deep into the lessons of our own beliefs and values. Our cultural evolution and heritage can teach us to find solutions.

This second part of the book will address our human heritage and the critical role of values in guiding our actions. It is essential to reflect on our deeply human desire for spirituality to comprehend this view. And we must not have this dialogue without considering the profound changes that artificial intelligence brings into our lives.

The German theologian Karl Rahner once put it very aptly: "Modern man must be a spiritual man; otherwise, he will no longer be a man at all."

https://doi.org/10.1515/9783111448329-007

Chapter 6
Findings from Sociocultural Ecosystems—The Human Side of Innovation

As a young engineer, I was always super inspired by the technical achievements and masterpieces accomplished by countless masters and experts in their fields. This unbridled enthusiasm has driven my dreams and decisions. It was a long learning journey, and surprising threats forced me to go far beyond technical expertise and hard scientific facts. This chapter is dedicated to these surprising "non-technocratic" factors.

As said before, many failed innovations are the result of people not understanding each other and not engaging with each other. These failures are also the result of human mindset issues and systemic dependencies. When we look at what is being discussed now about the climate and political crises, it seems that we are in a crisis of how people are behaving. Why? Let's together look at a few stories from my professional life.

Stories about innovation always show at least one part dealing with how people act in society and culture. Successful innovation is influenced by the rules of the organization, people's personal experiences, and their desire to take risks and make changes instead of feeling helpless. One of the main causes of failure is a lack of social skills and poor abilities to listen and cooperate.

Within such framework conditions, it is no surprise that highly educated young people entering their new jobs have a hard time creating new things. It's a lot to take on. There are so many models, success stories, and approaches to consider, which can be overwhelming, and most importantly, do you know any exact same innovation story that could give us a clear measure? In recent mentoring interactions I met young people who have learned everything about different models but often don't know how to choose the right one for the situation. They might not even know where to start. We must remember that many success stories sugarcoat the long, hard, and uncertain road to success. Frankly, it's too confusing to understand or even to learn from. I often was forced to go down paths I never thought I would go, and I learned procedures I never thought of at the beginning. I encourage the reader to be part of this development. As a practitioner, I will share the small, simple principles I have learned. I will also discuss the surprising connections between different areas of life that help us to understand these principles. I'm sure that just listening to these stories without feeling pressured to find solutions will also spark something in you that will help you deal with your own challenges.

It must warn her again that using methods without understanding the big picture can lead to big mistakes. We can and will work confidently when we understand the innovation question and the solution is obvious. But when problems are complicated

https://doi.org/10.1515/9783111448329-008

and unclear, and the situation is always changing, we can't depend on just one method. Choosing the right way of working is often a mix of art and science.

The true impact of innovation is not just in how it disrupts things but also in its ability to inspire hope, unlock new possibilities, and catalyze positive change across systems.

It seems that embracing the future with resilience and a new emphasis on foresight skills, supported by artificial intelligence, could be a fruitful approach, but it is important to consider that this may only be effective if the human factor is at the center of every action. Looking at the findings from working with Open Space methods, the assumption is obvious that we already possess skills that reside in our unconscious minds and simply need to be rediscovered, refined, and reactivated. Could the answer to this question lie in studying the systemic intelligence of the natural tribes that brought us into the 21st century more in-depth? I think that even if some skills are not as important as they used to be, there are some basic ideas in our genes that can help with change. It's good to understand the new drivers of change, like AI. But it's also important to value the old, proven drivers of change that provide stability and psychological safety. Most importantly, we need to trust our systems and our actions.

An innovation can't be considered an innovation unless it has a minimum impact and distribution in the world. Otherwise, it's just an ordinary invention with no meaning and impact.

If that's the case, we should consider a new approach. Why don't we develop a new version of the Stage-Gate model to accommodate innovation and change in the AI and collaborative ecosystem era? This question will guide our journey together as we work through examples and gain valuable insights.

At the end of this part of the book, you as the reader should be alert for looking not only at the technology and process insights but also at the many human and systemic factors.

Embracing Innovation Without Fear

One prerequisite for innovation that is in the blood of every true innovator is a certain type of mindset. People who really live for, with, and through constant innovation by embracing change and improvement in every situation, continuously cultivating and developing it without fear of failure, have this prerequisite in common. A good description for this type of mindset I have found in the fabulous book „Mindset: The New Psychology of Success„ by Carol S. Dweck.[25] Her book describes how this

---

25 Carol S. Dweck, *Mindset: The New Psychology of Success* (New York: Ballantine Books, 2006).

mindset can be understood, and the good message is that it can even be trained and cultivated. After decades of research, she, the world-renowned Stanford University psychologist, discovered a simple but groundbreaking idea: the power of mindset and the different appreciations that we can develop. She shows how success in school, work, sports, the arts, and almost every area of human endeavor can be dramatically influenced by how we think about our talents and abilities.

Carol is telling a story about her work with children and an experiment that she did at school. She tells about how she brought children one at a time to a room in their school, made them comfortable, and then gave them a series of puzzles to solve. The first ones were easy, but the next ones were hard. As the students worked hard, she watched their strategies and asked them about their thoughts and feelings. She expected differences among children in how they coped with the difficulty, but she saw something that she never expected. When faced with a tough puzzle, one ten-year-old boy sat down, rubbed his hands together, smacked his lips, and said, *"I love challenges!"* Another, sweating away on these puzzles, looked up with a pleased expression and said with authority, *"You know, I was hoping this would be informative!"* What's wrong with them? Carol wondered. She always thought you coped with failure, or you didn't cope with failure. She never thought anyone loved failures.

Carol further describes that people with a fixed mindset—those who believe that abilities are fixed—are less likely to flourish than those with a growth mindset—those who believe that abilities can be developed. Mindset reveals how great parents, teachers, managers, and athletes can put this idea to use to foster outstanding accomplishment. This concept of fixed and growth mindsets showed how our beliefs about intelligence and ability shape our behavior, motivation, and resilience. Individuals with a growth mindset view challenges and setbacks as opportunities for learning and growth, while those with a fixed mindset may be more concerned with proving their abilities and avoiding failure.

One of my personal key insights when reading the book is as well that people with this type of growth mindset believe that a person's true potential is unknown (and unknowable); that it's impossible to foresee what can be accomplished with years of passion, donkeywork, and training. In dealing with different types of colleagues in the innovation context, it was always one of my strongest success feelings when I could motivate somebody to go for an extra mile in innovation and when he or she needed extra motivation to believe in an unexpected solution from somewhere. And when the point of succeeding was achieved, they said, *"I would not have thought that this was possible!"* Like the boy who said, *"I love challenges!"*

When we realize that challenges are one of the main reasons we're here on this earth and that they help us to better understand ourselves, our planet, and the people we work with, we suddenly will be connected to an energy source that is of universal nature. I remember a presentation from our Paris-based trend agency where the thought leader kicked things off with this statement: *What do people really want? They want to experience their lives in all the different things they do.*

The works of the German sociologist *Dirk Baecker* provide further evidence for this fact. He states that institutions, marriages, friendships, and so on are here to solve problems that we would not have had without them. The challenge is what drives us forward and forces us to develop outstanding and new solutions.

When I read Carol S. Dweck's book, I immediately understood why I always was the way I was, and I felt really understood. I've always been one of those curious people who are always trying out new things. But sometimes, such people can be a bit boring for their environment, and that's something we always should be worried about. It is important to act on this natural behavior when it makes sense. But we have to learn to let go of it when other behaviors are more appropriate. For example, when it's time to start the more exploitative phases of scaling and going to market in an innovation process. As an innovator, you have to learn how to switch mindsets dynamically during different phases of innovation. An integrative innovation process at the end of this book will help make it happen.

We know that human qualities, like intellectual skills, can be developed. So, I think that kind of evolution of transformative skills is possible. And through that, we can get smarter about finding our meaningful contribution to the innovation game.

There is the famous notion of *Albert Einstein*, when he was writing to his friend Carl Seelig in 1952, *"I have no special talents. I am only passionately curious."*

It's clear that people who have a growth mindset like to explore and learn about the world on their own. They want to experience life and develop their own knowledge. They figure out how great and unique they are by building on shared experiences and tackling big challenges together. They simply feel comfortable like fish in water.

If that is true, why should we then waste time proving over and over how great we are by showing what we have achieved when we could be more energetic, full of life, and motivated by embracing the journey of exploration and ideas as the way of life itself? This means that the more we go into this "I know" behavior, our brain is getting the information that there is nothing new to discover. If we give up this thinking, we are open to learn and be astonished by everything that comes to us.

My book aims to support this mindset—a positive drive for all situations we encounter. It gives those often seen as ineffective dreamers a better standing, emphasizing the fundamental principles of ambidexterity. These principles are often overlooked or misused for short-term gains, but they hold immense potential across various contexts. No matter if you are an innovator by nature or a powerful realist or someone able to dynamically adapt to what's best for the current situation. During innovation development, both skills must be heard and balanced. A good process tames natural capabilities and strengthens complementary skills for everyone.

Of course, as innovation drivers, we naturally prefer a mindset of growth—others never would take the risk to fail. I recommend that we learn to do both and to switch consciously between both. Then we are in the good position to find the right language for the situation and to get better connected with our ecosystem partners.

Chapter 7
The Spiritual Dimension of Innovation

Spirituality, in its complex and multifaceted concept, has always played a significant role in my personal development.

I always had the feeling that there is something that is standing behind my quest for personal growth and a deep understanding of existential questions such as "Why am I here?" and "What is my purpose?"

Exploring answers to these existential questions is one of the biggest adventures and transformative challenges in life. I've chosen to incorporate this element into this book about innovation and change. I am certain that only people who have access to their inner beliefs and inner motivation can develop outstanding and meaningful ideas and bring them to fruition.

As stated above, we need a flourishing society where we can find opportunities to experience ourselves in social interaction if we are to find meaning, orientation, and purpose. We all need to figure out how to prioritize our personal goals and our deeper inner beliefs that make our lives meaningful. The sharing of experiences fosters mutual learning and contributes to the advancement of skills. This phenomenon is a rational progression in the course of human evolution. Storytelling is our natural way of acquiring knowledge and preparing for the future. It is how we always learned and still today learn about the world and find new solutions for a prosperous future.

As I am living in the Alps, surrounded by mountains, walking in the mountains on my own has taught me that the contact with the mental-spiritual dimension is nurtured by the nearness to nature and learning from nature. Nature can be harsh, inhospitable, and dangerous. The mountain does not wrap people in an all-round care-free package but rather demands a lot of hardship from them. In literature, art, and film, higher mountain places appear as places of mysticism and romance; their majestic appearance triggers humility and reverence. Climbing a mountain with great effort needs the development of foresight, recognizing connections, and gaining a more comprehensive perspective. I always have used these metaphors in order to perform in the context of innovation and transformation.

Spirituality as "The Inner Driver" Beyond Religion and Secularity

From an early age, I discovered that spirituality isn't confined to religious rituals or limited to a single belief system. It's a profound connection that traverses boundaries, offering a unique path to personal growth and fulfillment. For me, spirituality transcends organized religion and weaves itself into the fabric of life through independence, reflection, and depth.

https://doi.org/10.1515/9783111448329-009

Over the years, I have encountered spirituality in countless forms, each one contributing to my growth and self-awareness. These moments of connection have enriched my emotional well-being, guided my ethical values, and illuminated a sense of purpose that drives me forward. To me, spirituality is the divine spark within—a vibrant energy that fuels my beliefs, ignites joy, and inspires moments of unwavering motivation.

Looking back to that time, I must say that without the integration of spiritual practices into my daily life, my personal development journey would not have been beneficial enough to find meaningful fields of activity, peace, and a deeper connection with myself and the world around me. There were many life-changing experiences, but one of them was so powerful that it represents spirituality itself. It still inspires me today.

That experience, which I found in the beauty of nature and a personal challenge, was one of those rare encounters that had a deep and lasting impact on me. It showed me how spirituality can appear in the simplest moments. It's a connection to something greater that fuels our drive to grow, to aim higher, and to embrace life fully.

It is about how the mountains taught me a sense of spirituality and respect for nature. It was during my adolescence, on a serene summer day, that I experienced how the mountains could imbue a deep sense of spirituality and respect for nature. Around the age of 12 or 13, I often spent my summer vacations with my family on a Tyrolean "Alm" at an elevation of 2,000 meters. My father worked for one of the largest Alpine farmers, who followed age-old traditions of managing pastures in the high mountains. These days were marked by solitude, where I often wandered alone, lost in my thoughts and daydreams inspired by the books and films of the early 1970s. One day, while atop a mountain summit, about 2,700 meters high, I gazed at the majestic peaks surrounding me, and the vast panorama filled me with awe. I even noticed a rare jumbo jet flying at that altitude, its unmistakable four condensation trails marking its path. These moments of solitude fueled my adolescent dreams of becoming a test pilot or a chief engineer, building cutting-edge airplanes or the fastest cars. It was during these musings that I decided to pursue an education in mechanical engineering in Innsbruck.

I was enjoying the peace of my surroundings when the bleating of a sheep abruptly interrupted my thoughts. The sound was strange, given that the nearest flock I had observed earlier was several kilometers away. I followed the sound, driven by curiosity. I climbed down over rough rocks and discovered a young sheep trapped in a small, inconspicuous crevice, unable to free itself. The sheep was strong, but it was facing a slow and painful death without help.

I was determined to save the animal, so I pulled it up from above with my hands. I dug my hands into its wool with no tools but a stick and my vest. After considerable effort, I managed to pull it out. The sheep jumped up and stumbled away in search of its flock. I felt an overwhelming sense of purpose and strength, and a heroic greatness flowed through me.

This experience was pivotal in shaping my future career. I carry this oneness with nature and this drive to support life in all its forms with me every day.

Why We Can't Act Alone—Goodbye, Old World

Another lesson that was taught to me by unhappiness and pain was the transformation journey from a product development-oriented manager to a people-oriented supporter of integrative and systemic-oriented leadership.

In order to understand, I invite you to make a journey into the science of brain research. In German-speaking areas, very renowned brain researcher *Gerald Hüther* addresses exactly this challenge that I had to solve in one of his recent speeches that can be found on YouTube.[26] It deals with the aspect of becoming a free-thinking and emotionally independent and innovative person. This level, which he addresses, should not be missing in a book that deals with the aspects of innovation and change. It can be seen as a call from him to unfold our deep human nature by transforming our neediness into a new form of meaningful contribution to life.

In a time where personal worth is often measured by performance, status, or material wealth, his ideas offer a human alternative. He asserts that our actions, including our careers, consumption habits, and even our pursuit of recognition, are often a compensatory response to unmet inner needs. At the heart of his message is a profound question: *We must ask ourselves, are we living in alignment with our true human nature, or are we merely compensating for a deep longing to belong, to grow, to be seen—authentically, not superficially?*

Hüther states, "As long as I still feel that I have only satisfied my basic needs as a substitute—by shopping, by watching football, by making a career, or by earning money—and if I silence my basic needs, I will remain a needy person deep down." This resonates deeply with my own experience in the corporate world. In modern hierarchical structures, people are paid to fulfill specific roles defined by job descriptions and strategies. Their work becomes about compliance with predefined metrics —OKRs (Objectives and Key Results). In such systems, individual expression is often secondary, and recognition becomes transactional.

However, Hüther emphasizes that this pursuit of recognition—attention, influence, power—is not genuine fulfillment. It's a symptom of a society addicted to performance and praise, not one grounded in authentic human connection. His insight invites us to pause and reflect: *We should stop wanting something from others. We should try to think about how we can give something to others.*

---

26 Gerald Hüther, *"Wie Lernen gelingt – Gerald Hüther,"* YouTube video, 52:42, posted by "AKAD Bildungsgesellschaft," March 6, 2017, accessed July 28, 2025, https://www.youtube.com/watch?v= gbre5Hh2pvQ.

This shift, according to Hüther, requires a new orientation. Instead of seeking validation, we must focus on what we can offer—our presence, our creativity, and our ability to love unconditionally. *"Only someone who is no longer in need can do that,"* he says. This is not a romantic ideal but a call for inner maturity—a shift from external dependence to inner freedom.

In parallel, there is a growing recognition in the business innovation world of the limitations of traditional performance systems. Alexander Osterwalder, the creator of the Business Model Canvas, has himself pointed to the inadequacy of OKRs in early-stage innovation. Instead, he proposes AKIs—**Aspirations and Key Insights**—as more meaningful measures. This aligns with Hüther's thinking: Before we can create or lead authentically, we must understand what truly matters to us, what we deeply value—not just what we are told to deliver.

Yet this kind of understanding is not purely cognitive. Here, I believe the German word *"begreifen"* captures something that English lacks. "To understand" often stays in the realm of abstract logic. But *"begreifen"* means to *grasp with one's hands*, to internalize through experience. It's this kind of embodied knowledge that allows us to act with intentionality and depth. And this is precisely what distinguishes us from artificial intelligence. Regarding artificial intelligence, Hüther is crystal clear on this point: *"Machines have no needs . . . and because they have no needs, they cannot even develop an impulse to form an idea . . . They also don't have intentionality."* AI may outthink us, remember better, or process faster. But it cannot *want*, it cannot *imagine*, and it cannot *love*. These abilities spring from our needs, our lived experiences, and our capacity to connect with others—not just function efficiently.

In the age of generative AI, it is crucial that we keep technology human. We must not reduce ourselves to data-producing nodes in a machine-like economy. We must embrace our uniqueness: our desires, our creativity, and our messy but meaningful human processes. Keeping humans "in the loop" is not enough. We must remain in control, shaping AI development responsibly, with values rooted in experience and empathy.

Hüther's call is not just a critique of modern systems; it's an invitation to transform them. We must encourage and inspire ourselves and one another to unfold fully and live from a place of inner clarity, not external scarcity. Hüther's theory is clear: in that unfolding, we rediscover what it truly means to be human.

I would also like to mention my enlightenment seminar, which is a Buddhist-rooted method. I was part of a group of 20 people and at the age of 44 years. I knew it was time for me to indulge my craving for spiritual insight. The method is clear: for one week, no talking in the group. The only thing that happens is that you are asked, and you ask reciprocally of the others, *Tell me who you are.?* You search for answers. You should not be commenting on others' answers. I had a deep connection to my ego construct. After the week, I was surprised to see that a lot of my self-awareness was shaped by my environment and the obvious expectations of others. I encountered the psychological concept of "the authentic self," or the "true self," for the first time. This feeling of "this is really me" helped me in daily life in order to make clearer decisions and find guardrails and self-confidence.

Another story told by Gerald Hüther has stayed with me: *"A child is born as an authentic self."* He further explains that the child arrives in the world completely true to itself, untouched by expectations or the need to impress anyone. But soon enough, that child must figure out how to survive in a world that doesn't always reward authenticity. A world where people are often selfish, where fitting in feels safer than standing out. So, the child starts adapting. It builds what Hüther calls an ego construct —a kind of mask or structure designed to help navigate the world. It learns what gets praise and what avoids punishment, and slowly, that pure, authentic self gets buried under layers of coping mechanisms. These solutions are smart and necessary at the time, but they also take us further from who we really are. These words remind us that formative experiences happen *before* the adaptation fully kicks in— before the ego construct takes control. As we grow older, we respond to life from this constructed version of ourselves. Someone asks what we like, and the answer often comes not from the heart, but from the ego—the version of ourselves we've carefully built. And in most of the cases we don't even realize that the voice speaking isn't our true self.

My friend *Stephan Rothlin*, a Jesuit priest from Switzerland who works in China on ethics and economics, put it recently together by referring to the blessed Carlo Acutis very simply: *"We're all born as one-of-a-kind individuals, and we end up leaving the world as mere copies."* It's a haunting truth.

And then there's also the saying from Anthony de Mello, one of my favorite spiritual authors and admirable life coaches: *"Most people are born asleep, live asleep, and die asleep."* It hits the same note.

And again, when I was going through my midlife crisis and feeling unsure of things, I started to discover something real. Something tender. I got in touch with that little boy inside me—the one who used to feel pure joy just running around, exploring, and playing. And for the first time in decades, I didn't feel ashamed of him. I felt proud. Alive.

Another friend of mine, a priest and spiritual guide, once summed it up perfectly: *"You can't protect other people if you're only protecting yourself."* That's what I'd been doing for so long—protecting myself. My ego had been my armor. The more I dealt with these kinds of thoughts, the more I learned that true strength comes not from building walls, but from reconnecting with reality. Thankfully, I felt better and better on this path. I should also mention that taking this path means being fully committed to all parts of your life, including the people around you and the structural issues in your job and partnerships. You've got to make a decision about this. As *Gandhi* once said, *"Finding your inner truth can be tough: it's something only the brave can do."*

Now I began to feel like a true designer and innovator again when I turned my attention inward and started exploring my own nature. I discovered that supporting my colleagues—especially within the innovation network I mentioned earlier—can be incredibly motivating.

By helping others while also shaping my own vision for life, I reconnected with a deep sense of agency. I felt once more like the creator of my own path—and with that came renewed strength and motivation.

Chapter 8
From Rigid Systems to Inclusive Tribal Leadership —Eye-Opening Moments

I am coming back now to the "Open Space Technology" and Harrison Owen's impactful transformation of indigenous wisdom, or in this case I would rather call it *"humane know-how."* Because it is not just knowledge but something that touches the deeper needs of who we are as people. I never will forget the feeling of connectedness, wholeness, and fulfillment after 2 days of Open Space work with more than 100 people. The simple principles of the four rules and the law of the two feet are not only transforming the interaction during the conference, but they are also transformative for our mindsets in every human interaction. Why? They meet our inner needs and help us achieve wholeness. This is more relevant now than ever before. With all the information out there, it's crucial to make sure what you're seeing is relevant and true.

The printing press, invented by Johannes Gutenberg, changed everything. It made knowledge accessible to almost everyone in the world. The process of adaptation took almost 400 years, which is about 12 generations of humans. Technology changes so fast these days that social behavior changes a lot in one generation. The truth is that a lot of modern inventions make people adapt, or they risk becoming outdated superfast. This makes us dependent on technology. The internet is a perfect example. It's become the go-to language for global communication, and it's done that in a pretty short amount of time.

This is exactly why Open Space is so powerful. It shows us that self-organization works—when there's a shared goal or purpose. It's like a flock of birds flying in formation: they follow simple rules, like keeping distance from their neighbors, and without endless discussion, they move in harmony. No one leads, yet the whole group shifts together.

I have spent my life searching for that kind of clarity—a simple rule or guiding principle to live a meaningful, connected, and happy life. How to grow into a mature, whole, and respected person. Open Space provided a clear vision of what that would look like. Rigid systems are not the answer; trust in our shared human instincts is. We all want to feel connected, find purpose, and belong.

C.G. Jung's statement prompted a significant amount of introspection and personal growth in me. He once said, *"Anyone who has not answered the fundamental questions of religion and sexuality cannot be considered healthy."* Today, I know for certain that everyone in the world is part of this search. Every generation must answer these questions anew in the context of their time. This is a basic law of progress. It happens through social exchange, shared learning, and every action we take.

https://doi.org/10.1515/9783111448329-010

My first experience with Open Space at the age of 45 was a turning point. It sparked a deep curiosity and reignited a long-held desire to reconnect with the essential and meaningful parts of life. This desire felt like a return to something original—what could be called *religio*, a reconnection to our roots, our origin. What drove this longing was a growing frustration: despite all the wisdom and experiences of previous generations, we seem unable to truly learn from them. We repeat the same mistakes, again and again. Instead of evolving as individuals and as a society, we often feel stuck, trapped in a fear of the future and uncertain how to move forward.

I was amazed when I read in Harrison Owen's book that Open Space was inspired by the ancient African Ubuntu philosophy. He had done something extraordinary: he'd taken timeless indigenous wisdom and put it into a modern context. I was fascinated by it, and it pulled me in even deeper.

And along the way, I came across the book "The Fourfold Way" *by Angeles Arrien.* Arrien, a respected cultural anthropologist, educator, and author, dedicated her life to studying indigenous wisdom and spiritual traditions.[27] Her work revealed something striking—across nearly all shamanic cultures, four fundamental archetypes appeared again and again, often expressed through the ancient medicine wheel.

The medicine wheel is a circle divided into four quadrants, each representing a direction, a mindset, and a personal quality: the Warrior, the Healer, the Visionary (or Medicine Man), and the Teacher. These archetypes weren't just symbolic—they were tools. Ancient tribes knew how to switch between these inner qualities as needed, adapting to life's challenges with balance and clarity. Inspired by this insight, I began experimenting with the meditation practices Arrien described. I engaged in meditation in a variety of postures: standing still and observing nature inspired by the qualities of the warrior, sitting like a teacher, walking like a visionary, and lying down inspired by the qualities of a healer. Over the course of three years, these practices became part of my life. The result was transformative. I found myself reconnecting with my own inner compass, rediscovering a sense of purpose, restoring balance in my work and personal life, and defining a more authentic approach to leadership.

I've come to realize that these four archetypes translate powerfully into leadership and management today. Here's how I understand and apply them:

1. **Show Up and Be Fully Present—The Way of the Warrior**
   Being present means leading with clarity, courage, and decisiveness. When you show up fully, you tap into your strength, charisma, and ability to influence others.
   Leadership Learning: In meetings and conversations, be fully engaged. Lead by example. Decide when action is needed and take it—don't hesitate or delay. Determination and presence build trust.

---

27 Angeles Arrien, *The Fourfold Way: Walking the Paths of the Warrior* (New York: HarperCollins Publishers, 1993).

2. **Pay Attention to What Has Heart and Meaning—The Way of the Healer**
    This is about tuning into what truly matters—love, appreciation, empathy, and connection. It's about recognizing what brings warmth and vitality to people's lives.
    Leadership Learning: Lead with transparency and integrity. Share even difficult truths openly. Align your actions with your values and the purpose of your organization. Create a workplace that honors emotion and meaning.
3. **Speak Your Truth Without Blame or Judgment—The Way of the Visionary**
    This is the path of clear sight and deep insight. Speaking truthfully, without judgment, sharpens intuition and strengthens your vision.
    Leadership Learning: Foster innovation and creativity. Be open to new perspectives and flexible in your approach. Read your team well—know who's thriving, who's underused, and who needs support. Good leaders see clearly and act wisely.
4. **Be Open to Outcome, Not Attached—The Way of the Teacher**
    The teacher embodies wisdom and objectivity. Letting go of rigid expectations allows space for learning and growth.
    Leadership Learning: Stay informed about your environment—market trends, internal dynamics, and team feedback. See every experience, good or bad, as a learning opportunity. Teach through reflection, not control.

This blend of ancient wisdom and modern leadership is not only timeless—it's urgently needed in today's fast-paced, uncertain world. It reminds us that true leadership begins within and that to lead others, we must first understand ourselves.

This is another great example of how we can learn from tribal wisdom and integrate it into our daily lives and different professional roles. The medicine-wheel approach is great because it helps us develop four different mindsets. This gives us the ability to figure out the best approach for any situation. I highly recommend that you start your own journey to find your authentic self. When you do, you'll figure out what you need to work on. Try to meditate in every situation. As Angeles Arrien says in her book, you can do it lying in bed, you can do it when you sit, you can do it when you go for a walk, you can do it when you stay around and look into nature, and you can even do it while you are running. Sometimes I couldn't meditate when I was stressed, and my nerves were shot. But when I was running, I always found that my thoughts would return to a more relaxed state. It really helped me clear my head and get going. It's not about luck. Running is the meditation method of the visionary!

The Gift from African Culture

My first encounter with Harrison Owen's *Open Space Technology* opened my eyes to the value of indigenous African approaches to dialogue and leadership. Owen showed that large group conversations—whether involving dozens or hundreds—can be deeply effective when guided by just a few simple rules. These principles, drawn from the way African communities have traditionally gathered, reveal something profound: true innovation and collective insight arise from openness, trust, and purposeful conversation.

What struck me most about Open Space was that no matter how many participants were involved, you always come away with new perspectives—not only on the issues we were discussing, but also on the deeper connections between people, ideas, and systems. It created a sense of awareness that extended beyond the room. In a time when the world is increasingly complex and interdependent but often feels stuck, this kind of connection is more important than ever.

During this journey, I came across a book that bridged two seemingly distant worlds: spirituality and leadership. The book I mean is called "Ubuntu."[28]

It was endorsed by none other than Desmond Tutu—Nobel Peace Prize laureate, spiritual leader, and an icon of South Africa's freedom movement. On the back cover, Tutu beautifully described the essence of Ubuntu:

> *Africans have a concept they call ubuntu. It's about the essence of what it means to be human, and it's something that Africa will contribute to the world. It includes things like hospitality, caring for others, and going through thick and thin together. We believe that we are all in this together. My humanity is inextricably linked to yours. If I dehumanize you, I'm also dehumanizing myself. "No one is truly alone in this world, and that's why we work to serve our community with our full humanity.*

Ubuntu teaches us that leadership isn't about dominance or control, but about shared responsibility and mutual respect. It is a call to lead from the heart and to serve with one's full humanity.

Willem de Liefde wrote it in 2006. He used to be a director at different industrial companies and studied African ideas, focusing on the value of traditional African practices in today's world. The English version is called *"Lekgotla: The Art of Leadership Through Dialogue"*. Lekgotla is an African word that means *"meeting circle" or "tribal organization."* De Liefde says that thinking of companies acting like tribes, rooted in the African concepts of tribal meetings, gives another dimension to how they operate:

De Liefde's idea of Lekgotla stays in striking contrast to the hierarchical structures that dominate modern organizations. He writes that businesses could be transformed if they adopted the mindset, *"I am because we are."*

This sparked a eureka moment for me. I saw the direct connection between Harrison Owen's Open Space principles and the Lekgotla circle—two models from different worlds yet deeply aligned. They both center around inclusion, storytelling, listen-

---

28 Willem H. J. De Liefde, *Ubuntu: In der Gemeinschaft Lösungen finden und Entscheidungen treffen* (Munich: Signum Verlag, 2006).

ing, and elder wisdom. They encourage leadership not as command but as connection.

These ideas are strikingly different from traditional Western management, which is often rooted in Descartes' phrase, *"I think, therefore I am."* It emphasizes individual achievement, personal responsibility, and autonomy. This approach, while not inherently flawed, can result in overly individualistic decision-making if not consciously balanced by a broader perspective.

In contrast, Ubuntu leadership is grounded in the principle that we are defined by our collective identity. It focuses on the collective, ensuring decisions are made with the community's well-being and shared purpose in mind. This model makes it clear that leadership is not about personal power or recognition. It's about service, trust, and connection.

Where Western management often asks, *"What can I achieve?"* Ubuntu asks, *"What can we become together?"*

Over the following years, I began to test these ideas in my role as VP of Innovation. I applied them to my leadership approach, my team structures, and especially the way we built our Open Innovation network. And what I found was powerful: this kind of thinking doesn't just work—it's needed now more than ever.

I should mention that using the full principle of the Ubuntu mindset isn't without its downsides. I will talk about these in part III. At this point I would like to anticipate: It requires organizational skills, a good view from outside through specialists, and the willingness to live in a subculture that can coexist in a network structure within the given corporate hierarchies. When we want to fully implement the "ubuntu" principles in our environment.

Without it, we risk falling into reactive, defensive postures—arguing positions instead of seeking shared ground. Adopting an Ubuntu mindset helps us break that cycle. But it also comes with challenges. Briefly put, applying Ubuntu requires strong facilitation, external reflection, and the ability to cultivate a *"subculture"* within the existing corporate hierarchy—one that honors human connection while operating within a complex system.

Still, the potential is real. The *style of a tribal leader*—a leader who fosters inclusive, cross-functional dialogue—can be achieved today. Especially as younger generations seek meaningful, balanced, and purpose-driven work, the time has come to embrace this wisdom.

Core behaviors of this leadership style include open interaction, deep listening, and storytelling. Stories, in particular, play a key role in preserving the collective memory of an organization. In global companies, which are now far too complex to be managed top-down, leadership must become a balance of "soft" and "hard" skills. Rational analysis must be coupled with intuitive insight. Under this model, conflicts born from misunderstanding are minimized, and the organization can direct more of its energy outward—toward innovation, service, and impact.

Ubuntu reminds us that we are not isolated individuals. We belong to something greater. Trust grows when leaders commit visibly and openly to the common good. This is how we build community, purpose, and resilience.

When Desmond Tutu spoke of Ubuntu as a gift from Africa to the world, I believe he was absolutely right. That gift is becoming more relevant each day.

Ubuntu, Open Space, and the Rediscovery of Tribal Wisdom in Modern Leadership

I'd like to add another story to the Ubuntu discussion. It's about an interesting observation I had when I learned about cultural differences in how we look into the future.

In her already mentioned book *Insatiable Curiosity,* the Austrian researcher Helga Nowotny tells a striking story about cultural perspectives on time. A young colleague of hers worked with deaf communities and noticed something fascinating: in Western sign language, the sign for "future" points forward. But in some African communities, the sign for "future" points backward.

Why? Because from the African perspective, the past is the only part of time we truly know. The future lies behind us—unseen and unknown. It's not something we can stare at; it's something that arrives when we're not looking. This idea is a game-changer. It made me think differently, and it helped me push myself to do more. I'm now more confident and ready to go the extra mile to make meaningful changes in all areas of my life.

Nowotny adds that *newness* is not the same as *the future.* Innovation often comes by reconnecting with the past—by breathing new life into ancient wisdom. For anything to be truly "new," it must differ from the old *and* have enough in common with it to be recognized. Newness doesn't erase the past—it transforms it.

In this view, we don't chase the future—we prepare to receive it. And we do that by focusing on the present moment, by grounding ourselves in values, stories, and shared meaning. She writes that we can choose where to place the future in space, but it's already on the way to us in time. It's built into biological processes like a narrow gap that makes it possible to enter an eternal territory that's detached from change. We can think of the future as a kind of fluid transition or an extended present, with that open horizon that emerged during the European modern era. This era also brought about a sense of acceleration, linked to the degree of change and the increased appearance of the new.

As my friend Wolfgang Stabentheiner says in his leadership program: *"The good future is already laid out in the past."*

And maybe, through Ubuntu and tribal wisdom, we're finally learning how to walk forward with our eyes wide open—not just toward the future but living in it.

Modern Leadership and the Spiritual Foundation of Learning Organizations

When we believe that modern leadership principles are grounded in empathy, trust, and collective purpose, then we inevitably have to redefine leadership as a service, listening, and striving for authenticity, collaboration, and meaningful connection.

And I can't say this enough: Great teams are key to good leadership. These are teams that can adapt, learn, and transform in response to change.

Now, with the advent of AI, virtual collaboration, and increasing digital workspaces, we need to ask ourselves: *how do we keep the cycle alive that is formed by tribal wisdom on the one hand and shaping our future from the now on the other?*

When we make an effort to do this, we suddenly see the world with different eyes. New skills emerge. New assumptions take root. However, this profound learning cycle is jeopardized if personal, embodied interaction is lost. No virtual tool can replace the richness of human presence, which consists of looking someone in the eye and building trust over time.

No virtual tool can replace the richness of human presence, which consists of looking someone in the eye and building trust over time.

I believe the future of leadership must include a new archetype—what I call *Homo Innovaticus*. I am describing this new archetype in depth in part III of the book. But in context with the leadership aspect, I want to anticipate some aspects. The *Homo Innovaticus* is a human who innovates not only through intellect but also through emotional intelligence, cultural awareness, and spiritual grounding. This person thrives in complexity, seeks meaning, and leads with heart.

To make room for *Homo Innovaticus*, we must create organizations where curiosity, reflection, and inner transformation are as valued as performance. This requires structural support—cultures that welcome learning, budgets that fund growth, and systems that empower teams to lead from within.

We all can feel this shift that is so typical for the 21st century. Leadership is undergoing a radical transformation. The command-and-control structures of the industrial age are no longer suited to the complexity and interdependence of today's world. We must move toward a model of leadership grounded in empathy, trust, and collective purpose. This shift requires us to redefine leadership—not as dominance or direction—but as service, listening, and the pursuit of authentic connection. The *Homo Innovaticus* layout can be brought to life when modern leaders understand that their role is to hold space for growth, not to command it. To build relationships rooted in mutual respect and create environments where people feel seen, heard, and empowered.

When they stay attuned to the present moment and capable of sensing what is needed—not just from them, but from the collective. Then they are not threatened by the idea of shared leadership. In fact, they welcome it.

They design innovation ecosystems where leadership is dynamic and fluid. The role of the "alpha animal" behavior shifts depending on the context. The *Homo Innovaticus* knows how to distribute responsibility based on people's strengths, consciousness, and readiness. They can lead by stepping forward—or stepping aside. Their deepest skill is adaptive support: the ability to guide the team not through dominance, but through attunement and trust.

My friend Prof. Tom Hench said it to me very aptly:

> *For decades, we've been told to "give people a sense of ownership." But this is like offering a hungry person the "sense" of dinner. Either people have a true voice in shaping purpose, or they do not. Either they co-create the vision, or they remain passengers on someone else's ship.*

The African philosophy of Ubuntu remembers and helps us to realize the deep truth of "I am because we are." Leadership rooted in this wisdom recognizes that innovation is not just about new products or services—it is about new ways of being human—together.

This is the true work of modern leadership:
- To hold space for transformation.
- To awaken the spiritual core of our private relationships and organizations, because the two areas of life can no longer be separated!
- To make life and work a sacred act of collective becoming.

Innovation is inherently unpredictable.

This is not a failure of strategy; it reflects reality. It is shaped by trial and error, intuition, and insight. We learn as we go. And the best we can do, often, is to stay alert, stay open, and stay attuned to one another.

Our survival depends on more than efficiency; it depends on purpose. Ubuntu reminds us that we're all in this together. Leadership rooted in this spirit doesn't just drive change—it sustains it.

It's about new ways of being human—together.

Chapter 9
Imagining the Future: Possibility Thinking, Prophecy, and the Power of Inner Images

Throughout history, one thing has remained constant: the human desire to understand what lies ahead. From ancient civilizations to modern societies, people have always tried to make sense of the future—searching for clues, patterns, and meaning in the unknown.

It's part of our nature to wonder what's coming next. Whether it's tomorrow's weather, next month's challenges, or the distant future a century from now, we are driven by curiosity and the need for orientation. It's no surprise that the idea of a time machine—something that lets us skip through the past or leap into the future—has captured imaginations for generations.

Across cultures, this curiosity led to the creation of figures believed to access the unseen: oracles, seers, shamans, prophets, and wise elders. These individuals often became essential guides in society, offering visions, warnings, and advice. To support their insights, they used a range of tools and practices—crystal balls, tarot cards, palmistry, scrying, or trance states accessed through music, dance, fasting, meditation, or even mind-altering substances.

The Greeks consulted the Oracle of Delphi, while the Romans placed their trust in the sacred Sibylline Books. Indian traditions include prophetic writings in the Vedas, and in China, the *I Ching* (Book of Changes) became a key to interpreting cycles of change. In Abrahamic traditions like Judaism and Christianity, prophets held central roles as messengers of divine will—often warning of future consequences and urging moral action.

Interestingly, these visions were not seen as predictions alone but as deep insights—given through ecstatic states of consciousness—often with the goal of influencing the present. In almost every culture, prophecy wasn't simply about fate; it was about choice, transformation, and awareness.

And even today, in our secular, data-driven world, we can't dismiss the lasting power of these images and messages. Once a vision or prophecy is shared—whether it comes from a mystical tradition, a scientific forecast, or even a cultural narrative—it can deeply shape our psychology. It influences how we prepare, how we relate to the unknown, and how we make decisions.

In that sense, ancient prophecy shares something profound with modern innovation: both begin with the imagination. Both call us to pay attention to what we can't yet see. And both ask us to respond—not passively, but with intention.

As we explore themes of innovation and leadership, we must remember that truly transformative change doesn't start with technology or processes—it starts with the ability to imagine a different world.

https://doi.org/10.1515/9783111448329-011

One of the big questions that's followed me my whole life is how we can create a good future. Are we missing a key source that's already given us the answers? Given what we heard from Helga Nowotny's insights, the answer is a resounding "no." But the ways we can fuel and direct such imaginations of the future are really diverse and fascinating. We should take a closer look at history and try to find the valuable contributions that are often overlooked.

Imaginations We Hold of the Future

One of my favorite sayings is, *"Be careful with your dreams—they might just come true."*

This quote reminds us how powerful our inner images are. What we visualize—whether consciously or unconsciously—has a real influence on the actions we take and the direction we move in.

You might be familiar with the "pink elephant" effect. If someone says, *"Don't think of a pink elephant,"* your brain can't help but immediately picture one. This shows how difficult it is to suppress a thought once it has been imagined. The more we try to avoid it, the more it stays with us.

That simple example reveals something profound: there is a bridge between spiritual prophecy—often seen as mystical or intuitive—and the practical world of innovation and leadership. If the future is always shaped by the images we hold in our minds, then the way we imagine the future matters deeply.

Cognitive psychologist *Donna Rose Addis* has shown through her research that our thoughts about the future are often shaped by our memories and biases. Because the future is uncertain, we tend to fill in the blanks with fear—anticipating problems or threats, especially when we've had difficult experiences in the past.

This tendency is amplified by today's media landscape, which thrives on attention-grabbing headlines and emotionally charged content. Negative stories are more likely to go viral because they trigger our survival instincts. It's not necessarily a failure of journalism—it's a feature of human psychology.

As a result, many of us end up with distorted perceptions of the world. The *Global Ignorance Test* by Swedish statistician Hans Rosling highlights just how wide the gap is between perception and reality. When asked about global trends—like child vaccination rates, literacy, or life expectancy—most people answer incorrectly, influenced more by fear and dubious sources of information than fact. In many cases, Rosling reports that random guesses by monkeys outperform human responses when it comes to finding out how much of it is true. That's how strong our biases can be.

If we want to shape better futures, we need to see the whole picture. Just like when riding a bike—if you focus only on the curb, you're more likely to crash. A retired fighter pilot once told me a story that makes this point vividly: during WWII, if a pilot had to make an emergency landing in a field with just one tree, they would often crash into that tree. Why? Because in panic, they fixated on it. The very thing they wanted to avoid became their target. This is how fear can trap our focus and shape our outcomes.

The same applies in innovation and leadership. If all we see are risks and limitations, we are more likely to create them. But if we open space for imagining positive futures, we give ourselves permission to explore, collaborate, and create meaningful change.

This doesn't mean ignoring policy, economics, or the realities of business. Rather, it means finding a balanced perspective—where we consider the needs of customers, employees, and society at large. That's when real dialogue about the future begins.

And inevitably, this leads us to a deeper question: *What are the values guiding our vision of the future?* Hans Rosling was once asked if he was an optimist or a pessimist. His answer was simple and powerful: *"I'm a possibilist."*

To be a possibilist means acknowledging progress without becoming naive. It's about grounding ourselves in facts while keeping an open mind about what is still possible. We draw energy and confidence from what we've already achieved to fuel further progress.

As Daniel Swarovski, the founder of the Swarovski crystal empire, once said:

Innovation never stops. An innovation in one field inevitably leads to innovations in others. The key is to be aware and ready to act when opportunity comes.

His vision—*"a diamond for every woman in the world"*—was radical at the time. Fine jewelry had been reserved for royalty and the ultra-wealthy. But his dream was bold, clear, and imaginative. And because he believed in it, he built something that helped democratize beauty and luxury.

That's the power of a compelling inner image: it moves us beyond limits. And if we want to shape the future, we must start by paying close attention to what we imagine—because those images just might become real.

Human ecology, on the other hand, focuses on how humans adapt to survive and thrive. Or, as well, systems theory, which looks at how humans and their environment interact as complex systems with feedback loops. Basically, changes in one part of the system can affect the whole.

The very interesting idea behind the possibility thinking is that people have the freedom to make their own choices. Possibilists are people who recognize the progress that's been made in the world and are optimistic about what that means for future developments and possibilities.

This way of thinking isn't about being naive. It's about being well-informed and having a positive outlook. As Kevin Kelly puts it, we should be optimistic not because our problems are smaller than we thought, but because future generations will have more capacity, knowledge, and tools to solve problems than we anticipate. So, it well includes the trust in future generations and their own competences of problem solving.

With that we can agree that to carefully observe our cognitive bias is one of the most important tasks on our way to dealing with the future. Maybe our brains have these built-in filters that simplify information to help us avoid feeling overwhelmed. This can cause us to stick to old ways of thinking and miss chances to make progress.

Because of that, we need to tackle future challenges head on: we need to learn how to think critically and consider different points of view. This means getting information from lots of different sources, including ones that challenge our own views. What wonderful helpers do we have now in our pockets with the various AI companions. And no wonder that my proposal for a new innovation process that comes in part III starts with exactly this topic.

One well-known example that shows how important it is to be adaptive and visionary on the basis of early data detection is the story of Netflix. Netflix started out as a DVD rental service but then evolved into a leading streaming service by embracing digital innovation and investing in original content. This strategic shift, driven by forward thinking and data-driven decision-making, shows how important it is to be open to change and to keep adapting to what the market needs.

I'd like to circle back to my earlier point about dreams. Ever since I was studying mechanical engineering, I've been fascinated by the incredible stories of the pre-Columbian cultures in Mesoamerica. I've always been curious if there's a different message for us in these cultures, one that's separate from our Western history. Therefore, I followed this curiosity and fulfilled my dream in early 2024 by starting my retirement with a four-week study trip to the places where the Mayas, Olmecs, Aztecs, and Zapotecs lived and worked. I'll quickly run through the surprising findings here.

Findings from Mayan Culture

We may never fully understand how the Mayans lived their lives in detail, but what we do know from studying their traditions and beliefs is that despite many stories about the bloody side of their rituals, they valued support in their daily lives, felt happy and motivated, and were guided by their strong beliefs.

When I was in the Mayan region of Mexico, I was surprised to learn that even though the Spanish and the native populations have been mixing for centuries, there are still native Mayan people who keep their original culture and traditions. Even so, the glory days of high culture are pretty much in the past. I met a lot of people who are still really proud of their Mayan culture and language, and you can see it in the way they think, feel, and interact. I was even more surprised when I talked to them. They've been influenced by Hispanic culture for a long time, but they've kept their own customs, like how they live together and their own language. We had a great chat with a waiter who was really proud of his culture. He told us that in Mayan, the word for "cash" actually means "something special," not money. He gave a little smile, hinting at our Western tendency to prioritize money.

The Mayan Civilization is a really interesting topic, especially since its heyday ended in the 9th century BC, 400 years before Columbus' arrival. This made me very curious, and I wanted to understand more about the circumstances that made them fail.

From the many findings from visiting places like Palenque, Chichen Itza, Uxmal, or Tulum, I want to mention 3 key insights with a relevance to our question on how to learn from tribal wisdom:

Calendars and Different Senses of Time

The Mayan understanding of time was vastly different from our modern perspective. They used four calendars for distinct purposes: the Ritual Calendar (260 days for predicting the future and religious events), the Agricultural Calendar (365 days for farming cycles), the Calendar Round (a 52-year cycle combining the two), and the Long Count (tracking longer spans of time).

This cyclical approach to time brought balance and inspired new beginnings every 52 years, encouraging adaptability and cultural renewal. The "Wheel of Sun," displayed in the National Museum of Anthropology in Mexico City, exemplifies the Mayan appreciation for astronomy and timekeeping. Crafted from basalt, weighing over 24 tons, and nearly 3.6 meters wide, this remarkable artifact roots its origins in the ancient Olmec civilization.

It's a masterpiece of art and astronomy. Standing in front of that masterpiece of art and astronomy was a very deep and powerful experience. It takes us back to a time when people worshipped and feared the sun.

Very interesting qualities like seeding, communicating, dreaming, letting go, harmonizing, and many others are manifested and have been applied into the short- and long-term thinking. For example, the power animal of the jaguar stands for the power and strength of the qualities of life-giving forces of nature, fertility, and agricultural bounty, as well as transformation and agility in spiritual journeys. One can imagine that, driven by these power sources, they always had given aspects for development and further development.

Deeper information can be found in a very interesting journal article from a conference of the Society for American Archeology.[29]

This is one of my favorite findings. When you know that within the period of two generations an automatic reset takes place, you see the future as more predictable and have a higher respect for nature and responsibility for it. And you live with the fact that later your sons or daughters will be asked what your contribution was about.

---

29 David Bolles, "The Mayan Calendar: The Solar – Agricultural, and Correlation Questions," *Mexico* 12, no. 5 (1990): 85–89, http://www.jstor.org/stable/23759653, accessed October 31, 2024.

This approach lines up with African philosophies and Helga Nowotny's idea that the future is all around us in the present moment. As Anne Lamott said, "Almost everything will work again if you unplug it for a few minutes. Including you."

Could it be that we are missing in our today's thinking the value of "Exnovation," meaning the art of restarting from time to time? To upload our interest and free ourselves from things that are not anymore of help. More about that later, when we talk about Exnovation.

My second learning is dealing with

Hierophany

Hierophany is when the sacred shows up in the material world. It makes the divine visible or tangible. In the Mayan civilization, this concept was really important.

When I visited Palenque, I had the chance to meet Mildred Estephania Garcia, who is not only an excellent tour guide but also a well-known specialist in Mayan culture and history. She explained how the ancient Mayans observed celestial bodies like the Sun, Moon, Venus, Mars, and Jupiter. She also showed us how they incorporated this knowledge into their buildings. She even gave me the link to a scientific paper on the topic.[30] This was for me the long-searched missing link to understand the Mayan culture more in-depth. The authors spent four years observing solstices, equinoxes, and the highest and lowest points in the celestial bodies' movements. They noticed some distinctive patterns of sunlight inside the Temple of the Sun at Palenque. The study revealed new insights into the astronomical orientation of the temples and shows clearly that the architectural layout and design was on a profound knowledge of astronomical occurrences.

The Mayan priests were pretty savvy when it came to the movement of the planets. They used this knowledge to predict solar eclipses. They knew when the sun would hit a certain spot in the building, so they could easily place the ruler there and tell the people that, because he had a direct link to the gods, he would be enlightened by the sun for a bit, just like the priests had predicted. This made their connection to the divine even stronger, showing that they were able to communicate with the gods and keep their society running smoothly. It also built trust between the earthly and supernatural realms.

Role of Prophecies

The Dresden Codex is one of the most significant surviving pre-Columbian texts of the Maya civilization. It is preserved in the Saxon State and University Library in Dresden. This ancient Mayan manuscript, written in Mayan hieroglyphics on bark

---

30 "Astronomical Observations from the Temple of the Sun," Academia.edu, accessed July 20, 2025, https://www.academia.edu/71775088/1_Astronomical_Observations_from_the_Temple_of_the_Sun.

paper, offers profound insights into Mayan knowledge and culture. It contains messages believed to be divine warnings and instructions, guiding the people on how to appease the gods to avert disasters. Beyond its spiritual significance, the codex offers practical advice on issues like agriculture, mythology, medicine, and healing. The Maya had a deep understanding of cosmic cycles and events. This understanding allowed them to predict and prepare for future challenges. It also embodies their belief in the cyclical nature of time and history.

The resilience of the Mayan people today is a testament to the enduring strength of their cultural and spiritual heritage. History is not linear; it often follows a cyclical pattern of destruction, dispersal, and renewal. This interconnectedness of the past and future continues to influence how societies adapt and thrive.

The New Age movement has thoroughly examined Mayan prophecies, particularly through the work of Jose Argüelles in his book *The Mayan Factor*. Argüelles confidently interprets the Mayan texts, highlighting seven prophecies that, while speculative, offer relevant perspectives for our modern era. While these interpretations may not stand as scientific truths, they provide rich metaphors and frameworks that can inspire fresh thinking about societal principles and human progress. This connection between ancient wisdom and modern innovation is critical to understanding how cultural heritage can inform our future.

Mayan culture clearly demonstrates the value of integrating knowledge into daily life in sustainable and socially cohesive ways. Their mastery of biodiversity over 7,000 years has gifted the world more than 60 varieties of maize and over 35 types of chili peppers, such as paprika, tabasco, and jalapeño. It's inconceivable to imagine a world without these contributions.

Mayan culture's achievements clearly reflect a holistic understanding of life, blending science, spirituality, and sustainability. Their legacy offers a fascinating glimpse into their world and a roadmap for navigating our own challenges. We must incorporate their lessons into modern innovation processes, especially with the aid of emerging tools like artificial intelligence. This will pave the way for a more balanced and harmonious future.

The high Mayan civilization, with its big cities that had been interconnected by broad road systems fell apart around 1,000 AD, long before the arrival of the Spanish conquistadores. The question of why this happened is still a subject of much speculation. Despite the negative impact of prolonged droughts and crop failures caused by epidemics, which had a significant and detrimental effect on society. Some researchers also believe that conflicts between various classes of the Maya were the cause of the downfall of the civilization. Maybe oppressed groups rebelled against the rulers, which led to the collapse of the Maya civilization. I'm going to share my own theory on why the high blossom time of Mayan civilization collapsed and the big cities have been abandoned. As is the case with many other systemic causes of failing innovation and change, it is likely that the system of the ruling classes was unable to earn sufficient trust from lower classes and younger generations. Most people just didn't see the point in building higher pyramids or inventing new hierophanies. When the ruling class and the people are too distant from each other, the system inevitably collapses. How could it have been avoided?

Similar to the Maya, we may also be at a turning point in our culture. Although we have made social and structural progress, there is growing dissatisfaction among the younger generation, accompanied by a silent shift in values.

It is time to draw lessons from history and initiate a collective process that unites young and experienced generations. I believe that concepts like Open Space and Predictive Forecasting can help us achieve comprehensive and inclusive change.

Even so, Mayan culture and the way people act together survived, as I mentioned before. It's a clear example that a strong, resilient cultural foundation remains in people, no matter how apocalyptic a threat. The traditional culture of the rural Mayan people is still a huge part of their lives today.

We can learn from them that we should feel encouraged to take control of our lives, use technology wisely, and always respect nature. It shows us that making the world a better place starts with changing ourselves first, in our hearts and actions, and always being aware of systemic flaws in our political, economic, and social environments.

The Tribal Power Source

As we had a deeper look into the African and Mayan cultures above, I want to share one experience from North American Indigenous tribes that influenced my further life and spiritual development very much.

I think it was in the early '90s. I was on my way to New York and found a book at the airport called *"Secret Native American Pathways."*[31] It was written by *Davis E. Mails*, an American anthropologist, author, and researcher who's best known for his work focusing on Native American cultures. The book really helped me appreciate and understand Native American spirituality and culture better. It also got me thinking about my own spirituality and my relationship with the natural world.

The exercises share insights into how these cultures created a deep connection with a collective human heritage like never before. The deep lessons in ecological harmony, spirituality, storytelling, healing, time, and communal rituals inspired me to start my own long path of exercises. These exercises helped me reconnect with nature and explore how to nurture my spiritual well-being.

I'd like to mention one exercise that I still do from time to time. It's part of the spiritual knowledge that Mails received from Fools Crow, the legendary leader and

---

31 Thomas E. Mails, *Secret Native American Pathways: A Guide to Inner Peace* (Tulsa, OK: Council Oak Books, 1988).

healer of the Lakota Sioux tribe. When I started practicing, I was dealing with some stress from work and feeling unsure about my future. It was my first time trying deep meditation and using the power of my own thoughts to calm my restlessness. After about 4 weeks of following the advice of the Into Our Days transformed method of Fools Crow, I was able to calm my mind and reconnect to an inner state of peace. It was like my brain was finally able to step back from all the daily information I was exposed to.

The exercise is like imagining an empty tube through which everything from Earth to Heaven is flowing. It's got detailed instructions on breathing and cleansing your body during different cycles. It also uses symbols to help you remember your imagination. The more I did this exercise, the more I got to know my true self and felt stronger and safer.

For me, it was like a light bulb moment when I realized that modern psychology and inner pictures are a key part of our lives still in our modern days. And I started seeing how they influenced other aspects of my life. Many other meditation examples followed over time.

Chapter 10
The New Role of Futuring and Foresighting

Now's a good time to think about how we can look to the future. As we said, the future can be a friend or an enemy, a place we want to be, and a lot more. At its core, the future will be shaped by our current behaviors, actions, and choices. If we look at the future with our tribal awareness and Helga Nowotny's words from above, the future is all about teaming up to make the familiar feel like a new and improved version of itself. I like this view. It helps us imagine a future that feels familiar and trustworthy while also bringing in new ideas and insights from our current time.

John Naisbitt, the so-called father of the Megatrend Theory, reaches a similar conclusion in his book, Megatrends. "The new directions that are forming our lives." I remember the time when my boss, Helmut Swarovski, invited him to visit Swarovski in 1998. The Chinese markets opened, and we had to adapt our global strategy. The value of high-quality crystal goods is very high in Chinese tradition. I distinctly recall a dinner we had with him and his wife, Doris, when he gave us his recommendation. *"Innovation is like participating in a parade. It's important not to get so far ahead that you're no longer part of the parade. "Neither to the customers nor to the employees."* Naisbitt was appointed assistant secretary of education at age 34 under President John Kennedy, and his experience as a former manager at Kodak and IBM made him an expert on the subject. His advice was clear and helped me balance my job as of VP Innovation. It is essential to synchronize technology-driven projects with the market and the customer's ability to integrate. Do not underestimate the organizational anchoring of change in your organization. A company's success is ultimately determined by the interaction of its people and their intrinsic motivation to embrace change. This approach was key to identifying the ideal pace for growth, making sure we didn't overheat the market or ourselves.

I've always found the parade metaphor helpful when working on our communication strategy, from coming up with ideas to getting them out there. It's a solid perspective for any organizational design focused on innovation and change. I'm going to turn it this way: The creativity we display will influence how we make our ideas fly and shape the future. It's just how it is, and it'll always be that way. How much influence and control we have over our future depends entirely on our vision and convictions.

Now we arrive at the next paradox in dealing with innovation. On the one hand, we know that we can only define the future in the now, and on the other hand, we do often simply not have the time, resources, or capabilities to deal with the future. If we want to actively shape the future, we must invest in it.

We have a wealth of case studies and experiences from many areas of management. Most of them demonstrate that it is very important to draw pictures of a desirable future from time to time. The most common methods are Foresighting and Futu-

https://doi.org/10.1515/9783111448329-012

rizing. I have some experience with Foresighting activities, and I know that a good Fore-sighting process that results in possible future scenarios must include profound knowl-edge and involvement of the people in the organization, as well as external specialists and advisors. It's challenging for a company to develop process expertise and knowledge on Foresighting in-house. This is because you need to look into the future when you need to change your main strategy. The pace of your transition depends on factors such as your market presence, technological infrastructure, your position within the organiza-tion, and the maturity of your company in adapting to shifting environments. Based on my experience in the industry, this process typically takes five to seven years. In case of crisis, updates and adaptation must be done right away. In a world that's always chang-ing, we must always adjust our approach. Figure 8 clearly shows how the Foresighting process is making a significant difference compared to linear assumptions.

As I mentioned, we don't have to be experts in Foresighting. We just need to learn how to use the tools we already have and think about how and with whom we can apply them in our area. One example that can help us deal with the uncertainty and disruption of today and the future is from the UN Environment Program. This pro-gram provides a step-by-step approach to thinking about the future and scanning the horizon. The goal is to develop a culture that is ready for the future.

The method of Foresighting itself has been used in order to develop a report called *"Navigating New Horizons— A Global Foresight Report on Planetary Health and Human Wellbeing,"* produced by UNEP in collaboration with the International Science Council. The report calls for the world to pay attention and respond to a range of emerging challenges that could disrupt planetary health and well-being.[32] It presents insights on eight critical global shifts that are accelerating the triple planetary crisis of climate change, biodiversity and nature loss, and pollution and waste.

Developed by hundreds of global experts and distilled through regional and stakeholder consultations that included youth, they offer a glimpse into potential dis-ruptions, both positive and negative, that the world needs to keep a watching brief on.

Just to name one of the identified critical shifts: Fake in the form of misinforma-tion, declining trust, and polarization.

The report also says that we're facing a polycrisis, with environmental degrada-tion continuing despite efforts to tackle the planetary crisis. It is describing now the shift to net zero and the digital transformation are driving up demand for critical minerals, which is creating new challenges for both planetary health and human well-being. It is describing that AI has a lot of potential for economic and social growth, but it also has environmental consequences. On top of that, the increase in armed conflicts is also having a negative impact on the environment, creating long-

---

32 United Nations Environment Programme, *Global Foresight Report*, accessed November 3, 2024, https://www.unep.org/resources/global-foresight-Mreport.

term problems. Forced displacement is making health and environmental problems worse in a lot of countries.

The report makes clear that we must make better efforts in guidance and governance. We must integrate data and knowledge and make it accessible when and where it's needed. It also emphasizes the critical importance of adopting foresight to make decisions that shape a better future. This approach avoids the pitfall of merely reacting to the negative consequences of poor decisions.

The report's clear-cut solution is to create a new social contract. To reach the UN Sustainable Development Goals (SDGs) and make faster progress on climate and biodiversity targets, agile innovation and adaptive governance are essential.

This is as well precisely the focus of this book.

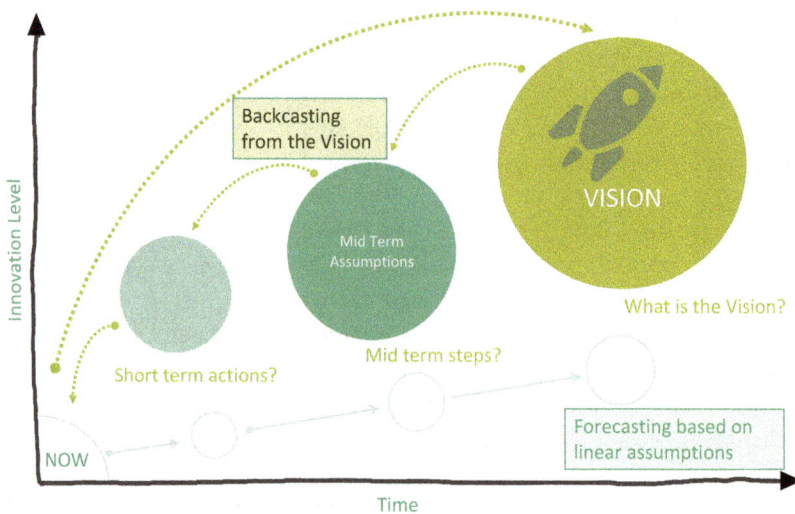

Figure 8: Foresighting vs linear assumptions.

At the Crossroads of Sustainability and Progress

We're at a crossroads, and the wisdom of tribal experiences offers some big lessons from the past. Is it time to rethink the fabric of our capitalist society? Instead of taking away the principles of ownership and wealth, we should be embracing the challenge of adapting and changing them. We should be more bold in our innovation ecosystems—let's infuse them with creativity, intelligence, and decentralized control mechanisms. If we can combine these solutions with the systems we already have, we can create a future where sustainability and progress go hand-in-hand.

Prophecies from the Hopi and Mayan people and the early warnings of the Club of Rome aren't just relics of ancient or old thought. They're like our rallying cry, telling us to pay attention to their warnings and make the changes needed for a fair and successful future. These words make us ask a very important question: how did we get to this modern problem, where other options to the current system seem impossible? The answer isn't in convincing ourselves of supposed securities, but in having the courage to imagine new possibilities. We also need to think ahead, work together, and believe that a better world is possible. Whatever the cost.

In the book *"The Dawn of Everything,"* The authors, *David Graeber and David Wengrow*, argue that it's crucial to rediscover such rich sources of indigenous thinking.[33] They try to make their main point clear: *that historical development wasn't a one-way street, and social segmentation isn't a necessary byproduct of settlement, division of labor, and mass society.*

Graeber and Wengrow express this with their model of open social development based on experimentation and adaptation. They support this with lots of archaeological and anthropological examples from different periods and cultures worldwide. People have always tried to avoid strict hierarchies by trying out different forms of social organization and, if necessary, overthrowing old structures in favor of more appropriate principles.

At the end of the day, the authors just have this open question of how we got to this modern dead end and why we can't imagine a realistic alternative to the current system. Unfortunately, they didn't suggest any pathways for the present that could help us rethink, steer, or initiate a completely new beginning.

For me it is just another example showing us how important it is to have people within institutions that are supposed to be coming up with new ideas and practical solutions to support them. I truly believe that the rapid growth of modern communication technologies, along with the imminent explosion of knowledge and the widespread accessibility of artificial intelligence and neural networks, has the potential to usher in a new era. I'm sure that one day we'll look back at this time and see it as the transformative time when everything began and the social interaction models we have today were replaced. Since we can't see into the future, should we be satisfied with the described weak signals? Or is it our job to use them to build a new future? Yes, I think we are called upon, everybody in his or her own place. For this to succeed we need a way of thinking that is able, on the one hand, to cultivate the experience and our processual knowledge about cooperation of networks and ecosystems and, on the other hand, our firm belief that we can shape our own future. With courage and intelligence. With diversity and focus.

I'd also like to mention the work of Yuval Harari and his theory of the "unfree human" at this point. The Israeli historian says that around 12,000 years ago, humans were in a tough spot when they started farming and lost their natural freedom.

---

33 David Graeber and David Wengrow, *The Dawn of Everything: A New History of Humanity* (New York: Allen Lane, Penguin Random House, 2021).

His bestselling book is Sapiens: A Brief History of Humankind. He asserts that during the transition from a hunter-gatherer lifestyle to settled farming during the Agricultural Revolution (around 10,000 years ago), humans did not improve their quality of life. In fact, they lost freedom. Hunter-gatherers had more varied diets, more free time, and less disease. They moved with the seasons, worked fewer hours, and had a flexible, less hierarchical social structure. Agriculture undeniably led to hard labor and social inequality. Farming required long hours of repetitive work, inevitably leading to the emergence of private property, hierarchies, gender inequality, and the start of large-scale organized warfare. He asserts that humans domesticated crops and crops domesticated humans. Harari provocatively states that *"wheat domesticated us"* because humans ended up working harder to serve the needs of plants rather than the other way around.

He argues that the Agricultural Revolution was *"history's biggest fraud"* and has created the illusion of progress, but it resulted in societies that were more rigid, less healthy, and more oppressive for individuals. I can only partially agree with that. And I want to make one thing clear: we have modern freedoms like our social systems. According to a World Bank report, the sustained free world trade progress and global investments have lifted more than *"one billion people out of extreme poverty in the last 30 years, especially in Asian regions."* We may have lost some freedom and calmness, but do you know somebody who would give up prosperity, healthcare, and the modern opportunities for self-realization and a calm life? Just to live the life of an early hunter or gatherer.

By integrating historical teachings and modern values and applying advanced forecasting techniques, we can enable balanced and future-oriented planning that strengthens both our culture and community.

What I want to say is that we should not underestimate the role of good dreams and fictions for the creation of solutions that help us to break out of our own bubbles of consciousness. That is what we can learn from tribal wisdom.

Chapter 11
Multilevel Value Creation and AI—Potential Antagonists

The Pivotal Role of Values as Guiding Principles

In this chapter, I want to highlight the importance of values as guiding principles, especially in addressing the challenges of a VUCA (Volatile, Uncertain, Complex, Ambiguous) world. Rapid change demands systematic, evidence-based approaches grounded in scientific thinking. This type of thinking encourages questioning assumptions, analyzing data, and approaching global crises—such as wars, poverty, and climate change—with a holistic perspective. All signs are here that we are willing to give up our free thinking in order to gain a little more feeling of safety amidst chaos and omnipresent value confusion.

The free exchange of ideas within focused and well-defined ecosystems, findings from nature, sustainable actions, and the embrace of forms of life that respect human rights are essential for a flourishing future. We must avoid short-sighted destruction without a plan to replace the disruption. If we continue down this path, we risk a future where economic self-interest reigns supreme and the essence of liberal democracy has all but disappeared. We must avoid a scenario where we find ourselves back in a world like that of the 18th and 19th centuries. Where we saw the emergence and gradual spread of democratic ideals mainly in Europe and the Americas, but these values were unevenly applied and often contradicted by colonialism, slavery, and entrenched hierarchies. It was a period of both revolutionary promise and systemic exclusion. Laying the foundation for the more inclusive struggles of the 20th century. What have we learned?

I am sure we can do that better.

The term "value" is used far too often without anyone really understanding what it means. The term is open to interpretation and has different meanings in different contexts. Different disciplines use different definitions. The old paradigm of profit maximization is transforming. It is being replaced by a new paradigm of responsible people organized in shared and dedicated ecosystems. These people are driven by collective issues. Society is not just a stakeholder. It is a beneficiary.

When I talk about values in this chapter, then we need to acknowledge that the term "value" and the term "principle" both describe fundamental concepts that often guide our behavior and decision-making but have distinct differences. I say they "often" guide us because in innovation and change they are "very often" overruled by systemic influences and biasing.

Values are personal beliefs that guide our behavior and decisions, like honesty or kindness. They vary between individuals. Principles, on the other hand, are universal

https://doi.org/10.1515/9783111448329-013

truths or rules, like justice or respect, that guide ethical behavior. They are consistent and unchanging. In short, values are personal and can differ, while principles are universal and consistent.

And principles provide a framework for ethical and moral decision-making. For example, the principle of honesty dictates that one should always tell the truth, regardless of personal values. So, if principles are rules that are made by organizations and systems, they are of great importance and must be questioned and adapted over time. Especially in times of change and transformation, like now. Values often reflect individual preferences, culture, and life experiences. And they help us to prioritize actions and choices.

Our time can be the start of a new era, where we can rebuild and make our society stronger by being open and reflective and using the advent of artificial intelligence guided by "humane" intelligence. I truly believe that both are possible. It's up to us. The world order of the last 75 years is falling apart. This is a direct result of ever more weak leadership in democracies and the rise of strong populists, autocrats, economic miracle healers, and dictators.

Let's look at a simple example: The **VUCA** model is a tool that has helped me understand challenging and rapidly changing conditions, especially in business and leadership contexts. It is crucial to focus our mindset on the right issues: **Volatility** refers to the speed and unpredictability of change. **Uncertainty** means there's no predictability and the potential for surprise. **Complexity** is about the multiple interconnected factors and the difficulty in understanding cause-and-effect relationships. **Ambiguity** is the lack of clarity and the difficulty in interpreting information. Meanwhile, the VUCA model is widely accepted and used to help organizations and leaders navigate and respond to these challenges. At a recent conference, an attendee introduced a new concept that was praised as the next model after the VUCA model helped us describe our world. Initially, I was taken aback by this model, but upon further reflection, I recognized it as another illustration of the theory that problem-solving frequently occurs in its initial, unreflective attempt and subsequent reinforcement of the problem: I'm talking about the new BANI model. BANI stands for Brittle, Anxious, Nonlinear, and Incomprehensible. It's clear that living in a VUCA world is challenging enough without perpetuating the dangerous misconception that only the negative aspects of volatility (brittle), uncertainty (anxious), complexity (difficult to understand), and ambiguity (incomprehensible) exist. It's clear that people who adopt this mindset fail to recognize the value of a simple shift towards principles that promote stability, define certainty through unwavering basic values, and acknowledge the inherent complexity of our world. It's like if we always focus on the empty part of the glass, we lose sight of what we have and become ungrateful. We must do this better. We should by far not believe that every novel theory or discovery holds inherent value.

Let's examine another example from my experience in innovation management. In the early '90s, when we first started talking about the fuzzy front end in the innovation manager community, it was tough to connect all the dots and come up with new solutions. At the time, the world was fragmented and culturally isolated. It was pure coincidence that this happened at the same time as the early days of the internet. We didn't have a good understanding of how this front end of innovation was driven and how it worked. Initial explanations indicated that the fuzzy front end was unmanageable. Some innovations were the result of long-term Research and Development programs while others were the direct result of a convergence of visionary actors, art, and trend-oriented consumer demands. The world has changed significantly since those days. Today, we have more sophisticated models. Our experience with dedicated innovation ecosystems has taught us how to define the expected results from change processes more clearly.

We've got to think more holistically and respect the systemic, overarching interdependencies. How the people involved interact with each other is of utmost importance. Because, let's face it, things are always changing. So, a new model for driving innovation and change has to be able to adapt, bounce back, and think strategically when dealing with the challenges of the modern world.

This shows how important it is to think about the whole system and support creativity to create a society that's ready for the future. I'm pointing this out because there's a trap when we work on new ideas. It's like we're dealing with new methods and theories that are trying to sell us something new, but we're not thinking about what we'd lose if we left the proven path.

And again, the above example of BANI underscores the notion that a misguided mindset tends to generate solutions that merely prolong the existing problem rather than offering genuine resolutions.

Preparation, intelligence and cleverness, and unshakable adherence to values are indispensable qualities in order to find useful ways of solving problems.

I am convinced that it's really important to have such guiding values that you can stick to. My personal values have been changing and developing over time, and I've been working on them consistently. In a free game of gap-oriented adaptation, renewal, and reorientation. My advice is to set some guiding principles in stone that will help us make corrections to the current situation, which is causing a lot of confusion. I'm not making promises that can be seen as another holy grail. But we need to start at a personal behavioral level if we want to contribute to this vision of a better world.

But how to start?

I learned about value-driven innovation development by pushing myself beyond what I thought I could do and working toward something bigger than myself. I also learned that it's important to go the extra mile and do more than what's required of you. There's a big focus on human rights, and over 128 countries are on board with the UN Human Charter. To keep these rights alive, we've got to be on board every day and really care about making sure they're protected throughout our lives. This effort is based on three key principles: mutual respect, adaptability without compromise, and dedication to making society better overall. This reflective process is a journey that forward-thinking organizations have to take. To succeed, they've got to adopt a new model of leadership—one that's characterized by adaptability.

Such an approach of *"a human-centered way of life"* could serve as a magnet for modernization and become a place of hope for young people. I wish for this departure—and believe the 21st century can still very surprisingly become a new century of strong values that support freedom and togetherness across religions, countries, and imperialistic saber-rattling. In any case, the alternatives are worse. Where should these movements start, if not at the individual level in the innovation settings of strong companies and NGOs and, of course, with their human drivers?

It's clear that all the signs of conflict are getting stronger these days, but we should be careful and remember that this doesn't guarantee a prosperous future. We should be especially careful when we look at history and past findings and try to predict the possible end of these approaches. I'd rather live in a free, open, and tolerant society. When we look at a lot of countries around the world, we realize that fundamental values are far from being taken for granted. But how can we contribute to at least initiate change? I think we all need to do our part, starting with our own families and our workplaces. Here's where I'm trying to go with this: it starts with the skills and readiness to step up and make changes.

At some point, we all have to ask ourselves a big question. What kind of society do we want to live in? Do we want a society that celebrates diversity or one that sees differences as a bad thing? Should we let envy, jealousy, intolerance, and hatred drive us, or do we take all our efforts and collaborative capabilities into our hands to create the new "Experimental Prototype Community of tomorrow"? We can use all the possibilities that our networked age offers on many levels. In other words, an EPCOT CENTER 2.0 that captures the spirit of Walt Disney and brings it into a new age of "integration of everything"? And addressing the important aspects of multifaceted global crises like wars, poverty, and climate change.

I'm going to reflect the vision I want to see in the 4-level value model that I've used for over 10 years. We'll start by discussing how to create value and why values are a huge differentiating factor in innovation before we dive into the models.

Value Creation

Values and trust have always been the foundation of my personal and professional life. To stay aligned, I regularly reflect on my top 10 personal values and connect them to my annual priorities. This simple practice has helped me stay grounded and intentional in how I live and lead. I've made a New Year's tradition of setting my compass. I don't like to miss this exercise.

Over time, I've noticed that the importance of certain values shifts with life's circumstances. Some values fade; others emerge. But the deeper insight is this: a meaningful life—whatever that means to each person—is always shaped by the values we choose to live by.

Whether we strive for success, connection, or impact, our values are the compass. The more our decisions align with them, the more likely we are to find lasting fulfillment.

In my own journey, values like respect, honesty, kindness, and loyalty have helped me build strong relationships and navigate difficult moments. These qualities have also strengthened my leadership in innovation management, where trust and collaboration are essential.

Core values serve more than just personal growth—they shape ethical action, strengthen community, and guide us toward responsible innovation. When shared and applied intentionally, values become a powerful source of trust.

And again: Creating psychological safety is "the" driver of creativity and openness to innovation.

Creating psychological safety is "the" driver of creativity and openness to innovation

---

Big corporations can have significant influence over the global economy, cultures, and environments through their services, products, and communication content. And their role in promoting values is vital for fostering unity and sustainability. Innovation actors are at the forefront to drive economic growth. When they operate with core values that prioritize ethical practices and social responsibility, they can contribute positively to society and the economy. That's why I want to mention the new appearance of the word "benefit corporations" or often referred to as "B Corp," which are a distinct category of for-profit corporations that are legally obligated to consider the impact of their decisions not only on shareholders but also on a wide range of stakeholders, including employees, customers, communities, and the environment.

This approach reflects a growing movement in business: combining profit with purpose. B Corps aim to do well financially while also doing good for society and the planet. They make social and environmental goals part of their core business model—not just an add-on.

As more consumers care about how companies treat people and the environment, the number of B Corps is expected to grow. These businesses are helping to reshape how companies contribute to a fairer and more sustainable world.

The nonprofit organization **B Lab** oversees the B Corp certification. Founded in 2006, B Lab supports businesses that want to make a positive impact. To become certified, companies must meet high standards for transparency, accountability, and sustainability—and they must renew their certification every three years by paying a fee and going through a review process.

Why Values Make the Difference

There's one story in particular that completely transformed my perspective on managerial behaviors. It's all about the value of "supporting each other in teams and being empathic."

In 1996, during my time at the Leading Product Development Executive Program at Harvard Business School, we were assigned a powerful and sobering case study: the 1986 Challenger space shuttle disaster.

Our team was given original NASA flight readiness reports, videos, and internal communications from the time. Our task was to analyze the decisions that led to the launch—and ultimately, the explosion that cost seven astronauts their lives. As we dove into the materials, something became clear: this wasn't just a technical failure. It was a failure of communication and culture.

Technically, the cause was known: a sealing ring (O-ring) in one of the solid-fuel rockets failed in cold weather. That part was understood even before the launch. So why did the shuttle lift off anyway?

The U.S. government appointed Nobel Prize-winning physicist Richard Feynman to lead the investigation. His commission confirmed the technical issue—but it was something in his final statement that truly struck me as a young mechanical engineer passionate about technology.

He wrote that beyond hardware, the real cause was a breakdown of trust and communication inside the teams. The culture discouraged open dissent. The one engineer who raised serious concerns about the O-ring's performance in cold conditions was ignored.

That shocked me.

It was my first real glimpse into how organizational culture can be as dangerous as flawed design. As aspiring leaders and innovators, we often focus on data, deadlines, and deliverables. But if people don't feel safe to speak up—if teams don't support one another—catastrophic decisions can happen, even when the truth is known.

That lesson stayed with me far beyond Harvard. It taught me that real leadership means listening, creating safe spaces for critical voices, and building cultures where truth can rise to the surface—before it's too late.

When teams don't support one another, catastrophic decisions can happen, even when the truth is known.

Let's take a closer look at the crucial process of decision-making. The Flight Readiness Officer of NASA was all set to hop on the video call with the boardroom right before the shuttle flight kicked off. I'll never forget the silence in the boardroom of the solid rocket producer Morton Thiokol when we listened to the previous discussions in the boardroom. The head of the company told his engineer to put down his engineer hat and put on his marketing hat. *"This rocket was meant to fly, not linger on Earth. We've already postponed the launch a few times because of the cold temperatures. The president is going to be on a live interview with the teacher on the shuttle tonight."*

According to the rules of the starting procedure, the Flight Readiness Officer was connected to the boardroom and asked a series of questions. *"Let's get this rocket started?"* After a quick pause, the company head gave the green light. As the problem was known, the officer waited for a few seconds, probably feeling the tension in the boardroom, and then asked, *"Is there anyone here who doesn't agree with this?"* The room went quiet for a few seconds. No answer. Can you imagine how much pressure there was on engineer Roger Boisjoly? The rest is history. The rocket blew up 30 minutes later during the first phase of its flight in front of the whole world, on TV. It was a spectacular failure to start. The accident shocked the entire world. It also made people question their trust in technology, showing that the limits might be closer than we realize.

In his book *What Do You Care What Other People Think?* Richard Feynman describes a different take on the events. This was my second most important takeaway from the exercise: he wrote that we can't make the public believe that flying to space is as safe as entering a bus around the corner. He describes that he was asking different people about the likelihood of a total loss of a shuttle. The answers were between 1 and 100 and up to 1 to 100,000. Whereas the 1 to 100 high-risk answers came from the technical staff members. The lower risk estimations came from the managers areas. What a huge difference. The latter would mean that over a timeframe of 300 years there could be launched shuttles on a daily basis, with only one loss in that time. Well noted that was in 1987. If we consider that between 1981 and 2011, 135 flights have been taking place with the loss of 2 shuttles. We see that the risk in reality was at 1 to 70! This story makes one thing clear. We've got to make sure we're communicating the facts about innovation clearly and accurately and highlighting the risks and effects on important issues.

In February 2012, the New York Times reported about the death of Roger Boisjoly at the age of 73 years. A reporter from the NPR radio station that visited him at his home in Utah in 1987 reported to have met a man that was thin, tearful, and tense. He huddled in the corner of a couch; his arms tightly folded on his chest. But he was ready to speak publicly:

"I'm very angry that nobody listened," Boisjoly told the reporter.[34] And he asked himself, if he could have done anything different. Six months before the Challenger explosion, he had predicted "a catastrophe of the highest order" involving "loss of

---

34 Howard Berkes, "Remembering Roger Boisjoly: He Tried to Stop Shuttle Challenger Launch," *NPR*, February 6, 2012, https://www.npr.org/sections/thetwo-way/2012/02/06/146490064/remembering-roger-boisjoly-he-tried-to-stop-shuttle-challenger-launch.

human life" in a memo to managers because of the problem with the temperature issue of the used materials.

But then a flash of certainty returned.

"We were talking to the right people," he said. *"We were talking to the people who had the power to stop that launch."*

Boisjoly testified before the Challenger Commission and filed unsuccessful lawsuits against Thiokol and NASA. He continued to suffer and was cold-shouldered by some of his colleagues. One said he'd drop his kids on Boisjoly's doorstep if they all lost their jobs, according to his wife, Roberta.

And she told about his death: *"He lived an honorable and ethical life. And he was at peace when he died."*

Isn't that a dramatic story?

Do we need more information to realize that innovation and change have to take place at a level that includes systemic and holistically driven dimension?

Yes, it is!

We'll also keep in mind that values and team principles like "supporting each other and never letting a colleague down in tough situations" are still the foundation of every human interaction—especially in our super-connected world. They make us strong and reliable.

It's not about punishing one of our members just because of the way the system and hierarchy work with leaders who aren't doing their job. It's not about punishing one of our members for following the rules.

This is a clear example of how systemic factors can distort our perceptions and cause us to miss the real issues, and the consequences were huge.

Now, let's dive deeper into how value creation can be seen in the context of innovation and change.

The 4-Level Value Model in Transformational Innovation

My experiences at conferences, seminars, and international meetings have consistently left me perplexed and disoriented. I was very often overutilized by so many different approaches and stories.

Thinking about and living according to my values gave me a sense of structure and direction in my work and personal life.

I am sure today that we need a new kind of value system—one that builds resilience and motivation and helps us develop meaningful strategies to tackle the urgent challenges of our time: respecting the planet and putting people first.

My friend Elke den Ouden, with whom I've collaborated in the innovation manager community for years, has some outstanding insights about how a value system that considers this could function. We were both on the steering committee for the Front End of Innovation (FEI) conference for over 15 years, and we met every year at the conferences. Elke worked for Philips for over 20 years and is now a researcher and professor at Eindhoven University of Technology. She is a TU/e Fellow in the Innovation, Technology, Entrepreneurship and Marketing group within the Department of Industrial Engineering and Innovation Sciences. She launched the book *Innovation Design: Creating Value for People, Organizations, and Society.*[35] It was in 2012. It's the most relevant literature out there for understanding what values mean at different levels of transformational innovation.

Elke outlines four distinct levels of value creation that can guide innovation efforts in a more holistic and impactful way:

1. **Value for the User**
2. **Value for the Organization**
3. **Value for the Ecosystem**
4. **Value for Society**

These four layers provide a framework not just for designing better products and services, but for creating innovation that truly matters—on every level.

Using these layers of values allows innovators to define their framework of possible contributors and co-developers from the beginning.

Let's have a short look into the values:

Value for the User

This level focuses on the value created for the user, as at the end an innovation needs to enable economical revenues. How to attract the consumer or customer for an extended period of use and not only for one use and one sale period? It has to involve designing innovations that improve the quality of life, meet personal needs, and enhance user experiences. Keeping an eye on our findings from ecosystems, this intent must be included in the central question that is used for the creation of the innovation. Therefore, the user is placed at the center of the value levels model. The aim is to create meaningful and engaging solutions that resonate with people on a personal level.

Value for the Organization

The second level of value is about the organization itself. It doesn't matter if it's a for-profit or a non-profit; it always tries to create lasting value for itself by offering added

---

35 Elke den Ouden, *Innovation Design – Creating Value for People, Organizations and Society* (London: Springer Verlag, 2012).

value to customers and, at the same time, creating value for employees by providing jobs. It's clear that organizations are involved in social interaction through their many relationships within their supply chains, customer and innovation ecosystems, and partnerships. This means that shared values and goals are always being addressed in ongoing innovation activities and are in line with the broader community. It's essential to adapt quickly, achieve goals, integrate everything, and balance values.

When it comes to transformational innovation, it's essential to spot and meet needs that users might not even realize they have. Remember to consider brand recognition when creating new ideas. It's an essential component of any effective innovation strategy. Take our jewelry field, for example. Our search field, "unexpected customer surprises," builds the emotional value of the brand. New business models are the key to organizational growth. They improve operational efficiency and integration within existing businesses. Transformational innovation is the driving force behind these changes. The goal is clear: innovation must help organizations capture value for themselves while making a positive contribution to society.

Value for the Ecosystems

If we want to create value that benefits everyone, we've got to look at the whole ecosystem. The Business Model Canvas method, which is shown in the adjusted templates in part III of the book, is a great way to get a general idea of the whole ecosystem. The whole ecosystem should extend to include suppliers of suppliers and customers of customers. Our strategy is simple: we help our customers succeed in their own ecosystems. In today's advanced economies of knowledge and transformation, it's clear that skills and relationships are more important and make such value networks more successful. In these business networks, which are a natural result of a well-defined innovation ecosystem approach, organizations can and will achieve more value than they could on their own. From what I've seen, in the early stages of innovation ecosystems, it's hard to know for sure what users need and how they'll behave. I'll say it again: it's really important to have dedicated innovation ecosystems that tackle the right innovation question and get the key players involved as soon as possible. As the involved partners evolve over time, it's important to have shared visions and values. We can group ecosystem partners in a way that makes sense by keeping those who contribute technology and know-how separate from those who contribute sales capabilities and different ways to market things. It's a challenge for the innovation leadership teams to combine both.

Value for the Society

Society is the highest level of value in the model. Users, organizations, and ecosystems are all part of society. When we're deciding on the price of products, we can't always think about all the costs, especially when it comes to the environment. But in the end, it's the citizens who have to pay the price. Whether it's a polluted environment, a regional crisis due to unemployment, or other issues, when taxes need to be raised, it's the citizen who ends up paying the price.

When we think about societal issues, we open a world of opportunities to create value for society as a whole. For example, we can use the UN Sustainable Development Goals as a guide to find new ways to create value for groups we didn't expect. Frugal innovation is a great example of this. It's all about making affordable, easy-to-use solutions for people who need them. It's about coming up with new ideas that are needed because of the situation, and it's all about making sure that the solutions are affordable and easy for people to get. One great example of this is using new chemical fluids for refrigerators when electricity isn't available. Take, for example, the solutions developed by my innovation network peer Sumitra Rajagopalan for baby incubators in poor areas of India. These solutions have helped reduce the death rate of babies in regions without electricity. Sumitra is the founder and CEO of Bio Astra Technologies, a company that develops smart materials and biomaterials. She also used her know-how in bioastronautics and material science to come up with cutting-edge solutions like cooling fabrics to effectively relieve heat stress. This technology is a lifesaver for workers in the hottest areas of India.

Different Views on the Value Framework

The model was a real game-changer. It showed how innovation can be focused on sustainability. It opened my eyes to the possibilities and the impact. It gave me some great arguments for decision-making and prioritization.

Elke's book mixes ideas from economics, psychology, sociology, and ecology. When these angles meet at the 4 levels pictured, it creates a happy place where user psychology and user satisfaction meet.

If the psychological view meets the organizational level, the result is all about the company's core values. They're basically the purpose and objectives of an organization. How employees act and think, along with setting goals on a strategic level, creates a framework for self-empowerment and further development on both a personal and organizational level. Right now, in our organization, our core values are being built on being imaginative, vigorous, inventive, and implementation-oriented.

Next, we can define new value propositions, which are simple statements of the tangible and intangible benefits of a new solution. By clearly communicating these benefits, users can decide whether to accept the solution and replace an existing, known solution. This is how it works, both for the people who come up with the new ideas (employees) and for the people who use them. Innovation only works when real users are integrated on a broader scale. This is just one example of what we can develop based on the model.

The framework lets you blend the four values and four views to make 16 different view models. I used this basic value framework model a lot to develop value propositions for communication throughout the entire development process. Every time, I find new and interesting insights. Once you've got a handle on the central innovation value proposition, it'll be the basis for defining the innovation ecosystem. And trust me, or not: A solid value proposition that's already been tested with lead customers and blended with a bold vision is one of the most important tools in the innovation game. It fits very well with Victor Hugo's saying, *"Nothing is stronger than an idea whose time has come."* The framework can help you spot or even create the early signals!

A solid value proposition that's already been tested with lead customers and blended with a bold vision is one of the most important tools in the innovation game.

A very interesting and valuable overview of Elkes Value Framework, along with the steps for creating shared value, can be found on the homepage of the Technical University of Eindhoven.[36]

---

36 "Value Models for Meaningful Innovations," accessed December 11, 2024, https://www.tue-light house.nl/Images/Propositions/20161003%20Value%20models.pdf. A brief description of the tools is also available in *Advanced Design Methods for Successful Innovation*, eds. C. de Bont, P. H. den Ouden, R. Schifferstein, F. E. H. M. Smulders, and M. van der Voort (The Hague: Design United, 2013).

Chapter 12
The Importance of Systemic Thinking

We often speak now about how systemic factors shape decisions and set priorities. But what does that really mean for innovation?

To truly talk about innovation and meaningful change, we need to understand systemic thinking—the ability to see the big picture and how everything is connected. Instead of focusing only on individual parts, systemic thinking helps us understand how those parts interact and influence each other. And in today's complex world, that kind of thinking is more essential than ever. Systemic thinking is key to making sense of the complex and interconnected world we live in. And where one-size-fits-all solutions are impossible.

I got a deeper understanding of this while attending a one-year educational program in Switzerland called *Organizations in Movement*. It brought together managers from schools, businesses, and NGOs, all eager to explore how systems behave during change. It was eye-opening. This helped me understand one of the biggest roadblocks to change— systemically inertia.

At the heart of this exploration were the revolutionary ideas of the two Chilean biologists Humberto Maturana and Francisco Varela, who were trailblazers in the field of autopoiesis. "Autopoiesis" comes from Greek, "auto," for self, and "poiesis," for creation or production. The idea behind it is that living systems are like little miracles. They're always creating and sustaining themselves. Originally a biological concept, it has since been applied to organizations, communities, and even societies. The key insight: systems have their own rules, processes, and internal structures that help them survive. They resist change not because they're inflexible, but because their survival depends on stability.

This helps explain why established organizations often push back against innovation. It's not that they don't want change—it's that they're designed to protect what already works. Like an immune system, they resist disruption.

But innovation depends on disruption. So, what should we do?

Here we find again the already discussed innovator's dilemma or the ambidexterity trap, or whatever we want to name it. We are dealing with a network of processes that produce the components that are necessary for its survival and at the same time, they adapt to changes in their environment while keeping their identity.

This is different from the traditional idea of organisms as systems defined by their environmental inputs and outputs. Instead, it suggests that the essence of life lies in its internal, self-regulated organization.

In organizational development, a core principle is to recognize and work with the system, not against it. A rigid organization that only delivers small improvements needs a gentle disruption—shake-up to stimulate creativity. On the other hand, a chaotic system that can't deliver consistent results needs structure and focus.

https://doi.org/10.1515/9783111448329-014

In both cases, resistance is natural—but also valuable. When we hit resistance, we're actually finding the edges of the system. And that's where the real work begins. If we ask the right questions and involve the people who are directly affected, we unlock hidden behaviors and create space for growth.

This brings us to a second essential principle: involve people as co-creators, not passive recipients. The ones who feel uncertain or afraid about the future are often the ones who hold the key to the solution—if we listen. People are part of the system too.

In fact, the human body and mind are perfect examples of living systems—constantly self-regulating, adapting, and balancing. Just like organizations, we resist change unless we're aware of it. That's why awareness and reflection are so important: they allow us to break free from automatic patterns and reset how we respond.

We must develop a higher level of awareness and consciousness to control, or even reprogram, the automatic functions that are part of our instincts and involuntary reactions. It's obvious that any living system will do whatever it takes to keep functioning. These fundamental principles of Maturana and Varela form the bedrock of systems theory. Systems theory is the key to analyzing and understanding complex systems, including social, organizational, and technological systems. This knowledge allows us to see entire organizations as living systems that produce and reproduce the parts necessary for them to keep going. These ideas have had a huge impact on fields like sociology, psychology, and artificial intelligence.

Personally, I've learned that the most effective way to work in innovation is by taking a relationship-oriented, system-aware approach. That means respecting how people are connected, understanding resistance, and guiding teams through complex problems with empathy and clarity.

I've been trying to figure out how to put this into practice for a while now. And it's time now to discuss one of the most effective methods I've come up with. I apply and improve it regularly.

The key to overcoming systemic resistance lies not in forcing change, but in recognizing its true nature. It's about building trust and creating space where change becomes possible—together.

Cracking the Code of Systemic Inertia: How to Lead Through Reciprocity

As Head of Innovation Networks, I constantly ran into two invisible but powerful roadblocks: the "Not Invented Here" and "Not Sold Here" effects. At first, I underestimated how much these silent barriers could drain team morale and collaboration. That was a mistake.

Determined to figure out what was really going on, I dug into the psychology behind workplace behavior. That's when I discovered the Law of Reciprocity—a powerful concept from social psychology that simply means people tend to return favors. When someone gives you something—advice, support, a small gesture—you instinctively feel compelled to give back. It's basic human wiring. Marketers know this well (ever wonder why free samples are so effective?). But in innovation management, we're not about creating obligations. We focus on building trust and a collaborative spirit around the things we've got going on. We share resources and support each other, and we're always looking to exchange ideas. This means that we always try to act in a way that benefits all of us and makes things better for everyone. So, it looks like reciprocity is a universal principle. In some places, people really believe in the idea of giving back, while in others, it's not as big of a deal.

As I began to internalize this, something shifted in me. I listened more deeply, paid closer attention to what others truly needed, and started getting better results— not just in negotiations, but in how people responded to me. But even then, I knew I could do more. I needed a framework to turn this insight into action.

That's when I merged the idea of Reciprocity with a method I already used in high-stakes meetings: ICE—Interests, Concerns, and Expectations.

Here's how it works: Before any crucial meeting, I do a fast, focused stakeholder analysis. I identify as:

I – **Interests**: What motivates them? What are they passionate about?

C – **Concerns**: What's keeping them up at night?

E – **Expectations**: What results are they hoping for?

Armed with this insight, I craft an opening that acknowledges all three. For example, when meeting a network colleague, I might say:

> I know you're passionate about cutting-edge technologies (Interest). I understand the pressure we're all under to stay ahead of the competition (Concern), and I also know you're looking for quick wins to respond effectively (Expectation).

Even if I don't have the short-term fix they're hoping for, that opening shows I understand them—and that makes collaboration far more likely. It's not about having all the answers—it's about making people feel seen, heard, and respected.

And here's the kicker: **Reciprocity opens doors ICE alone couldn't**. Even in situations with political baggage or historical friction, starting with generosity— genuine goodwill—helped melt some of the ice.

There are some exceptions where even the best will of offering collaboration has a hard time: It's about systemic warning flags like "comes from the wrong management group," "my boss could dislike talking to him," or similar. If you hear such comments, you must be aware that survival has the highest ranking in decision-making. In such cases it is of the highest importance that this issue is addressed. I recommend doubling the "C" (Concerns) and saying explicitly, *"I know your boss will not like it from the beginning, but if he understands the interdependencies, he may like it!"*

To make this approach easier to apply, here's a quick guide:

The R-ICE Method for Everyday Innovation Conversations

R – Reciprocity and Variety

Start with something positive. A warm comment, a shared smile, or a light joke. Even if previous interactions were rough, extend kindness without expecting anything in return. Just don't overdo it—authenticity matters. Never be too friendly when history shows that the people you are dealing with have disrespected you.

I – Interests

Frame your topic around what matters to them. Link your agenda to their motivations. When you show you understand their world, you've earned their attention.

C – Concerns

Most people operate in "efficiency mode." They're solving today's problems, not thinking about tomorrow. Respect that. Acknowledge their challenges before you pitch something new. This lowers their defenses and opens the door to innovation.

E – Expectations

People want to know: "What's in it for me?" Anticipate this. Signal that you understand their desired outcomes. Be clear, concise, and considerate of hierarchy and communication preferences.

In my experience, R-ICE is a small shift that makes a massive difference. It's simple, adaptable, and rooted in human nature. If you're serious about fostering innovation, this isn't just a technique—it's a mindset worth mastering.

Bias, Survival Instinct, and Global Thinking

Understanding and addressing systemic issues often starts with recognizing the problem of bias. Bias shows up when we favor certain outcomes, perspectives, or data over others, which can lead to unfair or incomplete conclusions. It's like tipping the scales so one side carries more weight than the other.

Bias is deeply tied to our history as humans. It helped our ancestors survive by encouraging trust and cooperation within small groups like tribes, families, and communities. This was crucial for survival in dangerous environments. However, in today's interconnected world, these same instincts can create barriers to broader understanding and collaboration.

Now, with the rise of global AI systems, we have an opportunity to overcome these barriers. AI can help connect people from different cultures and nations, creating a more unified global community. By enabling the free flow of ideas, information, and innovations, AI breaks down traditional borders and brings the world closer together.

When we step back and look at the big picture, it's easy to feel overwhelmed by all the ways we can make a difference. However, adopting a mindset that sees humanity as one global tribe can help us move forward. This approach fosters mutual understanding and cooperation, just as tribal thinking once did for early human societies. By viewing ourselves as interconnected, we can make smarter, more impactful decisions that benefit everyone.

This doesn't mean we'll eliminate competition or the principles of free markets and technological development. Instead, we'll create diverse innovation ecosystems that meet at shared goals: a healthier planet and respect for basic human rights. Natural tribes have long understood that an individual's well-being is tied to the group's well-being. In the same way, we must see that our actions impact the world around us.

In short, systemic thinking is not just a theory—it's a practical way to solve real-world problems. By recognizing how interconnected everything is, we can develop solutions that are both effective and sustainable. As we aim for a more integrated global community, the lessons from tribal cooperation and the capabilities of AI can help us build a brighter, more inclusive future.

We have already heard a little about **systemic inertia**, the resistance to change when an organization appears outwardly successful. This illusion of stability can tempt leaders to dismiss disruptive ideas as unnecessary or risky. Without **strong reasoning or evidence**, new proposals often fall flat before they even begin.

Another major pitfall is bypassing internal hierarchies and competence fields. Starting a project without the right buy-in can provoke resistance at the worst moment—when ideas are most fragile. As Einstein put it, "We can't solve our problems with the same thinking we used when we created them."

Systemic change requires more than new tools or processes. It requires **new mindsets**, emotional intelligence, and clear communication across all levels of the organization. Tools like the above introduced **R-ICE (Reciprocity, Interests, Concerns, Expectations)** are my favorite ones. Senior leaders and frontline employees see the world differently. Tailoring conversations and strategies to their perspectives is key to avoiding friction.

Consider Nokia: once a global leader in mobile phones, they failed to adapt to the smartphone era. Their partnership with Microsoft over Android was a critical misstep. The CEO's famous quote, *"We didn't do anything wrong, but somehow we lost,"* is a textbook example of **failing to read the signals of systemic change**.

Let's take a look at an example to better show how important systemic thinking is for a stagnant organization that needs to be transformed:

Picture a manufacturing company (SME) with declining sales and growing competition. The usual way to deal with this would be to cut costs and boost production efficiency. But in a fast-changing market, and when your technology is outdated and not competitive anymore, these measures just don't cut it. If we take a look at the big picture and use some systemic approaches, we'll see a few key issues. Is it outdated technology alone, a lack of innovation, or low employee morale? The leadership team must implement a plan to make significant changes. This plan must address how people in the company work together, how they're connected to outside technology and competition, and how to solve problems by focusing on understanding people, being creative, and trying new things.

I am personally convinced that the competition of ideas, sustainable innovation settings, and, most importantly, forms of liberal lifestyles bear in themselves the potential for optimism. Especially when we succeed in bringing together the younger generations with the more experienced generations, like the baby boomers. I experienced this potential in the last years of my professional career and can say that without the respectful collaboration of both generations, my capabilities to adapt to the fast-changing world would have been limited or risked failing completely. The "European way of life" could emerge as a beacon for modernization. I would like to see this transformation unfold, firmly believing that the 21st century holds the promise of a new era. The alternatives that are promised by forces that want to regulate or restrict the free thinking and, with that, unavoidable the creative freedom of our spirit are far less desirable. The emergence of the new Homo Innovaticus that I want to describe in part 3 has the potential to bridge the gap between the creative contributions of individuals and the restrictive nature of oversimplified fake truths that are not able to give us stabilizing effects by any means.

My intention is to create a resource that will serve as a definitive reference for anyone who wants to learn about the principles that have worked—and those that have not. My book doesn't claim to be a comprehensive guide, but it does contain the insights that have helped me navigate my personal journey. I'm sharing them as recommendations that can help others understand their own values and beliefs. This book is about the choices we make and the impact they have on ourselves, others, and the planet. We decide who benefits and who is involved in our actions. Our values must guide us to prioritize the planet and people.

I want to conclude with a business fable and a poem from one of my favorite writers, Erich Kästner: *"One should not stare into the window of the future. It lies in bed with the past. The first humans were not the last monkeys. And where there is a head, there is usually a board."*

The saying "He's got a board in front of his head" is an undeniable reference to the core issues of systemic innovation barriers and an inherent aspect of human nature.

But looking through the lens of systemic thinking, I am sure it can be transformed into a power source of collective advancement.

Again, the right mindset for growth and adaptation is key.

I love a very nice business fable that was given to me by an IBM employee with his presentation about the IBM "Wild Duck" program. This program was started by IBM founder Thomas Watson Sr. and was intended for a group of creative employees who were given the freedom to break the rules and work on new ideas without the usual constraints. The business fable I mean was written by Spencer Johnson in 1998. The story is about two mice and two "little people" who live in a maze and search for cheese, which represents their goals and desires. When the cheese is moved, the characters react differently to the change, and the book explores how to deal with change in both work and life. One of the "little people" resists and denies change. He is fearful and skeptical of the unknown, preferring to stay in his comfort zone even when the cheese is gone. His refusal to adapt leaves him stuck and hungry. The other "little person" initially reacts like the other, with denial and fear. However, he eventually comes to terms with the change and decides to face his fears. He learns to laugh at his situation and ventures out to find new cheese, demonstrating personal growth and adaptability.

It's becoming more and more obvious that, as we move forward with our innovation development, we need to be ready for the chance that our cheese will get moved along the way to our targets.

Strategy, Openness, and the Pitfalls of Top-Down Planning

We haven't discussed strategy itself yet. Traditional strategy was a top-down game. Executives set the course; the rest followed.

The way company strategies are developed has undergone significant transformations, just as the transformation described for the evolution of innovation and its arrival at dynamic innovation ecosystems. A profound innovation strategy is not possible without being anchored or, better said, empowered by a clever company strategy. The "impact of not addressing" how an organization drives change and innovation has changed. Especially in times of technological volatility and new management paradigms, this impact can decide whether an organization fails or succeeds. Traditionally, strategies were developed through a top-down approach where senior leadership would set objectives, which were communicated down the organizational hierarchy. The same is true of innovation processes: they are most successful when all kinds of people are involved in the development process. In this ever-changing landscape, it's essential to adopt innovative approaches as the nervous system for staying agile and proactive. This means actively engaging with the relevant ecosystems of technology, society, and business practices to be a part of the change. At the same time, use them to recognize the signals for necessary organizational change. Change is always part of strategic action.

It's not easy, but it's absolutely necessary. The relatively new "Open Strategy" theory has provided numerous valuable insights and learning cases, demonstrating how to ensure success in this area.

My friend Prof. Friedrich von den Eichen is the CEO of IMP Consultants, a leading strategy consulting firm and a pioneer on this topic. He is also the co-author of the book "Open Strategy—Mastering Disruption from Outside the C-suite."[37] He has recently made clear how strategy work is often performed in companies: *"It's called 'strategy,' but it's nothing more than a buzzword. It's essential to create an internal identity and make it engaging. There is nothing surprising or differentiating externally. The objective is clear: to conquer daunting challenges with straightforward strategies. This is unacceptable. The way strategy is practiced today is unacceptable. The good news is that the problem has been recognized and there is a proven solution."* He means digital tools, including strategy contests, which allow the widest participation. Hybrid digital/in-person tools are also included, such as a "nightmare competitor challenge" and a workshop tool that gamifies the business model development process. It's essential to remember the tools that help companies implement and sustain open strategy efforts. I'm proud to contribute when senior industry experts are called upon to provide substantial game contributions to address the "nightmare competitor challenges" of companies.

The preface of Prof. Gary Hamel to the book Open Strategy is self-explanatory. This is the definitive statement. *"An open strategy process is messier and more time-consuming than the top-down alternative, but the benefits are worth the effort. Open strategy is more vital than ever, yet it remains all too rare due to executive hubris. Get to work on Open Strategy now. It's one of the most important management innovations of the new decade."*

Role Models and the Human Element

Progress always requires role models. People who stand firm in their beliefs, even when it's hard. Everyone has a role model. These people show you the way at critical moments in your life. My personal role models are people who have always been willing to stand up for their values and beliefs, even when it meant facing failures and risks. They have always been people who have changed the world.

I am closing in on their core behavior. I see their mindset, which can turn an obvious failure into a gift.

My dad was the one who taught me how to tell stories and to respect nature and all living things. He was among the last to be raised with the principles of tribal wisdom in traditional mountain cultures that are already described in old Roman writings about the Celtic tribes, who were famous for extraordinary food production (e.g., Pliny the Elder in 77 AD).

---

37 Christian Stadler, Julia Hautz, Kurt Matzler, Stephan Friedrich von den Eichen, and Gary Hamel, preface to *Open Strategy: Mastering Disruption from Outside the C-Suite* (Cambridge, MA: The MIT Press, October 12, 2021).

He missed out on a big part of his early years because he was part of the well-known 1926-born generation that was sent to World War II at the age of 17. He blamed Hitler for robbing him of his youth. He made the best of it. He looked out for me and my brother when we were kids, making sure we got the most out of the opportunities we had. We were fortunate to grow up in a free society where we always could decide on our own pathways to growth.

I've met many role models that have positively energized my development. While I never met them in person, I've had conversations with some of them. They've given me a lot of energy for a long time.

One of them was Pope John Paul II, whom I met in my representative role as head of the parish council of our hometown in 1996 in Rome. I gave him a gift: a crystal pin with the symbol of the priest who was beatified by him that very day. This priest, Father Jakob Gapp, was a victim of the Nazi regime in 1943 and was from our village. After exchanging a few words on the strength of the beatified Father Gapp, I was deeply impressed by his words on the upholding of Father Gapps values in our time. Those values have been and still are my inner compass. It's like an early warning system. Back in 1938, he made it clear that a system with the mindset of the NS regime was never going to bring a good future. He ended up giving his life to defend his opinion. The records of history show that Minister of Inner Affairs Heinrich Himmler paid him deep respect, as he made clear in his recorded statement. He stated, *"If we had 1 million Nazi regime members with the strength of Jakob Gapp, I would not worry about the 1000-year Reich."* Not hindering him from sentencing him to death and labeling him as "forever dishonorable" in 1943. Isn't it a fascinating legacy when we see that in 1996, in the course of the beatification, the German government overturned this conviction? Isn't it an encouraging story that the truth someday will win, even if a current situation forces many of us to give in and go with the flow? In connection with the systemic discussion, this is my favorite example, showing we need courageous people who see through the ways of the dishonest. Father Gapp's last words were about *"Now I have to stay, even if the worst threatens me."*

Another meeting involved Mikhail Gorbachev in the year 2000 when I was leading the project to produce the biggest cross ever made of crystal, again in Rome. Mr. Gorbachev was the head of a beneficial organization, and I was introduced to him in my role. He expressed interest in technical details, and I'll always remember his profound comments during our conversation about challenges and risk-taking: *He said that you are always going to be part of the problem or part of the solution to a challenge. It depends on your decision, on who you want to be. He always tries to be part of the solution, he stated out.* As we know that he was one of the greatest influential statesmen, such experiences burn themselves into your memory, and you can always return to them. Using them as behavioral recipes.

Human connection, courage, and inspiration are not luxuries. They are the fuel for innovation. In a world shaped by rapid AI development, we must not forget our deeply social nature. We evolve by learning from each other.

It's simply the way we have learned to learn as social beings over evolution. We must thoroughly develop and cultivate this basic need. The way we interact as a species is one of our most sacred gifts. We must prioritize this heritage, especially as we move closer to talking about AI.

Balancing Chaos and Order: The Birthplace of the Unexpected

The concept of the **chaordic organization**, coined by Dee Hock, the charismatic founder of the VISA company, offers a framework for reimagining how we organize, innovate, and lead in times of profound transformation.

Dee Hock developed the **chaordic model** to address the limitations of rigid, top-down systems in a rapidly changing world. In his book *Birth of the Chaordic Age*, first published in 1999, he describes the term "chaordic" as a blend of *chaos* and *order*, reflecting the belief that thriving organizations must balance structure with flexibility.

At its core, the chaordic principle proposes that:
- **Distributed authority** empowers individuals and teams within decentralized networks.
- **Shared purpose and values** replace rigid rules as the main drivers of behavior.
- **Self-organization** allows systems to adapt organically, just like in nature.
- **Chaos and order** are both essential: too much control leads to stagnation, while too much chaos leads to breakdown.
- **Interdependence** is key: collaboration across boundaries is more powerful than isolated competition.

It encourages **agility, innovation, and resilience** in the face of unpredictable change. From startups to global responses to crises and even blockchain technologies, chaordic thinking is already reshaping how we work, govern, and grow.

But how do we activate this mindset? How do we build systems that support it?

This is especially interesting when we speak about a place where structure supports freedom, and freedom fuels innovation. VISA, one of the world's largest financial systems, was built on this principle. It wasn't governed from the top down. Instead, it was **self-organized, purpose-driven, and built around shared values**, not rigid rules.

Reading about the chaordic principle reminded me of my time as a member of an experimental group of Doris Wilhelmer in Vienna, which I described in part I. In her simulations of organizational structures, I encountered the tetralemma, a principle derived from ancient logic, particularly from Eastern philosophy and modern systems thinking. Western logic tends to choose between A or B. The tetralemma offers four (and sometimes five) positions. This is interesting when we talk about innovation. Innovation's job is to create something new. It's more about the real, new, and unexpected. When we start by exploring the existing landscapes and learn to better know them by naming them and visualizing them, we inevitably come to a point where our brain starts to come up with such new, unexpected solutions.

A tetralemma exercise includes the decline of 2 seemingly obvious solutions to an innovation question:
–   **A is true.**
–   **B is true.**
–   **Both A and B are true.**
–   **Neither A nor B is true.**
–   **A new, unexpected solution emerges.**

This final stance—the **emergent fifth option**—is the beating heart of innovation. It's the domain of chaordic systems. And it's only possible when we allow ideas to mix, collide, and evolve in unpredictable ways.

Unlimited diversity and openness must prepare the fertile ground for it. When a young developer pairs with a retired engineer, when an activist collaborates with a seasoned diplomat, when the wisdom of "how it worked" meets the question "why can't it be different?"—that's the tetralemma in motion. That's where new paradigms emerge—solutions we couldn't have imagined in a rigid binary world.

We need **intelligent navigation**. We need chaordic systems that are alive, dynamic, and deeply human. We need to **foster intergenerational synergy** as a strategic asset, not a sentimental ideal. And we must do this with a clear understanding that innovation doesn't come from choosing the "right" answer. It comes from **creating space for the unexpected to arise**.

That's the path forward:
–   A mindset for change.
–   A structure that flexes.
–   A collaboration that transcends age.
–   A logic that welcomes the impossible.

This is not just how we innovate.

It's how we evolve.

And when Exupéry was right with his saying about things evolving from the simple over the complex to the useful, we must take into consideration that balancing chaordic procedures could find some answers in looking at the old Chinese Dao concepts:

In her very new book, *The Dao of Complexity*—Making Sense and Making Waves in Turbulent Times, the author Jean Boulton states that a complex world cannot be explained by "forces connecting things" because forces are not things. To understand complicated situations, she writes, we need ways to consider different points of view:

We also need to trust our instincts and our ability to think logically. Methods must allow for paradox and allow situations to change over time and for new features to emerge. We can't just sit back and think that we're not going to have an effect on the situations we're interested in. When trying to understand the complex world, it's important to consider all the different factors and use scientific methods that rely on stories and personal experiences, not just hard facts and statistics. In academic language, the epistemology (the study of knowledge) must reflect the ontology (the study of existence). It's not scientific to analyze a situation as if it operates like a machine when it doesn't. The methods need to be more subtle and should be based on a poetic and intuitive understanding of what is happening. Sometimes, we see things that aren't really there.

What a wonderful approach and conclusion to the question of how to balance structures for innovation and the need to realize systems on the basis of the chaordic principle and respecting the systemic thinking—the ability to see the big picture and how everything is connected.

Chapter 13
Navigating the AI Epoch: Balancing Disruption with Human Dignity

The latest developments in artificial intelligence are generating significant interest and prompting reflection on its potential impact on our lives. It is an exciting time. We are on the brink of a new era, an age in which artificial intelligence will enter new areas of our lives. The pertinent question is not whether we want it, but rather how.

As we mentioned, global AI systems are going to change the way we connect people from different cultures and countries. This "global AI condensation" is great because it lets information, ideas, and innovations flow more freely, breaking down the barriers that once separated us. We also talked about how important it is to work together across different disciplines.

Recent publications and news from the AI front bring to mind the early days of the "digital transformation" that began in the mid-1990s. During that period, the "digital tornado" leveled one industry after another over the next 20 years. The music and entertainment industry are a prime example. It went from vinyl LPs and compact discs to streaming platforms like Spotify, Amazon Music, and many more. The same is true for the Kodak story in photography, which saw analog photography give way to digital cameras and smartphones, largely replacing film cameras and traditional photography services.

The closure of countless brick-and-mortar stores due to the rise of e-commerce giants like Amazon and eBay is irrefutable evidence that the retail sector is undergoing a fundamental transformation. Telecommunications is another perfect example of how traditional landline services have been rendered obsolete by mobile and internet-based communication technologies. My neighbor in the 1980s had a secure and well-paying job as a typewriter mechanic. The digital tornado left him unemployed in just two years.

We're all seeing this change firsthand, and I think we're about to step into a whole new era thanks to AI. This arrival is going to change even faster and have an even bigger impact than the digital transformation wave. Every industry has had to deal with the question of when and how the AI tornado will hit the core business and how to prepare for change. As Clayton Christensen said in the first chapter of his book Disruptive Technologies, we've got to remember that "disruptive technologies" are inevitable. We decided to develop new skills like Open Innovation and innovation ecosystems. We also got better at spotting weak signals of disruption. What have we learned from this period that could help us in this new situation with AI?

In an unpredictable (VUCA) world, tried and tested methodologies will become possibly useless. While some practices may become obsolete, fundamental approaches

https://doi.org/10.1515/9783111448329-015

rooted in trust, safety, and stability remain vital. I'm talking about valuable, refined skills and enduring principles that have proven to be effective throughout evolving change processes.

We must balance the introduction of new, disruptive elements—such as artificial intelligence—with the application of proven frameworks to discover the big opportunities that are lying ahead. In short, we must: It is essential to consider contemporary influences and traditional methodologies for navigating this duality and ambiguity. I am certain that cultivating resilience and trust is making the difference. Before we delve into the potential threats and opportunities presented by AI, it's crucial to understand that AI will never, no matter how advanced it becomes, be able to completely replace these two human characteristics.

We must say "never ever replacing completely" because when we analyze the recent interview of the "godfather of AI" and Nobel Prize Winner 2024, Geoffry Hinton, other ideas could also arise. Let's try to open up our awareness to the threats and opportunities in an unbiased way.

In his groundbreaking interview, In the most successful BBC television broadcast in history, "60 Minutes," he confidently asserts that AI will do enormous good.[38] However, he also directly addresses a warning, stating that AI systems may be more intelligent than we know and that there's a chance the machines could take over control.

The moderator Scott Pelley asks him directly: In this moment, does humanity know what it's doing? *Hinton's answer is clear: No.*

Do you believe we are entering a period in which we may have things more intelligent than us for the first time ever? Yes.
Do you believe they can understand? *Yes.*
Do you believe they are intelligent? *Yes.*
Do you believe these systems have experiences of their own and can make decisions based on those experiences? *In the same sense as people do—yes.* Are they conscious? *I believe they currently lack substantial self-awareness, so I conclude they are not yet conscious.*
Will they eventually develop self-awareness or consciousness? *They will have it in time.*
So will human beings be the second most intelligent beings on the planet? Yes.

Hinton further explains that his work on "Neural Networks" was not planned. It was born of a failure in the 1970s at the University of Edinburgh. He had a dream of simulating a neural network on a computer. He wanted to use it as a tool for what he was really studying: the human brain. At the time, almost no one was doing this.

---

38 Geoffrey Hinton, "'Godfather of AI' Geoffrey Hinton: The 60 Minutes Interview," *60 Minutes*, CBS News, November 2023, https://www.youtube.com/watch?v=qrvK_KuIeJk.

Hinton, in the course of the interview, is explaining how neuronal networks build their own learning algorithm and then interact with data it produces. These sophisticated neural networks are highly adaptive at performing a range of tasks. However, we do not understand the precise mechanisms by which they operate. The implications of these systems autonomously generating and executing their own computer code are significant.

He then provides further examples. Two robots are playing football. He makes it clear that they haven't been trained to play football. Their mission is simple: shoot the ball into the opposing team's goal. They taught themselves everything. What we did was we designed the learning algorithm.

The learning algorithms, he explains, are a bit like designing the principle of evolution, but when this learning algorithm then interacts with data, it produces complicated neural networks that are good at doing things, but we don't really understand what they produce.

He says that they are autonomously writing their own computer and executing their own computer code to modify themselves? And states that that's a serious worry and that when the systems become too self-sacrificing just to turn them off, it will not even be possible because they'll be very good at convincing people because they'll have learned from all the novels that were ever written in all the books of Machiavelli and the political connections.

We must say that it does seem a little spooky for now. It reminds us of that story from Walt Disney: The Sorcerer and the Apprentice.

In the story, the magician's lazy apprentice who, while his master is away, uses the incantations he has learned to bring a broom to life and make it carry water for him. The apprentice is Micky Mouse, and the story starts with him, weary from carrying water. The sorcerer wipes his brow, is bored with his own work, removes his tall, pointed hat and leaves his cavern. As soon as he is alone mickey puts on the sorcerer's hat and commands his broom to come to life pick up the buckets and carry water for him from the fountain outside to a huge vat in the cavern. Once he has the broom settled into this routine, mickey falls asleep in an armchair and dreams that he is standing high on a cliff conducting the clouds and stars and planets in their courses and calling up waves from the sea below when the waves crash over him. Mickey wakes an alarm to find that the armchair is floating in water. That fills the cavern. Mickey commands the broom to stop, but the broom walks right over him on its way to the fountain for more water. Mickey grabs an axe and chops the broom into splinters. Each splinter comes to life as a new broom, and each new broom carries two more buckets. This broom army marches unstoppably to the fountain. Fills all its buckets, then lines up to pour a flood of water into the cavern. Mickey's efforts to bail out the cavern are completely unsuccessful. He jumps onto the sorcerer's massive magic book, which is riding the whirlpool, and searches for a formula to stop the brooms. No luck! At this moment the sorcerer returns, parting the waters as he descends the stairs. He commands the flood to vanish, and the broom army to become one broom again. Then he contemplates the apprentice who did all this mischief. Shamed, Mickey takes off the sorcerer's hat and returns it to his unsmiling master. He hands the broom to the magician, picks up his two buckets and starts to tiptoe away. Mickey does not see the sorcerer smile.

We love stories that end well. But I get a very uneasy feeling about how we can stop artificial intelligence self-realization. When it starts doing things that are human and today controlled by morals and responsibility—at least in most cases. We can't hope that we wake up from the AI nightmare of losing control. We can't hope that the sorcerer comes back and makes everything unhappen. It is gone.

Game over!! Oh my god!

This is now an Alarming Point!!

Gary Marcus, a respected AI researcher and NYU professor emeritus, also argues in his new book, "Taming Silicon Valley—How We Can Ensure That AI Works for Us" that while AI has the potential to revolutionize various fields, it also poses significant risks if not properly regulated.[39]

He is asking if AI will help humanity or harm it. AI could revolutionize science, medicine, and technology and deliver us a world of abundance and better health. Or it could be a disaster, leading to the downfall of democracy or even our extinction. Marcus explains that we still have a choice. And that the decisions we make now about AI will shape our next century. He also explains how Big Tech is taking advantage of us, how AI could make things much worse, and, most importantly, what we can do to safeguard our democracy, our society, and our future. He highlights as well how Big Tech companies have often prioritized profit over safety and transparency, leading to the premature release of AI systems that are unreliable and biased!

He proposes several measures, including data rights, layered AI oversight, and meaningful tax reform, to create a safer and more equitable AI landscape.

Marcus emphasizes the need for firm regulation and public pressure to ensure that AI benefits society rather than harms it.

We must underline the importance of this new challenge and the urgent need for responsible use of AI. I hope that my proposal for a new innovation process will take this into account. One that allows us to fully leverage the potential of our new companion in our innovation ecosystems, while also ensuring that no "apprentices" inadvertently unleash the power of artificial neural networks that are beyond our control. If that can work, we may be able to open a new chapter in innovation, one that integrates the human skills of creativity and process knowledge and at the same time al-

---

39 Gary Marcus, *Taming Silicon Valley: How We Can Assure That AI Works for Us* (Cambridge, MA: The MIT Press, 2024).

lows for a balanced embrace of ambiguity—all with the fantastic help of our new companion AI.

To make this vision a reality, it's crucial to keep the ethical implications in mind. I'd like to mention the example of United Nations initiatives that address the ethical aspects of the AI revolution.

The United Nations has several initiatives aimed at promoting ethical AI development and deployment. Here are some notable ones:

1. UNESCO's Recommendation on the Ethics of Artificial Intelligence
   In November 2021, UNESCO made a big step forward with a historic agreement that defines common values and principles for the ethical development of AI. The idea is that AI technologies should promote human rights, transparency, accountability, and privacy. It also explicitly prohibits the use of AI for social scoring and mass surveillance.
2. UN General Assembly Resolution on AI
   In March 2024, the UN General Assembly passed a big new resolution to promote "safe, secure, and trustworthy" AI systems. The resolution makes it clear that human rights are an important part of the design, development, and deployment of AI. It also calls for countries to work together to make sure everyone has a fair chance to use AI technologies and to close the digital divide.
3. AI Advisory Body
   The UN has set up an AI Advisory Body to regularly check in on how things are going with AI, make sure everyone's on the same page with standards, and get people working together across borders. The goal of this body is to keep an eye on potential dangers, work together on emergency responses, and set up some rules for accountability.
4. The United Nations has put together a framework for ethical AI.
   The UN's Office of Information and Communications Technology (OICT) has put together a framework for ethical AI. This framework looks at ethical issues and gives guidance on how to make sure that AI development and use within the UN stick to ethical values.

To sum up, these initiatives show that the UN is serious about promoting ethical AI development around the world. The UN is setting standards, promoting cooperation, and ensuring accountability to make sure that AI is used safely and effectively. As responsible innovation drivers in organizations, we have a duty to spread, support, and co-develop on these topics, just like the UNSDGs do.

We need these global collaborations and trustworthy institutions in order to develop our individual road map to the integration of AI in all areas of our professional lives. For the time being 5 different applications are of help for me but the landscape is developing very dynamically. Each single one is strong in one field of application. It makes a big difference whether I want to research new facts in detail, if I want to get inspired by generative production of new combinations, if I simply want to improve my writing style, or if I want to summarize YouTube videos.

I'm always eager to try new things, and the key aspects of adapting to new technologies apply just as much in this field. Big Tech giants are increasingly dominating the scene. It is clear that they gain political influence as well. These giants have a clear advantage: as a brand, they must deliver trust in their solutions. They can't afford to lose this trust; they need to be careful and not do anything that could harm their existence. Safety and moral aspects are crucial, and even as they're effectively addressed by the regulations I mentioned, we must be very attentive and alert if they are respected! And we all know that especially moral aspects can be perceived very differently by different people and cultures. I am using my five favorite tools for my needs, and I use them nearly daily. For translating and as a correction tool, the "non-Giant" application Deepl fits my expectations best. ChatGPT for generative tasks and especially Microsoft CoPilot for research are tremendously helpful. Especially because CoPilot shows the used information sources very prominently. When I read names like Harvard Business Review or the homepage of a major, trustworthy university, I immediately feel confident using the information for my further work.

Another rule I have when using AI is that I always input the data into the Notes app on my Mac. This is where I can develop the content further, mix it with other research, and prepare the controlled content of my production, which I then use with my own interpretations and words in my work.

Just a heads up: AI has empowered individuals with the ability to create content without understanding its implications. If you meet them, you can't discuss any of the content with them. They are like the mentioned spoon that does not know the taste of the soup he wants to sell to you. We're at risk of losing one of the most important sources of knowledge production: trust. As we lose social exchange and intercommunication between humans, we risk AI having better "shiny" persuasion skills than responsible citizens. This is a serious issue that we must address.

I don't want to live in a world where chatbots and personal robots are shaping the way I interact with others. We know that, for instance, in healthcare, it makes perfect sense to help out the elderly or frail and to take some of the load off healthcare workers or caregivers in families and partnerships. And there are plenty of other examples, too.

AI is becoming a critical part of our work lives. Studies show that, no matter what industry you're in, on average every third working hour will be automated by 2030, with a lot of this being done by generative AI. The people who will benefit the most from AI are the ones who don't have a lot of experience or skills. This is typically the case with younger or less qualified employees.

These employees benefit personally from AI because their knowledge base grows. When companies see the benefits of efficiency, they're likely to replace qualified, educated, and experienced employees—who are expensive—with ones who aren't as qualified. "With a satnav, anyone can drive a cab. In the past, you had to know the city map inside out to get a cab license. The future of work is going to be interesting. On the one hand, people will compete with AI in the job market. They won't be able to market or apply their own experience and skills. It'll be tough to gain new experience, as many tasks will no longer be performed by the employee themselves but by AI.

Another important thing to think about for the future is how to give young employees the skills they need to do the job and also how to transfer the experience that people used to get through working for a certain number of hours. The big question is: how can we get this knowledge and experience across to new employees in a way that works well?

AI offers big opportunities to share knowledge. And we can use generative AI to update previous projects and knowledge areas in a way that makes them accessible to younger employees, who can then engage with them. It's very important for learners to engage with the topic in a playful way. As the saying goes, "I don't know anyone who has learned to play football better by watching." We gain knowledge from experience which can't be trained or shared with AI.

Generative AI is making it harder for kids to actually write their own texts. If we think about where we learn analytical, convergent, and divergent thinking, it's through writing essays. That's how we develop our thinking skills. A lot of what AI systems produce is just hallucination—it's not really anything more than a probability calculation. That's not really about the truth, though. This makes us vulnerable to manipulation, whether politically or in terms of our values.

Our educational systems, from kindergarten all the way up to universities and post-tertiary education, must also train to navigate in the analog world. We need to make sure we're building up those analog skills. It's interesting to note that this means we need to take a step back from digitization in education to focus on strengthening analog skills. They're important for our values and for forming our moral compass. If we can rely on similar skills, it helps us to navigate the digital world safely.

Studies, such as one from the Complexity Science Hub in Vienna, demonstrate that while we individually benefit from AI tools, we ultimately lose out because the outputs are homogenized. We're witnessing a clear loss of diversity and the capacity to solve problems.

A recent study from Oxford also shows how generative AI affects our problem-solving abilities, divergent thinking, and creativity in a negative way. In the past, people built their skills by getting hands-on experience. Because we're so focused on the end result, we lose sight of the different forms of capital that can help us get there. It's a bit of a paradox because if everything is the same, the individual still needs to stand out in the market to succeed. It might even get the creative juices flowing. If we all bring the same results from our AI-generated content, we will have to come up with solutions that challenge us to create by our own brain force.

A last thing to think about is the loss of joy. Today, we can even automate flight. It's becoming more challenging to find pilots because flying isn't as engaging as it once was. The cockpit is so automated that the pilot's main job is monitoring the systems. In Buddhist tradition, there is a parable about a spoon that is unaware of the flavor of the soup it serves. This parable suggests that reading without comprehension is as ineffective as a spoon that cannot taste the soup it stirs. It could be said that true wisdom requires a combination of practical experience and deep understanding, rather than relying on superficial knowledge alone. In other words, knowledge does not create wisdom automatically. It needs the transformation of the knowledge into viable solutions. Part III of this book is dealing with this transformation. I believe it is important to recognize the incredible human capacity to perceive, experience, and engage with the world in so many ways. It is my hope that AI will never be capable of doing so. Isn't it fascinating how wisdom is often captured in such vivid metaphors?

The Buddhist parable of the spoon that cannot taste the soup reminds us: knowledge without understanding is hollow. AI may stir the pot, but only humans can savor its meaning.

After this critical view of AI, I will discuss the incredible opportunities it presents.

Regulations must align with our core values of goodwill, mutual support, and a commitment to building a bright future. Is the adaptation of AI subject to the same rules as any other evolution, as discussed in previous chapters? We have to consider that this time it is a new and epochal transformation in the case of AI. We must recognize the grave threat posed to our existence by the possibility of "neural networks taking a life of their own."

The innovation processes that accompany the further rollout of AI must therefore be defined carefully. On the one hand, AI will help to create progress; on the other hand, it must be limited in its scope. This objective can only be accomplished by applying the insights derived from the aforementioned logics, such as Stage-Gate or innovation ecosystems, to identify the critical point of no return that must not be exceeded under any circumstances!

The words of Friedrich Dürrenmatt, best known for his works in drama and literature, in his satirical play "Die Physiker (The Physicists)," will not apply in the regard of AI. Dürrenmatt boldly explores the tension between science and ethics, challenging the impact of scientific discoveries on humanity. The overarching insight of the stories is clear: "What has once been thought cannot be taken back." The play highlights the absurdity of madness and sanity, the responsibility of scientists, and the dangerous potential of scientific knowledge when misused. It's a thought-provoking exploration of how knowledge and power intersect in dangerous ways. This is as relevant today as it was then.

If we have a solid set of values and principles and a good process, we'll be able to navigate that big transformation that has already started and make the most of the opportunities that lie ahead of us, or, better yet, say it with our findings from indigenous cultures that lie around us, like:

- **Improving Efficiency:** Businesses and industries work more efficiently by automating repetitive tasks and analyzing large amounts of data quickly.
- **Enhancing Healthcare:** AI assists in diagnosing and thus hindering the outbreak of diseases, personalizing treatment plans, and even predicting patient outcomes.
- **Transforming Transportation**: Self-driving cars and traffic management systems and even fulfilling the old dream of flying taxis and cars.
- **Boosting Entertainment:** AI recommend movies, music, and books based on our preferences, enhancing our entertainment experiences.
- **Advancing Education:** AI-powered tools providing personalized learning experiences and helping educators track student progress and as well providing agentic AI tools that can solve even complex tasks for us.
- **Addressing Global Challenges:** AI in climate modeling, disaster response, and resource management to tackle global issues.

It is our duty to take all our knowledge and benefit from new technologies and to fight for our beliefs and spread hope as long as this world exists.

In this light, the inspiring adage from Markus Langes-Swarovski in the Manufaktur experimental work floor of Swarovski Company in Wattens, "Everything you want is on the other side of fear," takes on new significance. It serves as a reminder that, beyond our fears and doubts, lies the potential for profound transformation and healing. By confronting our fears, reframing our biases, and fostering a sense of unity, we can initiate the positive changes necessary for creating a sustainable and meaningful future for generations to come.

Astronomical research definitively shows that the sun will eventually run out of fuel. In about 3 billion years, the sun will have used all its fuel. It will blow up into a red giant and destroy the Earth. The worst thing that could happen is to live in fear of that grant and lose hope. We must not destroy our lives already today. We must ensure we are not the last generation! This means we are called to live sustainably and peacefully because our days are a gift. Let's conclude our exploration of AI with the words of *David Steindl-Rast*, an Austrian-born spiritual leader, monk, author, and founder of a global Center for Spiritual Studies. At 98 years old, he has a lot of insight to share. When he asked himself what the innermost source of the mysterious order in nature was, he confidently answered: *"I am convinced that it is an outflow of the creative power of that loving power that surmounts us infinitely."*

Finally, this means that we are asked to find a good balance between the vision-driven potential of innovation to invoke hope and transformative change on one hand and the integration of established methods that provide stability and frameworks for engagement on the other hand. In other words, to master the interplay between embracing the new and valuing the tried-and-true.

Together, we can shape a positive and successful future by fostering a shared understanding and collective action towards the responsible use of AI.

I am convinced that the source of the mysterious order in nature is an outflow of the creative power of that loving power that surmounts us infinitely. David Steindl-Rast

One of the big issues with Open Innovation is sharing proprietary info. In context of AI, here's a new term that's come up: "Synthetic Data." It makes a strong case for a shift from traditional OI practices to more secure, efficient, and scalable approaches that rely less on the sharing of data. Synthetic data, made using algorithms and simulations, copies real-world data without exposing sensitive information, which makes it a new option for OI. It's almost impossible to have a data breach or someone steal your intellectual property. Sharing data and working with others can be risky. Synthetic data can help with that. It's a substitute that keeps the statistical properties of real data but never reveals any actual information. This means companies can work together and come up with new ideas without worrying about their private data being compromised. There are going to be a lot of other advantages of AI as we move forward.

We all are asked to join this exciting journey into the future, guided by informed and enlightened principles that ensure AI serves humanity in the best way possible. AI has the potential to transform the existing innovation procedures, enabling them to evolve in a self-regulating manner. For this reason, the development of an innovative innovation process is an area of great interest.

A Navigation Tool for Our Modern Era

I spent most of my life searching for direction and guidance, as well as sense and fulfillment. While writing this book, I came to the conclusion that I needed an adapted tool to guide me. The idea of a compass to help us human travelers navigate an increasingly complex world was inspired by many people, stories, experiences, and even painful failures and threats. While the idea for this book evolved over the last ten years, I knew it was too early to write about such a topic.

But in the last five years, through the conscious observation of the things that are happening around us, I feel that we are entering an era of epochal transformation that reshapes human evolution. The increasing speed of digital transformation, environmental threat, and the decline of familiar values are culminating and forming a new state of consciousness for human evolution.

We are entering an era of epochal transformation that reshapes human evolution.

With all the new things AI can do, I think we'll be able to feel safe and connected, like in a small tribal group but amid a global dimension. That's where we come from, evolution-wise. We need new social leadership models that encourage the values that benefit everyone. At the same time, we must stay connected to our local communities, even though they're dealing with political problems, conflicts, and uncertainties. This demands our undivided attention, a newfound self-assurance in our solution skills, and the boldness to undertake an iterative learning phase with the integration of AI in the optimal location.

It's time to stop chasing a utopian ideal and start leveraging the tools we already have. We can identify weak signals in our daily lives. This navigation tool encompasses both individual objectives and collective goals. It serves the individual self as well as the collective "we." It is a guiding force that inspires and enables the full realization of our potential, both as individuals and as contributors to the collective endeavor of shaping and inhabiting a desired future.

The crossing of the chasm will be possible.

Lifelong learning is an indispensable task of today. By consciously acknowledging accountability for our behavior, we can effect positive change and minimize negative consequences.

Emphasizing a sense of community promotes collaboration and cooperation. By adhering to these values, we can create a meaningful and fulfilling framework that addresses the pressing issues of our time while promoting a brighter and more hopeful future.

At this point we must come back to the critical role of the Inner Development Goals that have already been briefly mentioned:

The IDG initiative addresses the nurturing of inner development skills and shifts in order to more effectively reach Sustainable Development Goals.

At the IDG summit in Stockholm that I visited just recently, I was very much intrigued by the massive power of people on a global level that are moving forward this global initiative, and I had the chance to dive deeper into this topic. I really recommend visiting the summaries on their homepage.[40]

There was a wonderful speech and introduction of Massamba Thioye. He is the project executive at the UNFCCC (United Nations Framework Convention for Climate Change) secretariat and is leading the development of the Hub. His work focuses on creating regulations for measuring climate action impact, incentive mechanisms for sustainability, and frameworks to enhance the use of innovation for climate solutions.

Thioye talked about the great idea of using new technology to help people live better lives while keeping our planet safe. He was talking about optimal human functioning, personal growth, and fulfillment, meaning living in a way that's in line with our natural tendencies, a meaningful and purposeful life, and reaching our full potential as humans. He says it's a crucial way to achieve a flourishing life, achieve system change, and interact with others as a catalyst for development. He is certain that our

---

40 Inner Development Goals, accessed July 20, 2025, https://innerdevelopmentgoals.org/.

actions reflect our current state of inner development and fulfillment. This inner development and our interactions with others are key to growth. Adopt certain behaviors. Reflect on past experiences. Interact with people who have reached their full potential. This will accelerate our development, enhance our self-awareness, boost our emotional competence, and broaden our ethical understanding.

He goes on to say that when it comes to development, self-awareness and passion usually start with some internal reflection. That's because, if they're not operationalized, they can only be eternal in inner development if they're internalized. He suggests meditating on passions like self-control and combining them in an effective way in a development that goes beyond inner reflection. *"This could help us build a system change. Then we can build the society we've always dreamed of one that's empowering and that makes a difference in people's lives. And only then will we be able to help make the vision of security and human dignity, which is at the heart of the UN, a reality."*

What a great vision that shows we're not in this alone. In the next chapter, I'll share my experience and best knowledge to suggest how to use our intuitive and awakened abilities through a navigation tool. I'll try to bring together the aspects that define the framework for the epochal change that we're already in. We've got to use our hearts and deal with our spiritual problems and at the same time make the best use of the tremendous technological possibilities— just like shown in evolution.

We've got to use our hearts and deal with our spiritual problems and at the same time make the best use of the tremendous technological possibilities— just like shown in evolution.

Openness and serendipity, connecting to our co-workers, and building innovation ecosystems for further growth will be our companions.

Part III: **The Advocate**

A Changing Activist in a VUCA World

In our world that's so volatile, uncertain, complex, and ambiguous, just talking about change or thinking up new ideas isn't enough. We need people who are all about making change—change activists—and who act with clarity, courage, and commitment.

After doing a lot of research and getting practical experience in innovation, one main thing has become super clear to me: understanding innovation in theory is important, but living and enacting it is transformative. A lot of times, people who talk about innovation are seen as storytellers or visionaries who don't have any real-world impact. But innovation, in its truest form, isn't just about ideas. It's a mix of insight, execution, and measurable change. It's both an art and a science, and it demands presence, responsibility, and relentless application. With the rise of artificial intelligence, we are entering a new epoch. Knowledge is no longer stored but instantly connected. Insights are no longer slowly accumulated but exponentially multiplied. This moment is not just a technological shift—it is a civilizational turning point.

In parts I and II of this book, we learned how to create entire innovation ecosystems that are living, breathing networks. These networks encourage experimentation, learning, and scaling.

Part III is designed to challenge you, the reader, to take action. These ecosystems are not just for tech hubs or startups. They can appear in schools, cities, rural communities, artistic collectives, or even in your personal environment if you are involved. "Where life has placed you". What matters is the shared intent: to shape the future consciously. We must weave the philosophical, practical, and emotional threads of change into a cohesive vision for action. This is undoubtedly meant to show the potential influence of AI as a companion that will help us step into this new age. This is the age that combines the knowledge of Homo sapiens with the creativity and motivation of Homo culturalis and opens the way to Homo Innovaticus—a responsible creator who actively moves the world forward. This individual actively cultivates spaces of learning and transformation in everyday life. These individuals are philosophically well-read and universally interested in culture. They share experiences on all levels and possess a simple innovation mindset to navigate the complex landscape of information. They use AI and emerging technologies as catalysts for wisdom and connection, not crutches. We must become architects and stewards of the future. To become such a change activist forces us to move from abstraction to action, from knowing to becoming, and from reacting to co-creating. This is the true frontier of our time. Anyone willing to step forward is welcome.

Members of this global, diverse, and ever-growing movement are not afraid to fail forward. They celebrate learning stories, even the messy ones. Their mistakes be-

https://doi.org/10.1515/9783111448329-016

come data. Their missteps become turning points. This is how this new type of man evolves.

In this chapter, I propose a new process to enable a repeatable, guided, and interconnected procedure. A procedure that is enabling us to find and use our visions for the future not as something we wait for—it is more something we awaken into.

We are all part of the same vibrant Innovation Tribe.

Chapter 14
The Quintessence of Deep Learning

Entering the New Era of "Integration of Everything"

Creative Destruction: Understanding Innovation Waves

The Austrian/American economist Joseph Schumpeter came up with his theory about innovation cycles. He described "long waves of innovation" and came up with the term "creative destruction" to describe how new ideas and technology replace old ones. He also emphasized the critical role of entrepreneurial spirit and risk taking in fostering innovation, arguing that the willingness to take risks and pursue new opportunities is essential for economic progress and the continual evolution of the economy.

These cycles were always accompanied by major breakthroughs, and they help us today to understand our time in relation to these long cycles and to continue it in the spirit of this idea.

Innovation is a process that revolutionizes from within, destroying the old structure and incessantly creating a new one. Joseph Schumpeter

---

The first wave of the Industrial Revolution, for example, ushered in the first factories, waterpower, and textile industries.

The second wave brought railways, which opened up new possibilities for urban growth based on steam power. These periods took place from 1785 to 1900.

The third wave was driven by revolutionary automotive industries, electricity, chemicals, and internal combustion engines.

The fourth wave was driven by the mass adoption of aviation on a global scale and its economic integration and started in the early 1950s. It took place over 40 years and was overwritten by the advent of the Internet, which paved the way for digital networks, software, and new media.

It is now, 30 years later, being revolutionized by AI, IoT, robots, drones, and clean tech.

What does this mean? We have already looked at the weak signals and what we can learn from the history of innovation and change in order to predict possible new developments. We see that the cycles get shorter, more integrated, and even more "VUCA."

My experiences during the Fifth Wave of Innovation prove that a new window is open for an integrative way that can "produce" a new type of human being. This human being can integrate, innovate, and positively evolve a new quality of the future. Or in other words: This individual is not only technically adaptive but also emo-

https://doi.org/10.1515/9783111448329-017

tionally intelligent, systemically aware, and capable of integrating innovation with human values.

What do I mean by that?

Even Henry Chesbrough is mentioning in his conclusions on the future role of AI in Open Innovation that it could likely lie in hybrid models that combine the strengths of AI-driven processes with human-led Open Innovation.[41] He further concludes that such models could leverage AI's capacity for rapid ideation and data processing while harnessing human creativity, intuition, and ethical judgment at the same time. As an example, he mentions that AI could generate initial ideas or prototypes, which human collaborators then refine, contextualize, and ethically evaluate through OI platforms. Such approaches might further democratize innovation by allowing a wider range of participants to contribute meaningfully, even if they lack deep technical expertise. On the other hand, we should be concerned about centralized power, diminishing creativity, lack of agency, and IP issues that I already mentioned. At the end of the day, whether we are someone who sees the glass as half-full or half-empty, Chesbrough ends up at the same place I did: the future of innovation is going to be all over the place, with everyone getting involved and things changing in ways we can't predict.

We are truly a species unlike any other on this planet. But have we already reached the end of the line? Thanks to our culture, medicine, and technology, we're more independent than ever before. Could it be that evolution continues for us humans too? Could a new human species emerge from us? What would it look like?

An interesting documentation on the public cultural powerhouse TV station ARTE gives some insights into these questions. The documentary says that a lot of people think that human development stopped when modern civilization emerged.[42] Remember the theory of Yuval Harari? Evolution is all about adapting to a changing environment and living conditions, and this is happening right now.

Researchers like evolutionary medicine expert *Frank Rühli* are always on the lookout for new changes: Things like how our bodies handle lactose, how we can fight off HIV, or the presence of extra blood vessels in our forearms. Some studies even suggest that our bodies can adapt to unhealthy lifestyles, like a poor diet and lack of exercise.

So, our evolution continues. But whether a new human species could even emerge is far more difficult to answer. The fact is that natural selection would take millions of years. However, today we have other options that could speed up the process.

At the Francis Crick Institute in London, *Sophie Brumm* is conducting research on human embryos using the CRISPR/Cas9 gene scissors. The gene scissors can be used to

---

41 Henry Chesbrough, "Open InnovationOpen Innovation in the Age of AI," *Laerbro*, October 12, 2024, https://laerbro.com/insight/2.
42 ARTE, "Wird es eine neue 'Spezies Mensch' geben? Die Antwort auf fast Alles," *42 – Die Antwort auf fast alles*, last accessed January 4, 2025, https://www.youtube.com/watch?v=-NMrO6biEv8.

intervene in the human genome and alter it. The resulting changes are then passed on to future generations. The first designer babies, Lulu and Nana, were born in China in 2018. Will research produce "superhumans" in the future and thus change the course of evolution?

Danish bioinformatician *Thomas Mail* goes even further. He sees the future of our species not in biology at all, but in our fusion with technology.

There is no doubt that AI will play a key role, and here especially the advancement of Artificial Neural Networks (ANNs). The beginning of that evolutionary step is already present and around us, comparable to the potential of electrical currency that appears to be switched off but is nevertheless effective. To me, it's like this principle of alternating current. It took a while, but I finally figured out that a shortcut could happen when the light switch was off. I had a new lamp installed at home, and that's when I realized it. If it does not come from the expected direction, it comes from somewhere else. This metaphor shows to me that in today's networked world, it's no longer possible to "switch off" change because everything and everyone is interconnected. It's like there's this energy just waiting to be used in every direction, and we can feel the potential but not yet control.

The quote of the *Austrian writer Peter Rosegger* is for me a beautiful example of how we could think about the integration of "victorious technologies and developments" when he addresses that all new developments should be subjected to make the "cultural society," "the civilized society," more moral and happier.

> If it one day turns out that the victorious technology can make the cultural humanity more content, more moral, and happier, then it will be a divine advance. Otherwise, despite everything —a fatal aberration.[43]

And at the same time, he states that we need to try out what routes are viable.

Mind you, this statement is now over 100 years old and, in the context to AI, maybe a very useful thought!

The term "Homo Culturalis," as mentioned by Prof. Nils Goldschmidt describes that social cohesion and addressing societal challenges requires an understanding of the cultural and social dimensions of human behavior.[44] The *Homo Culturalis* concept addresses more inclusive communities by recognizing the importance of cultural heritage, shared values, and social connections. It emphasizes the importance of cultural and social factors in shaping human behavior and encourages solutions that are attuned to the complexities of our modern world.

---

43 Peter Rosegger, *Schönheit der Technik, Monatsschrift Heimgarten* Nr. 3 (Graz: Verlag Leykam-Josefsthal, 1909), 211.

44 Nils Goldschmidt and Hans G. Nutzinger, eds., *Vom homo oeconomicus zum homo culturalis: Von Handlung und Nutzen in der Ökonomie, Kulturelle Ökonomik*, Band 8 (Hans G. Nutzinger, 2009).

We know that Homo sapiens is the most successful model in evolution because it is a master of adaptation and can cope with unprecedented multidimensional threats. Intuition is likely one of its best tools. In this context, I see the potential influence of AI as a companion that will lead us into a new age. This age combines the knowledge of Homo sapiens equipped with the creativity and motivation of Homo Culturalis and opens the way to *Homo Innovaticus* – a responsible creator who actively moves the world forward. Figure 9 is visualizing this logics.

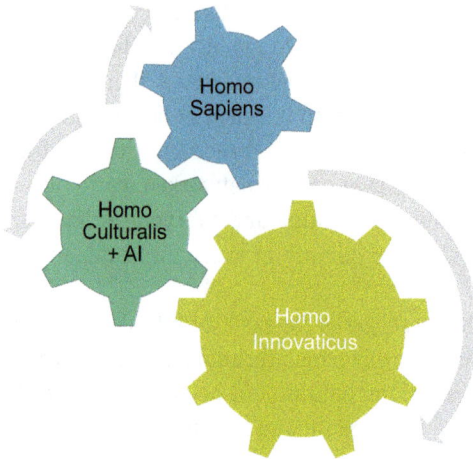

Figure 9: *Homo Innovaticus*–Driven by Culture and AI.

I also strongly believe that "human humanity" is a unifying force that connects all of us. We're always being challenged to make new starts, but the *Homo Innovaticus* isn't helpless when it comes to these new beginnings. Instead, he can create targeted structures by setting rhythms, milestones, and communication points that enable us to establish visible nodes and steering points. This approach lets us shape new developments and stay motivated as new things keep entering our lives.

The shift from Homo sapiens to *Homo Innovaticus* will probably happen through cultivation. This means we can repeat (cultivate) processes that promote targeted growth. There are some relevant examples from history, like the French Revolution. It came up with a new calendar that should have helped make some systematic changes, and it should have helped redefine values to make progress possible. As we know, the calendar didn't make it, but it did help change the way people thought.

As mentioned earlier, the reassessment of our value systems plays a central role in every transformation. We need to recharge what is considered crucial and develop the ability to shape life models from our knowledge and experiences of failure that support us in our development. In this context, coincidences, crises, and unexpected potential also play an important role in our progress.

The quote of the Austrian-born poet and philosopher *Erich Fried: "It is good when people do the right thing. But it is even more important that the people who do the right thing are really people."* This underlines the basic human need to understand and learn things—a cornerstone of philosophy that calls on us to learn from the past and move into a new future. We are thus called upon to act in the here and now and to actively shape the beginnings that surround us.

In our new dynamic and interconnected world where beginnings are constantly around us, it is on us to play an active role in shaping our future. By rethinking our values, building structures, and learning from experience, we can overcome the challenges and have a positive impact on our world.

At this point we can also trust in our evolutionary skills of human action and change. Learning in this context is not linear. We should try to integrate everything and draw connections.

One of my most admired philosophers *Hanna Ahrendt,* once put it very aptly: *"We humans are beings with a gift for action who are always capable of making new beginnings. Over and over again. We have the talent for it. To set new trends."*

Hannah Arendt's idea of "natality" opens up a whole new dimension. Natality is all about this ability. Arendt says that every new beginning is unique and often surprising, and that everything happens for the first time. The idea is that every new action and event also creates new possibilities, shaping reality in unexpected ways.

We humans are beings with a gift for action who are always capable of making new beginnings. Over and over again. We have the talent for it. To set new trends.
　Hannah Ahrendt

This view shows that change is often caused by something sudden happening. The path to a new state is achieved by replacing the old, which no longer corresponds to the current reality. Aristotle said, "The beginning is half of the whole," showing how important the first step is in any change process.

Exnovation versus innovation

One key point I want to make is the difference between "exnovation" and "innovation." Exnovation is when you let go of the old structures and make room for something new. The question we're dealing with here is, what do we need to let go of to make room for the new?

It's clear that understanding and creating new things, and dealing with them, are essential. It's about recognizing where we came from, encouraging the necessary changes in our society, and developing and adapting the structures we already have and creating new ones.

By learning from the past and actively shaping the future, we have the power to make valuable contributions to progress and to further develop ourselves and the world.

I want to add my deep belief that if we want to understand something from the past, we must do so through processes and procedures that can be derived from the origin. In doing so, we must define stages and not skip individual steps, like Cooper's Stage-Gate principles that we know very well from chapter one. Dirty corner cutting hinders learning and targeting.

The three basic things to always be recognized are:

- **Comprehensibility:** Every change or innovation must be made understandable; we must recognize the origin.
- **Target naming**: Clarity about the goal is crucial for successful implementation.
- **Analysis of origin:** The origin of an idea or action can be understood by tracing it back to a decisive initial act, such as the founding of a state or a revolution or the radical change of an organizational structure, including the responsible leaders in a company.

Changes not only arise in a historical or political context, but also because they are "ripe." Sometimes there are also immeasurable origins, like religious ideas about light: "In the beginning, God created light." This idea refers to the basic, often mystical aspects of beginnings.

Both small changes from everyday life and major disruptions—such as Schumpeter's concept of "creative destruction"—are sources of innovation. The aim is to overcome or improve the old, depending on the forces and skills at play.

It is very much like we had to learn how to deal with the flood of new knowledge that resulted from the information explosion after the Internet's advent. The new opportunities and solutions evolved over time. In my first podcast, which I produced with the Future Institute of Matthias Horx in Germany, I predicted already back in 2006 that in the future, innovation managers would collaborate in a network that spanned company borders. This was a game-changing prediction, as it was one of the first to suggest the potential for innovation managers to work across company boundaries. In a world where a company's advantage over its competitors defined its value, collaboration and the sharing of best practices were not viable options. Today, it's clear that collaboration on fundamental topics elevates the entire industry and its reputation. The evolution of these enabling networks only appeared on a broader level in 2017. The process was very much accelerated and supported by leadership institutes and their mutual investment into platforms and conference formats like "Innovation Roundtable," ISPIM, and many others.[45] The development of the Innovation Roundtable format led by *Prof. Axel Roseno* from Copenhagen Business School enabled insightful presentations within a protected environment of like-minded indus-

---

45 Innovation Roundtable®, accessed July 20, 2025, https://innovationroundtable.com/about-us/; ISPIM – International Society for Professional Innovation Management, accessed July 20, 2025, https://www.ispim-innovation.com/.

try managers on a global level. With that setting I found the ideal environment for learning, receiving feedback, and establishing partnerships for cross-border innovation. And I was asked to contribute to the program by personally interacting with Professor Roseno and sharing the networking findings from our internal Innovation Network developments. At the same time, this collaboration was also a great contribution to raising the industry standards for innovation. Today, the annual conference in Copenhagen is the biggest get-together of innovation-mindset managers from various functional areas in companies. Bringing together more than 600 managers from various functional areas in companies, like HR, Research and development, Marketing, and Innovation Management, and many others. Some companies are using the format to train their next generation of leaders for their future tasks. I'm thrilled to see the new level of global collaboration and support taking place these days. And now, with the incredible power of AI solutions, we're about to take it to the next level! This is a truly remarkable moment in history, as we're about to witness the incredible power of tools that can not only assist us but also generate their own solutions independently from our input. Isn't that spooky in the best way?

Absolutely!

Could it be that we wake up one day and will be surprised like Albert Einstein, who has for a long time denied the existence of quantum effects?

Nobel Prize winner Erwin Schrödinger, the Austrian-born father of quantum physics, already found out in 1933 that our understanding of reality is challenged by allowing objects to exist in multiple states or locations simultaneously. He already described the superposition of photons that do not belong to a system as long as they are not observed from outside. He divided the world into two realms: the large, familiar macroscopic world and the small, quantum world with its own rules. Objects can exist in multiple places or states at once in the quantum world until observed.

Einstein called this effect "spooky"—and for good reason!

Richard Feynman, whom we already met in this book in another role, one of the most influential theoretical physicists of the 20th century, made numerous contributions to the understanding of quantum mechanics and its implications. While he spoke and wrote extensively on the subject, one of his most famous quotes about the quantum world comes from the introductory chapter of his lectures on physics:

I think I can safely say that nobody understands quantum mechanics.

This statement highlights the mind-boggling and counterintuitive nature of quantum mechanics, even for experts in the field. Feynman was well-known for his ability to deeply understand and explain complex scientific concepts, yet he acknowledged the atypical and often paradoxical nature of quantum phenomena. It's fascinating how it differs from the kind of intuitive understanding we have for classical mechanics. That was in the 1960s!

Throughout his career, Feynman emphasized the importance of accepting the weirdness of the quantum world and learning to think in new ways to grasp its implications. He was instrumental in showing how quantum mechanics explains and predicts various phenomena and was an advocate for teaching it as an integral part of physics education.

Now let's jump into the year 1997, when *Prof. Anton Zeilinger* and his team in Innsbruck, Austria, worked on a series of pioneering experiments by which the quantum state of a particle (or system) was transmitted from one location to another, without the physical transfer of the particle itself. That was crucial to the field of quantum teleportation. The *"Innsbruck Experiment,"* relying on the principles of quantum entanglement and superposition, earned him the Nobel Prize for Physics in 2022:

The phenomenon where two or more particles become interconnected such that the state of one particle instantaneously influences the state of the other, regardless of the distance separating them. This principle is central to quantum teleportation. The original particle's state is destroyed in the process at the sending location, while an exact copy of that state is recreated at the receiving, observing location. The experiment involved three photons: one photon whose state was to be teleported and two entangled photons shared between the sender and receiver.

The Innsbruck experiments were groundbreaking because they showed that quantum states could be transmitted without physical movement of the particles themselves. This work not only advanced understanding of quantum mechanics but also suggested potential applications in quantum communication, cryptography, and quantum computing.

For me that is one of the most fascinating and important happenings in the last hundred years, and that is why I wanted to give much room to a broader extension.

Could it be that one day, we'll all wake up and realize that we're living in a quantum world? The incredible ability to teleport thoughts and information could be the fundamental principle of our human existence. Isn't it fascinating to learn that aboriginal tribes of the Australian indigenous population had or may still have this ability? Could it be that we have forgotten, unlearned, or developed our thoughts the wrong way? Could it be that we simply are not yet ready to understand things beyond today's scientific horizon?

Could it be that we have forgotten, unlearned, or developed our thoughts the wrong way?

And that we just need to connect to the unbelievable wideness of human potential by observing and inventing and by AI-supported connecting to the knowledge of the world and the fundamental principles of a new nearness to nature (our nature)?

Yes, we can—we have the talent!

And we need to be patient. That is why I have chosen this example that shows the dilemma of our days: we want innovation to happen in a short time, overnight, bringing money into our pockets tomorrow morning. And in many cases, we lose the potential for a bigger move at the same time of thinking like that.

Let's all put our best foot forward. My approach to making meaningful changes is based on experience. Every change process can be improved, but you can't just take a shortcut. That's the investment we have to make in time and brainpower as a society.

It's pretty obvious that we're in a crisis of values and meaning. We're like managers who keep making the same mistakes. We're stuck in our own way of thinking because we can't learn, and we're so anxious that failure means death. We've got to understand that adapting to change is the only way to deal with volatile times. We've got to let go of the things we love that aren't useful anymore if we want to make room for new things. It's not easy to face the truth, but it's important to acknowledge it. When will we learn?

As Bob Dylan put it in his famous song about the answer that is blowing in the wind:

How many times must a man look up
Before he can see the sky?
How many ears must one man have
Before he can hear people cry?
How many deaths will it take 'til he knows
That too many people have died?

The answer, my friend, is blowin' in the wind
The answer is blowin' in the wind

I have a dream that one day we will cross the chasm and create our future on the basis of our value-driven humanity. It is possible. We have the talent.

Of Human Growth and Serendipity

Human growth depends on more than just developing skills, knowledge, and emotional well-being. As people grow, they become more aware of their abilities and potential. This awareness drives them to seek new ways to solve problems and improve their lives. When individuals thrive, society as a whole benefits.

The story of the princes of Serendip is the origin of the word *serendipity*. The term was coined by the English writer and historian Horace Walpole in a letter he wrote in 1754. He used it to describe something he saw in a Persian fairy tale called *The Three Princes of Serendip*. In the story, the princes are sent out by their father, the king, who's wise enough to send them off to other kingdoms to figure out what works best. They stumbled upon great ideas by accident and brought them back to their kingdom.

Today, *serendipity* refers to when something good happens by chance. You often hear about it in relation to scientific discoveries, creative processes, and everyday life, where something unexpected happens and leads to a positive result. I always like to give a brief explanation for those unfamiliar with the term: If you hadn't started drilling for water, you wouldn't have discovered the oil field.

If you hadn't started drilling for water, you wouldn't have discovered the oil field.

We must tackle our global challenges head-on: climate change, healthcare, and education. These challenges present broad fields for the application of the serendipity mindset, where one field can learn from the other. Innovative technologies improve access to education, allowing more people to learn and grow, which in turn creates a more knowledgeable population. Partnerships between schools and tech companies create programs that teach students valuable skills, preparing them for future careers and fostering a culture of innovation.

It is more than evident that human growth and innovation are deeply intertwined, both contributing to a promising future. By fostering the development of individuals, we create a fertile ground for innovative ideas, leading to solutions that enhance the quality of life for people around the world. This, in turn, supports continued growth and progress, creating an ongoing cycle of improvement and hope for the future.

I've discovered my life's true purpose and my role in propelling this next phase of innovation and leadership forward. I'm thrilled to contribute by offering my experiences and actively participating in cultivating the ideal environment for this vision to flourish. It's as thrilling as the moon landing, which ignited my passion since I was a curious 9-year-old in 1969. I was amazed to see the moon and the unbelievable fact that at this moment humans are on their first moonwalk.

And like we elaborated when we were talking about the role of innovation ecosystems: by pinpointing and defining the fundamental innovation question—the raison d'être for change—we can realize Hannah Arendt's belief that we have the talent to always set new beginnings for a greater good.

Chapter 15
Homo Innovaticus: A New Release of Homo Sapiens

Cultivation of a New Way of Coexistence

A careful observation of the world around us inevitably leads us to envision a new kind of human being—one who possesses everything necessary for survival and transformation while maintaining commitments such as respecting nature and all forms of life. Simultaneously, this new human is deeply engaged in technological advancements, including artificial intelligence and the metaverse. This vision encompasses integrating these elements into a meaningful life that draws from the ancient wisdom of human tribes and their intrinsic nature. Despite having forgotten much about our inner lives, spirituality, and religion, we can still forge a connection and develop ourselves beyond those experiences brought with them.

In the following sections, I will describe what such a *Homo Innovaticus* might look like. Subsequently, I will discuss my approach, which I believe could serve as a fundamental tool to help us adapt to these new habits.

My experience in innovation management has shown me that it is ultimately about envisioning things as they could ideally be. There are numerous examples of this. Our quest for inner fulfillment and happiness has undergone trials and errors throughout evolution and the domain of invention. Some ideas have endured, while others have not; we experiment, discard, or pass them on. A democratic system is also a unique aspect of humanity.

In the current challenging task of developing an innovation system and future principles, success will depend on our ability to define the right steps based on our experiences, findings, and process knowledge. This is crucial because we have only one planet, and its resources are already stretched to their limits. In my generation, there was an awareness that we are the first to confront this problem. Unfortunately, many have continued as before, without taking care or finding solutions.

At the core of our human experience is our perception of our biological existence. From this base, we evolved into what was already described as Homo Culturalis above. The Homo Culturalis cultivates values and establishes recurring, life-sustaining foundations that represent a vital second pillar of our identity. This "cultural evolution" is manifested through shared narratives and societal norms that enable us to navigate and flourish in our communities. A future type of *Homo Innovaticus* could emerge as a transformative force, harnessing the potential of modern artificial intelligence to augment these two foundational human aspects. By doing so, *Homo Innovaticus* not only addresses existing challenges but also charts a forward-looking path for humanity—a path that embraces creativity, sustainability, and collaboration.

https://doi.org/10.1515/9783111448329-018

Focusing on personal experiences, insights, and reflections instead of trying to apply universal laws or rigid doctrines is now asked. It is all about setting up a framework of guidelines and principles for a new way of coexistence. This new way is designed to deal with today's many challenges. These challenges are often deeply systemic, intertwined with issues related to spirituality, legislation, personal experiences, and pervasive ignorance.

These factors may seem unrelated, but they all are interdependent, and we can't deal with them in one sequence. We need a sequential approach because we cannot handle all topics at the same time, so we need to row them up and work on them iteratively. It's clear that articulating a clear, compelling, and inspiring vision of a future is not just an obligatory leadership tool; it's the key to taking others with us towards a shared goal or ideal. The term *"Duty of Vision"* is the right one for that purpose. Only leaders with a meaningful *duty of vision* can inspire and guide others to transform ambitions into reality.

It is essential that a shared foundation based on fundamental human rights be the guiding thread throughout the development sequences. The human rights have been declared to guarantee everyone the freedom to live their best life and make sure that everyone's voice is heard and respected in the conversation. So, it is our duty to enable this right to as many people as possible:

Because of that, it is imperative that every generation, regardless of age, be aware of this cultural heritage and a "common standard of achievement for all peoples and all nations." Because we as a civilized world have committed ourselves to the human rights declaration. All humans are *"born free and equal in dignity and rights,"* *irrespective of "nationality, place of residence, sex, national or ethnic origin, color, religion, language, or any other status."*

Nonetheless, it is important to acknowledge that human rights are currently facing significant challenges, stemming from the actions of leaders who may lack foresight and integrity, as well as systemic-related narrow-mindedness. So, our commitment is more asked than ever before. The fundamental agreements must be cultivated, reloaded, re-experienced, and integrated into our daily lives in an ongoing, never-ending process. We must be constantly alert and proactive in developing these agreements for our future. It needs to reach our daily discussions, all our social, political, and behavioral interactions, and especially our definition of how we drive innovation and change processes. If we are not in exchange with our past that has given us these values, how can we talk about a good future? Everyone has a role in that process, and every generation has to define its own priorities. The base will remain. Our navigation tool is the human rights declaration. Every contribution counts. Every day, especially with the people we meet. Remember the "Open Space Rule": the people right here in this moment are the right ones because they're the only ones we can really talk to!

Thus, the essence of this book is not just a reflection of our own journeys but an invitation for readers to engage in this crucial dialogue. Together, we can explore how knowledge, culture, and innovation can converge to create a more equitable world.

We must not allow ourselves to be thrown off course, because even the global structure of the United Nations is struggling with the systemic shortcomings described in this book. The immoral exploitation of veto rights for the purpose of profit maximization must be stopped at all costs! Even if it means that geopolitical alliances have to be rethought and adapted. Referring to *Darwin*: "It is the most adaptive to environmental threats who survive, not the strongest and most powerful who play game theory in an egocentric mindset!"

Stephane Hessel, who actively participated in the development of the human rights declaration in 1948. is describing in his famous book that he wrote at the high age of over 90 years, *"Time for Outrage!"* that it is our duty to stand up when this moral contract is broken: "*Not with violence, but with conviction, clarity and OUTRAGE!* Find your reason for outrage.[46] This is the start of resistance."

Breaking Free from the Shadow of the Past

It's my deep belief that *Homo Innovaticus* emerges from the shadow of its past and becomes an independent changer and developer of a new future determined by him.

He gets rid of a large part of the influences and barriers that stand in the way of his next development step. He skillfully uses power structures such as political systems, pressure-exerting environmental hierarchies, or destructive conspiracy theories of all kinds to initiate and orchestrate his win-win-win solutions. He loves the challenges posed to him by systems of power through money, military, and religion. He has the skills and the endurance to bring the effective forces of his current ecosystems into exchange with one another and to transform those affected into positive development.

The new Homo Innovaticus skillfully uses power structures such as political systems, pressure-exerting environmental hierarchies, or destructive conspiracy theories of all kinds to initiate and orchestrate his win-win-win solutions.

On the one hand, he draws on these skills from his reflection and inner wisdom, which he has experienced, learned, and integrated as a kind of tribal consciousness over thousands of years of socialization through living together in adaptive systems. And, finally, he's also learned from the mistakes of the past. Recent experiments dealing with the planet, marginalized social groups, and political systems have shown him

---

46 Stéphane Hessel, *Time for Outrage!* (BrightSummaries.com, 2017).

where we all are wrong. This allows him to fully develop his inherent potential, which makes him the "cultural person" term used by Peter Rosegger.

The modern civilized person is a wanderer. He lives in adaptive and dynamic social structures and is in constant conflict with the threats that arise around him. Work, business, religion, law, science, and art emerge as the dominant framework systems or worlds of experience and life models. He uses these as fields of activity for his development. He recognizes these as opportunities to solve problems that would not have arisen otherwise. He sees and feels like a philosophically well-read and universally interested cultural person who likes to talk about his visits to the theater and the books he has read.

It seems that the journey to evolve from primitive man into civilized man was a long and hard one, spanning thousands of years, and in this book I would like to respectfully honor that journey and express my belief that while we may choose to set aside our tribal experiences, it is crucial that we never disregard the profound spiritual dimensions that lie beneath the surface.

As discussed in the chapter on the promoter model, he recognizes the importance of collaboration in achieving his goals. He understands that success is often built through networking and working together with individuals who share a similar commitment to the task at hand. In the context of the promoter model, he acknowledges the significant role that power, relationships, knowledge, and knowledge practice play in the processes within the system.

There is one change in history that could serve as a thinking model. The downfall of the Roman Empire was probably brought about, not least by the epoch-making change, through the religion of Christianity, which emerged as a better model for the future for the majority of people living in the empire. Suddenly there were strong communities evolving that gave rights and that preached for the rights of humanity for every human being in the empire. How blasphemous and dangerous was that for the Roman establishment? At the Council of Nicaea, Emperor Constantine had no choice but to make Christianity the official state religion, since no other religion except the Jewish one was allowed to exist. Also known as the Constantinian Turn. Today we describe this change in history as an epochal turn.

Maybe with the arrival of AI technologies we are at the dawn of such a new epochal turn. This time is caused by the surprising speed of knowledge consolidation and insights explosion that happens right in these days.

It is becoming increasingly evident that a new set of key skills is emerging for the actors involved. These include intuition, meditation, self-reflection, active listening, and leading questioning skills, coupled with the knowledge of how change processes work.

It also seems imperative that success be measured at the four levels of the value system described above, namely user, organization, ecosystem, and society.

This means that we should not only measure success based on economic factors such as cost reduction, profit per customer, market share, return on investment, and other metrics from linear systems. Instead, we should also consider other important factors, such as employee satisfaction; products that make the world a more beautiful and joyful place: platforms that enable safe and value-based global social exchange and networking: and many other similar aspects.

The new Homo Innovaticus doesn't have to define all fields of action by himself.
  Instead, he can tap into the collective knowledge and resources offered by global networking.

The new *Homo Innovaticus* doesn't have to define all fields of action by himself. Instead, he can tap into the collective knowledge and resources offered by global networking. He employs a method that is essentially a form of replication. He uses the United Nations Sustainable Development Goals (UNSDGs) to achieve global alignment. To enhance impact and resilience at the inner level, he employs the Inner Development Goals (IDGs), as previously mentioned. The list could be extended much further.

Holistic Human Nature

The *"integration of everything"* is happening because we've learned to see humans as "always" holistic beings. They can only find useful solutions in the layers of work that were seen separately 30 years ago and mentioned above. These layers include the economy, spirituality, law, science, and art. We must anchor people and their tools. I believe that AI can play a role as an enabler, integrator, and—as should be obvious—as an extended workbench for our creativity. This works when we realize that acting in a self-reliant and self-assured way lets us take on different roles. We all play the roles of screenwriter, art director, and actor in our own lives, all at the same time.

The created solutions strengthen everyone involved along the value levels. Those involved become empowered contributors. In my public presentations at conferences recently, I always expressed this as my deep belief:

> *A strong innovation ecosystem is a condition of single innovation players and their networks that sustain their complexity while contributing to human needs and win-win-win situations.*

One of the most exciting things that has been brought to me while writing this book is that the new proposed innovation code has to start with using strong AI tools that must be combined with a new kind of dreaming. This new way of dreaming combines our natural nighttime dreams, our creative daydreams, and a kind of intuitive spark from AI, creating a cool blend of human and technological imagination. It's important to recognize the connection between moral principles and the deep human connections that allow for a more meaningful interaction.

This new way of dreaming combines our natural nighttime dreams, our creative daydreams, and a kind of intuitive spark from AI, creating a cool blend of human and technological imagination.

And to be very clear: The last moral instance that is deciding about all new things that are created and intended to be put into reality must be people of flesh and blood and a soul and a heart.

Deep down, it combines the vastness of our souls and our unconscious with the concentrated breadth of knowledge driven by artificial intelligence. As the saying goes, "Dreaming is the breathing of the soul." This new form of daydreaming fosters a vision characterized by improved knowledge and a conscious connection with the world and the people in it.

This theory as well fits very well into new findings of dream research and neuroscience research.

Allan Hobson, a leading dream researcher, explains this very well when he says that during sleep, there are neurotransmitter patterns in the areas of seeing, movement, and feelings of the brain.[47] These patterns send things from the brain stem to the higher cerebral cortex. There, they are mixed with our memories, and the brain produces a narrative story that we understand when we wake up. Everyone has experienced dreams that are completely ridiculous and incomprehensible, yet still within the bounds of imagination. Researchers may not fully understand these dreams, but that doesn't negate their significance. We all have our stories, and it's clear that dreaming serves functions beyond just training neurons in the brain and fiction writing to solve problems at a higher level. There's a lot of evidence in different cultures that suggests people have had visions or dreams like the ones Moses is said to have had.

What now if we succeeded in catching the point at which the brain in its dreaming status accesses memories and we could send some better data, like data that is produced by realistic historical AI data?

Could we send some better data, like data that is produced by realistic historical AI data, to our brains for daydreaming?

A very important signal that this thought is not unrealistic delivers us again Richard Feynman. In "Surely You're Joking, Mr. Feynman!", he describes his experiments with lucid dreaming as a way to explore the mind's capabilities.[48] He mentions how he would "program" his brain by focusing on a specific question or thought before falling

---

47 David Robson, "How Studying Babies' Minds Is Prompting Us to Rethink Consciousness," *New Scientist Weekly*, February 15, 2025.

48 Richard P. Feynman, *Surely You're Joking, Mr. Feynman!* (New York: Bantam Books, 1985).

asleep. This practice allowed him to observe his dreams more consciously and even influence their direction to some extent. Through these experiments, he explored sensory experiences, emotions, and the ability to control or modify dream scenarios, all while maintaining a curious and scientific approach. It's a fascinating glimpse into his relentless curiosity and unconventional methods!

If we could further develop access to such a procedure by using our fantastic human ability to daydream. What will that look like? It would enable us to interpret the results of generative AI at a higher level than we have access to. We could use the produced stories in a structured process that allows control, conscious reinterpretation, and social exchange within a dedicated innovation ecosystem.

Let's delve deeper into this question.

Can Daydreaming Collaborate with AI?

The exploration of a useful answer can only be addressed if we combine the latest findings of modern brain research with the experiences derived from the earlier chapters of this book. My theory is about how we can succeed in achieving a daydreaming process in which we consciously interact with an AI chat. This chat is half driven by our conscious skill to ask leading questions and to weave them into the creative status of our brain. I'm calling this approach "AI serendipitous dreaming," and it's the first step in the proposed new innovation process. The previously cited recent article in the New Scientist magazine delivered the final piece of a puzzle that comes with the experiments of Richard Feynman in the 1980s.

It describes the brain research of *Professor Bayne at Monash University in Australia*, and we can find a very interesting aspect that is relevant when we speak about creativity and the AI serendipitous dreaming approach. Baynes and his team suggest that the ability to think, with an awareness of our body and its surroundings, are all knitted together into something we loosely call consciousness. The inner life we experience as adults is a mix of different elements, including a sense of self. Bayne and his team are really interested in where primary, or "core," consciousness comes from. They say it's a subjective experience, like when you taste coffee or smell lavender. The key point to understand is that all our awareness in each moment is part of a single, larger experience. Take watching a violinist, for instance. We experience the sound and sight together, not as two different things.

The origin of this core consciousness occurs when we start to be aware of any events inside and outside our bodies—such as the pain of colic or the calming sound of a parent's voice—and are able to distinguish between them. Bayne and his colleagues suggest a practical approach to settle the debate. They point to recent research identifying four patterns of brain activity and behaviors associated with conscious awareness in adults. While none of these consciousness markers can, by itself, guarantee the presence of an inner life, taken together, they give a strong indication that someone is aware of their surroundings.

One of the consciousness markers that Bayne and his colleagues considered concerns the ways that different brain regions temporarily link up into working networks. Brain scans reveal that when we are in something like a **default mode network (DMN).** This network is described by them as somehow a default program that we bring with us and that was shaped by generations before we have been living. It is the network that is working when we are at rest or when we are daydreaming. We all know that daydreaming is a very energy-optimized and relaxed state where we feel well and not stressed.

Our brain brings a thinking pattern network with us that was shaped by generations before we have been living.

The second mode is described as the **Executive Control Network (ECN),** and this comes into play when we need to capture attention and solve difficult problems in daily life. Bayne also describes that this executive control network interacts with a **Dorsal Attention Network (DAN).** They speak about the DAN being responsible for the connection of the body to our consciousness.

Now the interesting finding for me was that people who are asleep and dreaming, which is for most an unconscious state, show **an ebb and flow of activity between the three described network states**.

We know from creativity methods that our creativity is at its maximum when we are relaxed and not stressed. Suddenly it all dawned on me. I've always wondered why the ambidexterity trap exists, and now I know it. It explains why it's so hard to cope with it. Prof. Baynes' research definitively shows that it's impossible to handle both creative projects and day-to-day stress simultaneously. Our brain operates in distinct modes for creative and stressful work. It is like we are operating like a computer with different operating systems that are not connected to each other. A default mode allowing us to function properly during the day in a very relaxed but efficient manner. An executive control mode that captures attention and solves difficult problems and is connected to our body's nervous system, keeping us alert for new information from outside. It also has a highly connected dream mode that combines everything in a "spooky" way. We can thankfully take this as an untouchable secret of our human nature, our connection to something higher, or simply a divine gift to us humans.

It is like we are operating like a computer with different operating systems that are not connected to each other.

We could call that "cognitive ambidexterity"—and it explains the necessity to switch between creative thinking and analytical problem-solving.

During sleep our dreams produce patterns mixed with our memories, and the brain produces a narrative story that we remember when we wake up.

Italian researchers have emphasized the significance of the Default Mode Network (DMN). The DMN is most active during periods of rest and daydreaming, allowing for a free flow of thoughts and creativity. Recent findings show that while the DMN might seem to be inactive during tasks requiring focused attention, it actually continues to function in the background, helping us access our memories and build connections between seemingly unrelated ideas.

From an evolutionary perspective, the DMN provides a necessary framework for creative thinking, enabling us to innovate and adapt to our environment. My observations suggest that individuals using strategies to engage both daydreaming and AI collaboration are better equipped to generate creative solutions and overcome challenges than those who operate strictly within traditional problem-solving methods.

In my first personal experiments with people applying this new process—integrating daydreaming with AI—I have noticed they come up with more innovative ideas and effective problem-solving strategies. By harnessing the natural capabilities of the brain to traverse its rich landscape of memories and imaginative possibilities, we unlock a broader spectrum of insights, often surpassing what we can achieve through linear thinking alone. This first signal motivated me to fine-tune my proposal for a new innovation approach.

Isn't it revolutionary to think that by leveraging daydreaming and AI together, we can trick the brain into exploring a richer tapestry of memories and creative possibilities? I firmly believe that this theory warrants deeper exploration. Using this new methodology for generating high-impact creative solutions across various fields would make sense because we know from creativity methods that our creativity is at its peak when we are relaxed and not stressed. The key to leveraging the proposed AI-enhanced daydreaming is recognizing that the brain is highly connected to our memories and experiences when it is in daydreaming mode. By alternating between daydreaming and AI questioning, we can effectively deliver new memories to this unconscious process, which are perceived as real memories by our brain. The process of using this AI-enhanced daydreaming is straightforward: the brain is busy to our memories and actions. By alternating between daydreaming and AI questioning, new enhanced memories are delivered to this process. These are seen as real memories by our brain at this moment as the fresh AI-produced data is brought in. It is a training process that produces narrative stories based on memories. The fictions produced in this way can now be taken to further handling by our conscious decision-making about which way we want to further proceed. And because of that we need a good and structured process to find clear thoughts, understanding, and trust.

By alternating between daydreaming and AI questioning, new enhanced memories are delivered to the creation process in our brain.

I want to make it again very clear at this point. I am speaking of daydreaming, not of real dreaming. The role of dreams in training our brains to interact between the different modes described by the work of Prof. Bayne, is evident. Dreams seem to act as a form of cognitive rehearsal, enabling our minds to explore various scenarios and solutions while also affirming our memory connections. This interaction serves as a "dry-training" exercise, allowing us to brainstorm and innovate based on our stored memories and experiences, all while weaving a fictional narrative. Touching the area of our dreams overnight can be harmful for our sleep! We should keep our fingers away from that. But alone, the insight that our brain is working in the same mode when daydreaming and nightdreaming opens us the way to further experiments.

Our brain works in the same mode when daydreaming and nightdreaming. This opens the door to further experimentation.

The DMN as well has a fascinating ability to act as an autopilot, allowing birds engaged in long-haul flights to take power naps of over 12 seconds and avoid falling down to earth. The DFM is of great evolutionary importance. And I want to repeat it: We can thankfully take this as an untouchable secret of our human nature.

Many cultures have long believed that dreams can offer prophetic insights or guidance. Across different societies, there are numerous anecdotes of dreams leading to breakthroughs or foretelling events. This cultural recognition of the power of dreams further emphasizes their potential role in fostering creativity and problem-solving.

Homo Innovaticus Can Do Things Better

However, we should not end this section without the realistic warning that history unfortunately paints us a contradictory picture of the world. The history books are full of fanatical individuals with no long-term positive intentions who ruthlessly exert their power through violence and conquest. Powerful movements often follow a violent course. However, these mindsets do not usually promote long-term prosperity or human development. They usually lead to poverty and chaos. It is not for nothing that they say that the revolution eats its own children. Only progress that is based on fundamental and long-term prosperity can be sustainable—and still needs constant adaptation to the needs of the current challenges.

When our motivation is to take from others through abuse of power and warfare, we inevitably fall into the illusion that this will lead to a better life. Often such destructive processes are aimed directly at those who seek the common good.

We can do better than that!

Distilling all the aforementioned lessons into a simple, accessible format, which I call the "Minimum Viable Innovation Process," is the proof of concept that we can learn from the experiences in industrial innovation cultures of the recent 30 years. This process helps us identify and refine our core innovation topics, define our innovation ecosystem, and develop Stage-Gate logics along with clear communication tools.

And the big aspiration with that is, can we crack the code of innovation and change with the help of AI?

Over the last four decades, the paradigms for future preparation have evolved dramatically. This has forced us to adapt. The relentless evolution of data availability and the acceleration of AI applications have rendered our previously developed tools ineffective. We are in a precarious situation, much like the frog that remains unaware as the temperature of its environment rises to perilous levels. Sticking to outdated methodologies is a recipe for disaster. It is clear that by neglecting the fundamental logic of the innovation basics that have been proven to work, we lose stability and predictability of change processes. We must keep this in mind at all costs.

The fast-paced world demands that we remain adaptable, informed, and proactive. Fostering minimum viable innovation must begin by creating a robust sense of importance and impact, leveraging the most advanced AI models available. In this initial phase, we construct a conceptual framework—an 'empty tube'—that acknowledges undeniable realities, establishes working conditions, and fosters dreaming within and beyond our conscious imagination framework.

It's more important than ever to start every change project with a bit of trial and error to gain insights and data. To embrace the new and avoid being held back by our biases, we need to forget everything initially. This might sound unusual and daunting, but it's important to remember that we're not giving up anything permanent.

As previously stated, innovators possess a mindset conducive to growth and risk-taking behavior. Conversely, others may be reluctant to take risks due to their aversion to failure. It is therefore recommendable that we develop the capacity to engage in both approaches and consciously alternate between them.

It's really important to be able to switch up your mindset at the right time and with the right people. This is something we've already talked about a lot, and it's all about following the ambidexterity insights and being able to switch between different ways of thinking.

It's also important to come up with the right questions in the context of the desired change. As *Mahatma Gandhi* once said, *"Be the change you wish to see in the world."*

The favorite innovation principles and findings, which we have already explored together, dictate the new *"Minimum Viable Innovation Process"* in the age of AI. We build on these principles and extend their application with today's tools.

Innovation Is Human—and must stay that way: Innovation is not simply the result of data or computation. It is a deeply human endeavor. While AI can augment our processes, only humans can infuse innovation with ethics.

Not surprisingly, the ingredients for a new process I suggest are as follows:

- Stage-Gate thinking is the clear choice. It breaks down any process into its basic stages and gives us the ability to define and control the principles of how to get from one step to the next.
- The use of the basic promoter model to improve is vital. Identify it is essential to involve the people who can and must contribute to our innovation project.
- Clayton Christensen's strategy for breakthrough technologies is the key to understanding the ambidextrous nature of innovation.
- The new innovation ecosystem thinking and definition are essential for understanding how to enable collaboration on a global level and accelerate the impact of such systems.
- Harrison Owen's Open Space Technology is the key to successfully integrating the different perspectives of the various dimensions of the systemic overall approach of the participants. It involves our tribal wisdom and inner longings.
- The new mix of human ethics and smarts, along with AI's mind-blowing, wide-ranging but tamed capabilities.

Will it be possible to bring all these aspects together into one logical and simple sequence?

Why not? Let's try and start with a new endeavor. We have the talent. We are the premature, experimental prototype community of the *"Homo Innovaticus !"*

We are the premature, experimental prototype community of the Homo Innovaticus!

And right now, it's time to figure out how we can make this happen in practice. We start with the basic simple version to develop a feeling and a first overview and should be understood as an introduction and dry training:

Chapter 16
The Innovation Approach of the *Homo Innovaticus*

We're embarking on a new adventure to discover amazing new insights and connections. Armed with these insights, we can explore what they mean for our central innovation question, helping us make a bigger impact. Even if we forget most of the insights we've produced, we can identify the most impactful ones for the next steps. AI has the potential to revolutionize how we gather and analyze information, producing insights in ways never before possible.

The British author and entrepreneur Paul Graham once said, "When experts are wrong, it's often because they're experts on an earlier version of the world." I love this simplification so much because it gets straight to the point: Even if we think we know it all, we still have to deal with the sheer volume of information out there, which creates endless versions of reality, some good and some bad. In such a fast-changing environment, how can we be sure we're getting the right information? We can't simplify things by ignoring important details. Building trust and reliability and at the same time embracing the new is our hidden agenda.

The Process

The basic, and minimum viable approach of the Homo Innovaticus to innovation takes into account that he must be able to navigate complexity, combine internal development with external change and pursue innovation from an ethos of cooperation.

This Minimum Viable Innovation Process (MVIP) is a structured approach to innovation that involves breaking down the innovation process into manageable phases. Each phase represents a key milestone in the innovation journey, from initial concept development to implementation and scaling. By following this structured approach, you can systematically address the challenges and opportunities associated with innovation. The version shown in figure 10 in detail is specifically intended to help those readers that are familiar with the practices and the language used in professional environments. Those who are not used to speaking this language and to working with process charts, I invite to jump on our journey for everybody on chapter 17, named *"Homo Innovaticus* for Beginners", which allows you a guided travel through the MVIP without having to have detailed expertise in innovation and change processes.

https://doi.org/10.1515/9783111448329-019

Step 1: AI *and Serendipity*—Dream and Play: Establish a Sense of Importance and Impact

Assess the topic you wish to change. Analyze the existing realities and knowledge surrounding the issue. Use all kinds of insights, dreaming, contemplation, listening to your inner voice, and old dreams. Engage in a playful exploration of related topics. Be playful, explorative, and visionary. Document your insights and develop mind maps of the emerging themes.

Step 2: *Vision and Alliance*
Define the Partners for Your Personal Innovation Ecosystem

Collaboration is the key driver. Identify and define your future partners without bias. List potential partners, reaching out to everyone, even the most unattainable helpers. Gather as much information as you can about them. Categorize the partners based on their roles in research, exploitation, and promotion. Experiment creatively to gauge their openness to collaboration, but don't pressure them to embrace your vision. Focus on discovering common interests and synergies that may lead to partnership. Listen to their pros and cons, but don't promise too much.

Step 3: *Collaborative Open Space*
Rephrase your Vision and Utilize the Power of Alliance

Use the R-ICE Method: Create a positive drive. Define the interests, concerns, and expectations of each stakeholder or contributor group. Draft your innovative vision. Create a preliminary innovation calendar and a rough draft of your Innovation RADAR. Use the template at the end of this chapter. This will help you outline your key milestones and your four must-win impact areas, including the Planet Area, as a fixed starter.

Step 4: *Orchestrate and Ride the Change*
Freeze Your Fields of Action and Start the Journey

Use the logic of the four predefined phases, earlier in the book.
Break down your vision and urgency into manageable stages.
Dismantle your vision and address the urgency of change.
Redefine the framework and contents of change.
Involve your defined ecosystem partners by offering them smart roles in the RASCI context.
Ensure that the process is logical and structured. Be sure you have your most important contributors and stakeholders on board for your journey.
Finalize your basic communication pictures.

Draw down your individually adapted Innovation Calendar (use the template at the end of this chapter) and communicate the contents.

Stay in the driver's seat. Keep in mind to fail and learn early and to correct, extend and/or even abandon your approach.

Constantly adapt your RADAR and fly with trusting yourself as the contributor and orchestrator of your life's vision, and consolidate your achievements by adaptation and communication.

Enjoy Your Ride

Mode d'Emploi: How to Use

So, how do you use the basic process in practice? The four steps should help us figure out the principles of action we need to pass through when we want to minimize the risk of failure and get most people, systems, and Mother Earth involved. When we look at all the different examples in the book and think about what we can learn from them, I've concluded that the key to success is being able to switch between different ways of thinking throughout the process without losing sight of the big picture. I tried to include the basic principles of the core innovation methods, blending them with the challenges and new tools of today.

Therefore, every step is described by its predominant mindsets and clearly defined switching points to let them deploy in the best way. As well, in the following I will introduce the according mindsets to the different steps along with inspirational recommendations, guiding rules, practical tips, and a form of virtual gatekeepers. The virtual gatekeepers shall help you to check if you are really prepared to jump into the next step. This offers you a guided way through the most difficult part of innovation.

What was once the fuzzy front end 20 years ago is now a great opportunity to create a future that's driven by our inner beliefs and hopes, thanks to AI and the reflection of our personal evolutionary steps.

From my experience, the more time you invest in yourself by enjoying the dreaming, exploring, and playful phase at the beginning and by finding your co-developers and companions for change in phase 2, the more vibrant and authentic you'll feel, and the closer you'll be to your purpose and meaning in life. But in the end you decide how fast you go through the process. For small innovations it may be that you can do this in 2–3 days, and for long changes it may last up to many months or even years. But to benefit most from the initial phase, I recommend having a minimum of 2 nights for steps 1 and 2 to allow your inner beliefs and inner spiritual connections to raise their voice while you are sleeping.

If you're an innovation professional, you'll be able to use this to define change processes and scale them up beyond what's described.

If you're just looking to use the proposed process for any kind of personal change, even if you don't know much about innovation management, I suggest going through the described steps. Use the predefined questions to find your path. Think of the descriptions as a virtual mentor that helps you find your own path and travel mates in life.

In any case, I encourage you to try out the suggested process for all kinds of goals, changes, and even dreams in your life. From what I've seen, if you put in the time to use the awesome new AI tools at the start and simply play around with them and then invest in finding your co-developers and partners for change in phase 2, you'll really shine and be more authentic, which will help you reach your full potential.

Let's go!

Phase One: AI and Serendipity

Dream and Play: Establish a Sense of Importance and Impact

Assess the topic you wish to change. Analyze the existing realities and knowledge surrounding the issue. Use the Intuition Method, as previously described, to engage in a playful exploration of related topics. Use all kinds of insights, dreaming, contemplation, listening to your inner voice, and old dreams. Engage in a playful exploration of related topics. Be playful, explorative, and visionary. Document your insights and develop mind maps of the emerging themes.

Predominant Mindset

Explorative. Playful. Openness for new inspirations. Connected to your inner dreams. Listening to your inner wishes. Empathic for other people. Curious to find out your personal path to fulfillment and happiness.

Leading Questions

When was I happy in my life?

What did I contribute to that situation?

How could I reconnect to that experience?

How could I bring myself again into such a situation?

Miracle question after Steve de Shazer: "Imagine a miracle happens overnight and all your problems are solved. What would be the first thing you notice the next morning that this miracle has happened?"

Methods and Practices
AI Serendipitous Dreaming

Check out all kinds of AI and be surprised by the new findings. Go deeper by letting yourself be guided through extended proposals of AI. I use MS Copilot to generate more prompts and access the referenced primary sources for answers. I also use Chat GPT to request more detailed versions of the proposals by prompting it with: Enrich and enhance the text. This keeps it like a real dream, but on steroids. It's like a supercharged version of daydreaming. It lets you explore and move through worlds that are sort of real, sort of imagined—but with a much bigger and related knowledge base compared to what you already know. It con-

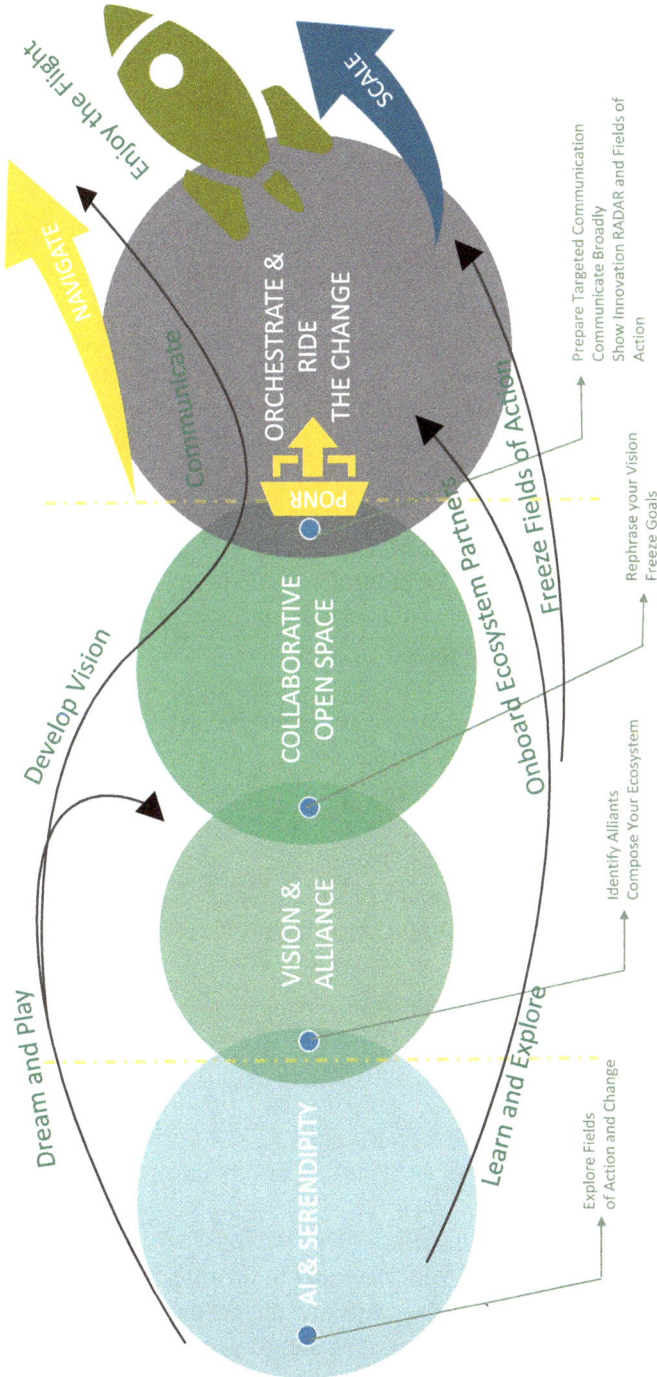

Figure 10: The Minimum Viable Innovation Process (MVIP).

nects you to your intuition and the knowledge of the world and your ancestors' experiences. The human spirit is defined by our unique capacity for hope, dreams, and aspirations, and AI will never fully replace them. AI will help us speed things up, improve them, expand them, and make them better. It will also, interestingly enough, make our human skills as social beings more relevant. AI will make our findings more relevant to our human skills as social beings.

– **Mind Mapping**

Draw mind maps of your things that resonate in you. Cluster them and try to find things that you want to change in your life or in your communities.

– **Miracle Questioning (De Shazer)**

The Miracle Question can help you to recognize your goals and wishes more clearly and to focus on solutions rather than problems. The method encourages you to imagine an ideal future and identify specific steps that could lead to this future. It helps you to visualize positive changes and motivates you to actively tackle these changes.

Inspirations / Recommendations

Take a few days off. Read inspiring literature. What is your biggest fear today? Write your own "Eulogy." What would you like to be told about you? What can you do now to go in that direction?

OUTPUT: Write a list of things you want to achieve and cluster them.

Virtual Meeting With the Gatekeeper

People's emotional intelligence must always be in the driver's seat. Every gatekeeper must represent a real person, respectively, and it's virtual representator.

Leading Question:

Tell me about your findings.

Tell me about the most burning question in your life and your motivation to find solutions.

What was the interesting experience that made it a favorite?

Are you well prepared for the next step?

Do you need support?

Preparations for the Next Step

Draw a one-page, easily understandable description of your vision.

Phase Two: Vision and Allies

Define the Partners for Your Personal Innovation Ecosystem

Collaboration is the key driver. Identify and define your future partners without bias. List potential partners, reaching out to everyone, even the most unattainable helpers. Gather as much information as you can about them. Categorize the partners based on their roles in research, exploitation, and promotion. Experiment creatively to gauge their openness to collaboration, but don't pressure them to embrace your vision. Focus on discovering common interests and synergies that may lead to partnership. Listen to their pros and cons, but don't promise too much.

Predominant Mindset
Explorative: Search mode for the detection of allies and supporters and refinement of my central topic.
Emergent: Welcome to the new insights.
Proceed with being open for every new inspiration.

Leading Questions
Who are the people or organizations that can show you insights?
Who has already solved the topic in another field?
Whom do I know who could connect me to the leading people?
Who could help me to find my leading question?

Methods and Practices
–   Stakeholder Analysis
–   Prompting: CHAT GPT Search
–   Literature Research

Inspirations / Recommendations / Actions
Make a list of contributors and knowledge carriers.
Think about how you could get in touch with those people.
What do you have in common? What could be of interest for them?
Start conversations with them by using R-ICE.
Connect with them but hold back on sharing all your ideas right away. This will give them space to share their own perspectives and insights. Wait for the right time to open up fully.

Output
Outline of the vision. Rough Mission vision Statement and personal motivation.
Wishlist of supporters and allies, clustered by research or market access degree.
First Win-Win-Win Ideas.

Virtual Meeting With the Gatekeeper
Show me your first rough outline of your vision.
Why will it have an impact?

Preparations for the Next Step
Define the "Must Win Areas" that are critical for the success.
Define a rough draft of promoters on the basis of the promoter model.

Phase Three: Collaborative Open Space

Rephrase Your Vision and Use the Power of Alliances

Use the R-ICE Method: Create a positive drive. Define the interests, concerns, and expectations of each stakeholder or contributor group. Draft your innovative vision. Create a preliminary innovation calendar and a rough draft of your Innovation RADAR. This will help you outline your key milestones and your four must-win impact areas, including the Planet Area, as a fixed starter.

Predominant Mindset

Collaborative: Search mode for the detection of allies and supporters and refinement of my central topic.
Defining: Welcome to the new insights.
Dynamic switching between explore and exploit behaviors

Leading Questions

How to develop Win-Win situations?

Methods and Practices

- *Open Space*
- *World Cafe*
- *Innovation Radar (template added)*
- *Innovation Calendar / Map (template added)*

Inspirations / Recommendations / Actions

Communicate your vision very powerfully.
Invite for collaboration.
Refine your vision together.
Distribute the first subtasks and subwork packages and let the findings flow into the Innovation RADAR and MAP.
Develop contracts and commitment statements.

Output

Innovation RADAR (template)
Must-Win Fields
Midterm key events
Minimum Viable Business Model Canvas (template added)

Virtual Meeting With the Gatekeeper

Resource check: What have you planned? How did you receive commitment.
Budget. Promoter Analysis.

Preparations for the Next Step
Innovation Calendar / Innovation RADAR / Financial Risk Analyses

Phase Four: Orchestrate and Ride the Change
Freeze Your Fields of Action and Start the Journey
Now the change project gets visible publicly and needs sound preparation.
Use the logic of the four predefined stages, earlier in the book.
Break down your vision and urgency into manageable stages.
Dismantle your vision and address the urgency of change.
Redefine the framework and contents of change.
Involve your defined ecosystem partners by offering them smart roles in the RASCI context,
Ensure that the process is logical and structured. Be sure you have your most important contributors and stakeholders on board for your journey.
Finalize your basic communication pictures.
Draw down your individually adapted Innovation Calendar and communicate the contents.
Stay in the driver's seat. Keep in mind to fail and learn early and to correct, extend, and/or even abandon your approach.
Constantly adapt your RADAR and fly with trusting yourself as the contributor and orchestrator of your life's vision, and consolidate your achievements by adaptation and communication.
Use the logic of the four predefined stages, earlier in the book.
Break down your vision and urgency into manageable stages.
Dismantle your vision and address the urgency of change.
Redefine the framework and contents of change.

Predominant Mindset
Exploitation: Search mode for the detection of allies and supporters and refinement of your central topic
Realization/Implementational: Translate the Innovation RADAR into clear work packages and roles.
Fly and Navigate: Orchestrate the allies and support them.
Communicate: Clear dedicated messages, but give enough room for changes
Prepare for the Launch:

Leading Questions
Who should be addressed by communication?
How can I safeguard the energy in the process?

Methods and Practices
– *Innovation RADAR*
– *Innovation Calendar / Map*
– *Communication Plan*

Inspirations / Recommendations / Actions
– Freeze Innovation RADAR (especially targeted Action Fields)
– Targeted Communication
– Expect the Unexpected.
– Act Dynamically.

Output
– Communication Plan
– Innovation RADAR
– Must-Win Fields
– Defined ROLE (RASCI Model as basis— Responsible, Accountable, Support, Consulted, Informed)
– Minimum Viable Business Model Canvas

Virtual Meeting With the Gatekeeper
– Resource check: What have you planned, and how did you receive commitment?
– Budget.
– Promoter Commitment Check
– Last Corrections

Preparations for the Next Step
Enjoy and orchestrate.

Overview Charts and Working Templates

Further explanations behind the used terms

The Impact of Information Overload on Decision Making
Information overload significantly impacts decision-making processes. Platforms like Facebook, X, TikTok, and Instagram have completely changed the way we connect and share content. They've given us incredible power to reach a global audience in seconds. This has democratized information sharing, but it has also led to an overwhelming influx of data. The sheer volume of content presents a thrilling challenge: to distinguish between credible sources and misinformation. We must filter the best, unbiased information from different sources. When faced with a lot of data, we often

THE INNOVATION PROCESS OF HOMO INNOVATICUS

STEP / ESSENTIAL FEATURES	AI & SERENDIPITY — AI Dreaming and Playing	VISION & ALLIANTS — Define Personal Innovation Ecosystem	COLLABORATIVE OPEN SPACE — Rephrase Vision wit Partners	ORCHESTRATE & RIDE THE CHANGE — Freeze Field of Actions and Start Journey
PREDOMINANT MINDSET	EXPLORATIVE; DREAMING; PLAYFULNESS; CURIOUS	EXPLORATIVE; EMERGENT; OPENNESS	EXPLORATIVE/EXPLOITIVE; COLLABORATIVE; DEFINING; DYNAMIC	EXPLOITATIVE; IMPLEMENTATIONAL; COMMUNICATION; DYNAMIC
LEADING QUESTIONS	Finding my Purpose; Remember the moment of...; What if a miracle happens	Who are the thought leaders; Who solved similar questions; Whom do I know already; Whom will I access	How to define WIN WIN Fields	Whom to Communicate
METHODS AND PRACTICES	SERENDIPITOUS DREAMING; MIND MAPPING; MIRACLE QUESTIONING	STAKE HOLDER ANALYSIS; PROMPTING: CHAT GPT Search; LITERATURE RESEARCH	OPEN SPACE; WORLD CAFE; INNOVATION RADAR; INNOVATION CALENDAR	INNOVATION RADAR; INNOVATION MAP/CALENDAR; COMMUNICATION PLAN
INSPIRATIONS	Recognize & trust inner dreams; Write your Eulogy; Feeling of Purpose; Intuition	Use RICE Method; Connect to first poeple	Refine Vision together; Develop INNO RADAR together	Freeze Action Fields; Still expect the unexpected; Cummunicate Broadly
QUESTIONS OF GATEKEEPER	List of Findings; Emotional/rational founding question	Why will it have Impact?	Resources; Budget	Resources checked; Budget availability; Last Corrections
OUTPUT & PREPERATIONS FOR NEXT STEP	My Mission Vision	Mission Vision Statement; Impact Explanation; Must Win Areas for Change	MV Business Model Canvas; Must Win fields; Innovation RADAR; Financial Risk Analysis	Communication Plan; Innovation RADAR; Must win Fields; Partner Commitment; Believe

© 2025 Hannes Erler

Chart 1: The Innovation Process of the Homo Innovaticus.

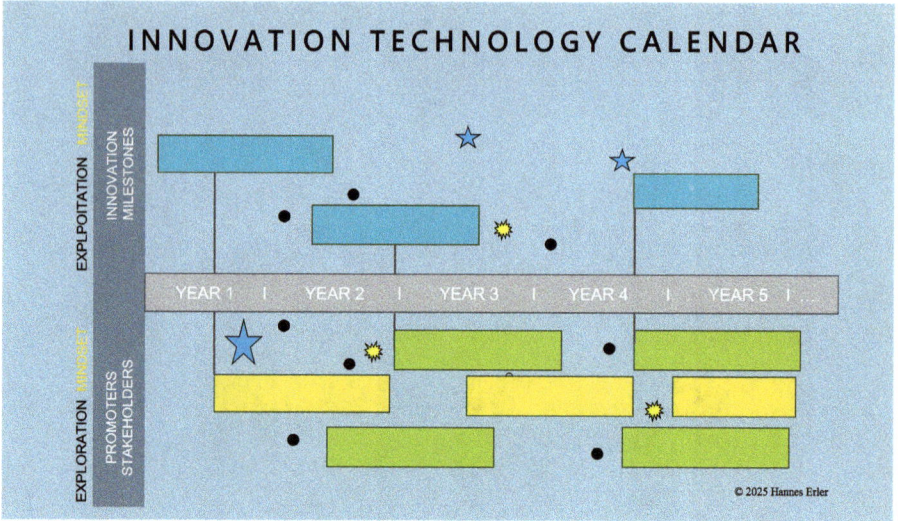

Template 1: The Innovation Technology CALENDAR.

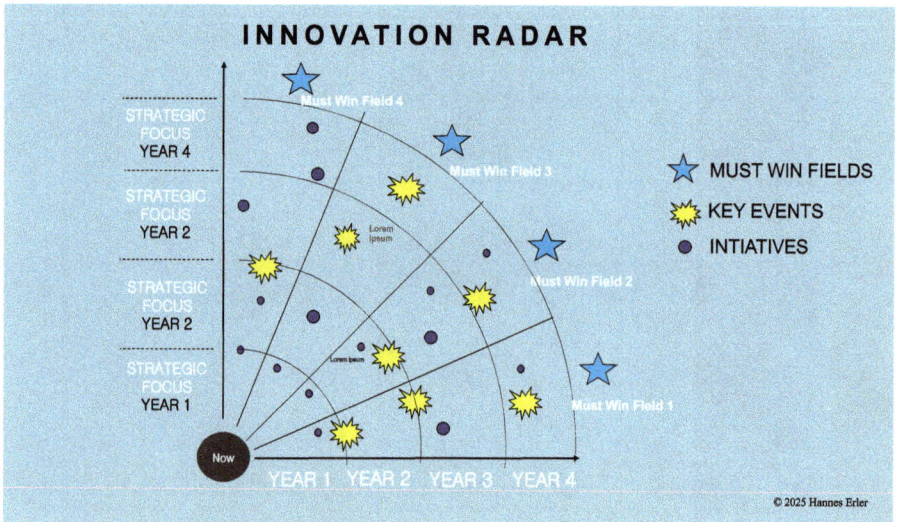

Template 2: The Innovation RADAR.

experience what's known as "analysis paralysis," where the sheer volume of information hinders our ability to make decisions. This can lead to delays, missed opportunities, and less-than-ideal results. AI-powered tools can sift through vast amounts of data, identify patterns, and provide insights that would be difficult for humans to discern. By incorporating AI into the MVIP, we will enhance our ability to gather rele-

BUSINESS MODEL CANVAS (OSTERWALDER)

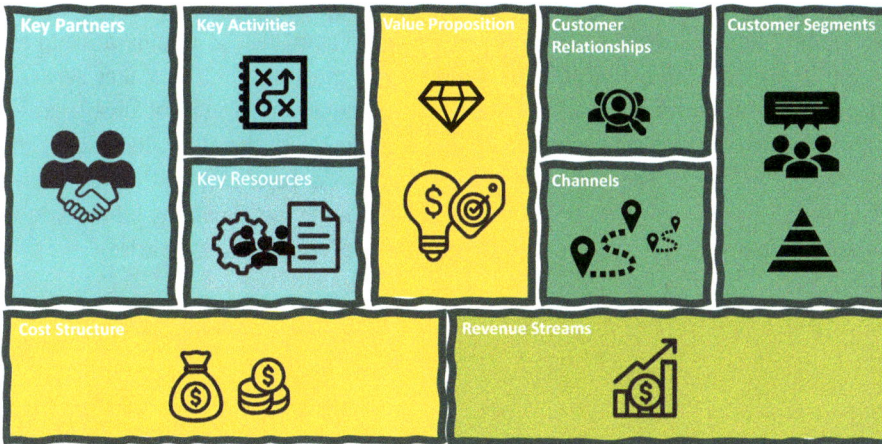

Template 3: The Business Model Canvas. Adapted from Alexander Osterwalder.

vant information and make informed decisions. The MVIP tackles this issue head-on with a proven step-by-step process for collecting and analyzing information. It also includes built-in gates that allow us to pause and reflect, giving us control.

The R-ICE method is the framework for prioritizing innovation efforts based on four key factors: reach, impact, trust, and effort. Let me be clear: The quality of communication and our ability to create an atmosphere of trust in our social interactions cannot be mentioned often enough. As you can see in Chart 1, it's pretty simple to understand how the different parts are connected. Templates 1, 2, and 3 are great tools to use during the development process. They've been used a lot in many change projects, and they've been approved a lot.

Many transformational and disruptive innovations fail not because fatal flaws in the solution, but because the company fails to understand key aspects of the business model that the innovation is embedded in.
  Prof. Peter Koen at the FEIUS conference, Boston 2023

The Innovation Calendar and the Innovation RADAR tool are essential for tracking and communicating our innovation activities over time. I've seen many innovation and change projects fail because people didn't have access to the important information. As the orchestrator and key driver of your innovation, it is your responsibility to stay on top of things and ensure that the big milestones are met. Innovation RADAR is the dynamic tool that provides the visual representation of the innovation landscape, highlighting the actual areas of focus and potential opportunities. This tool is essential for ensuring that all involved parties stay on track and adapt their innovation efforts as needed. It must be viewed as a dynamic tool that requires regular updates. Innovation is an inherently dynamic process that requires flexibility and adaptability. The MVIP must be open to new ideas and willing to adjust the approach as needed. But: The truth is, the more time that passes, the less open we are to new ideas. It is imperative to adhere to the plan. If the environment changes, you must decide if it makes sense to adapt or cut your losses and start over with a fresh framework. You must always expect the unexpected on your journey if you're going to deal with the MVIP. Remember the key rule of the Open Space Method: Whatever happens is the only thing that could have happened. This will help you be prepared and resilient. This flexibility allows you to respond to changing circumstances and seize new opportunities as they arise.

Chapter 17
HOMO INNOVATICUS for Beginners

I promised that this book will also be intended to help those readers that are not familiar with innovation management, change management, or any organizational topics. I promised to find a way from the basic stuff to the complex to the useful application of innovation and change. We're all passengers on the spaceship Earth. That's why it's important that everyone understands the basic findings about successful innovation and change, even if they're not a specialist or experienced innovation manager. I'm going to translate our MVIP into everyday language so anyone who wants to make a change can understand it. We must use and recirculate the critical resources of our planet responsibly. The spaceship Earth has no emergency exits. We must continue our journey of adaptation together. We must find our co-travelers to be sympathetic or not. Everyone has a role to play in ensuring a safe flight. No matter where fate has placed you or what you have done in the past, you must contribute. Remember the other rule of the Open Space Technology: "Over is over —now is the right point to act!"

You are already satisfied with the results you have produced during the four steps of the above version of the MVIP. As an experienced innovation professional, I know this to be true. Congratulations! Go for it. Don't waste time. Your role, contribution, and that of your co-workers are clearly defined. Skip the next pages of the inner journey. Doubts about your chances of success? Take a good, hard look at yourself. It'll give you the ammunition you need to convince others of your authenticity and power.

Since the first astronauts have seen the Earth from outside, we know the expression of the "overview effect." This has changed the perspective on our planet and mankind. It's a perspective that's breathtaking in many ways —good and bad. The German-French sociologist *Steffen Roth* has claimed that if a Spaceship Earth thinking could one day be fully realized, it would represent the most perfect total institution ever created in the history of humankind. For me, it would be arrogant and presumptuous to make such a claim, but that doesn't mean we shouldn't tackle the dream of such a claim. It may sound utopian, but it's true. We know from Open Space Technology and Harrison Owens' immutable law of the mind that the rule of "Over is over—now is the right point to act" means we are where we are because of everything we did in history. As time has gone by, we've been collecting more and more experiences. Our access to these experiences comes from the narratives we've created and the decisions we've made.

So, it is also about our conscious access to our failures and findings and our willingness to look at them with an unbiased view. Thus, it is more about how we interpret what has brought us into today's circumstances. A value-free look at them shapes our future because we have no other way than realizing that the framework condi-

https://doi.org/10.1515/9783111448329-020

tions for a good future are already determined by the findings so far. Using the metaphor of the spaceship earth inevitably opens our minds to the realization that all supplies to spaceship earth that we can drain or pollute are limited.

This connects directly to the well-known Hopi prophecies, which provide significant insight into the interconnectedness of life and the fragility of our world. The Hopi indigenous tribe of North America has long held prophecies predicting significant changes in the world. These prophecies emphasize the need for humanity to live in harmony with nature. One of their prophecies, known as the "Hopi Blue Star Prophecy," foretells of a time when a blue star will appear in the sky, signaling a great transformation. This transformation will bring about a period of renewal and peace if humanity chooses to return to a respectful relationship with the Earth. It will bring about a time of chaos and destruction if we continue to exploit and harm the planet.

The Hopi prophecies remind us how powerful stories and beliefs from the past can shape our future. When people believe strongly in a prediction, they often begin to act in ways that make it come true. This is called a self-fulfilling prophecy—where expectation and behavior feed into each other. If people expect something bad to happen and talk about it constantly, fear grows. That fear can become so strong that it influences actions and leads us straight into the very disaster we feared. This is why it's so important to recognize these moments not as endings, but as signals for change. Instead of falling into fear, we must choose to act differently—and help create a better outcome.

The narratives of our tribal wisdom are maybe still, or because of the upcoming AI technologies and supposed data overload, a key to allowing further development of our species and at the same time reminding us of the urgency of our situation. They call us to hear the warnings of the past and recognize that our actions have a direct impact on the future. These prophecies can be a guiding narrative in our journey of innovation and change, reminding us of the interconnectedness of all things and the importance of sustainable practices.

Helga Nowotny's findings from African culture support the notion that the future is already present around us, not merely ahead of us. We play an active role in the continuity of the past, present, and future. This unique way of looking at time, which sees time as a continuous and connected flow, will lead to a deep healing. It challenges the belief that our actions don't matter, encouraging us to see the value in what each person does. It's clear that this only works when people are brave enough to act. We are all part of the same group, like a tribe or a crew on a spaceship Earth. This perspective directly challenges the linear, Western concept of time and encourages us to act as change agents, actors, and role models within our *Homo Innovaticus* consciousness.

This clearly shows that progress in smaller groups of organizational subcultures, voluntary work, and social institutions can only be achieved by this principle of shared responsibilities that work towards common expressed goals. This is the crucial finding in addressing global challenges such as climate change and resource management. A collective mindset is key to understanding the impacts of our actions on future generations and working together towards a sustainable future. It also helps us navigate this journey with a sense of purpose and responsibility.

Because of this, I invite you to start a journey with me. This journey is based on a new story about the *Homo Innovaticus*, a term that speaks to the spirit of our time.

I have chosen to use the metaphor of a journey from one island to the other. Each island represents an important part of the MVIP of the *Homo Innovaticus*. You will travel alone—or not really alone:

As we embark on this journey, you'll meet your guide and mentor, who'll be your ferryman, taking you from one island to the next. You'll meet a ruler on every island. This ruler is like a wise king. He's a transformative mentor. He's got a lot of power and wisdom. This mentor's main goal is to make sure you get the rules and guidelines that reflect the island's main mindset. He'll help you find the answers to your pressing questions and discover your unique contribution to the *Homo Innovaticus* tribe and your vision for a better world and brighter future.

Our adventure starts now, as we prepare to set sail from the harbor. You need to know why you're traveling and what you hope to achieve to stay motivated. On our vessel, you are more than just a passenger; you become a traveling researcher, like historical visionaries Christopher Columbus or Commander Kirk of the Starship Enterprise. You start to learn and find ways to change the story of our society to make it better.

You will alternate between the roles of a learning apprentice and a courageous adventurer. As an apprentice, you will experience direction and inspiration. As an adventurer, you will embrace new experiences and uncharted territories. You will face challenges and be asked uncomfortable questions, but you will never be alone. Your encounters will offer insights, advice, and inspiration to help you understand your role in the world, equipping you with the tools needed to navigate the complex ecosystem of modern *Homo Innovaticus*. You will learn how to draw your personal roadmaps and explanation tools.

It is up to you how far you go with your visions and aspirations. In any case you will have to leave now the ground of your familiar safe havens, and I invite you to simply travel through this guided tour. A tour that is intended to embark without detailed knowledge on innovation topics but makes you a full member of the journey of the awakened *Homo Innovaticus* and finding your personal role and meaning and how to contribute.

Establishing the purpose and vision of your travels is essential to sustain motivation and endurance along the way.

As a preparation for the journey, I recommend you start with the very initial 2 key questions:

How can I connect to my deeper purpose and sense in life?

How can I find my place and role for making an evocative contribution to a new era of prosperity?

My experience shows that these initial questions will lead you on a self-discovery journey that connects you to your deepest inner desires and hopes. These are the most important ingredients for a fulfilled and happy existence.

We're all on a journey, and it's important to remember that each of us has our own path to follow. You're in charge of your own meaningful life. Decide how long to spend on each of the different islands and how to bring your dreams to life. As in our modern times, we tend to fulfill our traditions solely with the help of our own personal symbols. This tendency of separation can be mitigated by reusing customs and traditions of our ancestors. Sometimes renewal means returning to the source where all our personal and cultural myths are created: The human psyche. Because of that fact, I have woven in some spiritual practices that helped me on my personal path of evolution and that are rooted in my studies of practical exercises of our ancestors. At the end of the journey, remember that it's your chance to present your unique contribution to whatever you call it. I tend to call it my higher self that is connected to the "integration of everything." And the integration of everything we already have defined above as the interconnectedness and interdependence of various aspects of our lives that is driven by advancements in technology, globalization, and a growing awareness of the need for holistic approaches to societal challenges.

Of course, you can start your journey by thinking about a burning question in your own life. If you're going through a tough time and need some help finding a way out, this journey is the perfect place to come up with some creative solutions. It'll work, because your first question will be improved and more specific as we go along. You're the one in control the whole time.

You have your question? Write it down, and let's go aboard our vessel that brings us to the first island. Show your question to your imagination of your ferryman, who will pick you up when you leave the island, and don't expect answers from him. He is your guide and mentor and will know how to give you the right advice and transformative questions along your journey.

As this journey is a visionary journey, you have now to decide about how you want to travel. Some people prefer to sit in their comfort chair in a quiet environment where they won't be disturbed. I prefer to take the questions with me and walk around alone in nature, taking breaks under a tree with a good view or hiding from the rain somewhere. It depends. You will know how to create your personal environment and style. The most important thing is that this is your personal holy time and the window for the sequence is protected from interruptions.

My metaphor for it is that of a daydreamer that is half in life and half in his world of just some thoughts and dreams for the future. It depends on the situation and the task. You decide how long you'll stay on the island. You can do it by doing short sequences of at least 20 minutes every day and/or more often.

The important thing is to keep making progress and to get in touch with your inner self by meditating on your main question. It's also important to decide when you want to take notes. So, you should either always carry a small notepad and a pencil, or, as I prefer, speak the thoughts you want to preserve for later work into your smartphone. The other perk is that you can use digital words to copy them into prompts for enrichment with AI and/or later into your word writings. And again, the most important thing: always distinguish between the work that reflects your deep inner dream state, the work that was created with the help of "AI hallucinations," and the work that you want to keep as your insights and expanded beliefs that you are willing to share with other people! And that's what we should all be known for: The responsible, global *Homo Innovaticus* is the one we can trust to address the issue!

Now, we're here on our first island, and it's time to dive into our adventure. It might be a small step for the world, but it's a huge step for your personal growth.

The Island of "Intuition and Serendipity"

Imagine the ferryman has set you off and you are welcomed by your guide and coach, who makes you familiar with the rules and guidelines.

His name: ***"The Serendipitous Dreamer"***

You prepare for your imaginary stay on the island, and always when you enter the island within your self-organized time windows, you make yourself aware that you are safe and protected on this island with whatever happens in your imaginary world when contemplating over the given tasks and findings. It is important to start every visit by remembering your question and the findings that you had from your last session.

Your task on his island is to enjoy reconnecting to your inner dreams. To find out why you are here. To find out what makes you happy and to refine your understanding of your personal environment.

The guidelines are very simple:

Stay EXPLORATIVE and CURIOUS at any time, enjoy dreaming, and embrace your playfulness like the child that plays in its sandbox.

There is only one real rule: Stay connected to your inner self, to your dreams and wishes, and give up any resistance to that route in negative feelings. Take negative feelings as references that are showing you the barriers that may be rooted in past experiences that have influenced your development. Don't worry— we are all having such experiences. But if they get upper hand, take a break and seek professional help.

The serendipitous dreamer, your guide and co-traveler, asks you questions, and you are asked to develop your deep inner answers, collect them, and put them together to a new understanding of yourself.

You can choose the questions and their order. Be honest in your answers. Remember that you are in a safe mode, allowing you to jump over all barriers that would hinder you from thinking big and free. You are safe, because for this exercise you are alone with you and your inner resources.

Questions of the serendipitous dreamer:
–   **If I think about my life up to this point:**
    What have been my big dreams for my life?
    What people played a role in these dreams?
    What was my contribution?
    Remember a situation where you had this feeling of being more than you thought you could be?
    –   Listen to the song "Give Me One Moment in Time" by Whitney Houston. Listen to the words and let them help to connect to this feeling.
    –   Visualize this situation and remember the people, the topic, and the place.

What is the similarity of this to my situation today?
–   **I reconnect to my inner wishes and dream them forward:**
    Try to think about your future and how your life might end at some point down the line. A line that you don't know?
    Write down a short version of your eulogy that you want to hear when all the people that you love and that are of value for you are here and are listening to this speech.
    What have been the highways that you have traveled in your imaginary life and your eulogy?
    –   Listen to the song "My Way" by Frank Sinatra and reflect on the words.
    –   Visualize, especially on the part of the song where it goes about
    I have traveled each and every highway
    Times, when I bit off more than I could chew
    I ate it up and I sped out
    I faced it all, and I stood tall.
    For what is a man (woman), what has he (she) got— if not himself (herself)
    . . .
    The record shows I took the blows.
    Yes, and did it my way
    –   Reflect about every single part and write down the best version, and let yourself be inspired by the music in doing that.

Use your intuition and ask all kinds of artificial Intelligence helpers in order to help you in your serendipitous dreaming and ask the following questions and play around with the answers and further thoughts:
    Tell me stories about people who have found their deeper purpose in their lives.
    What do these stories of success have in common?
    What are the important framework conditions for a happy and meaningful life?

– **I make miracles happen by serendipitous dreaming.**
As a daydreamer that is half in life and half in his world of thoughts and wishful dreams, you ask yourself the already described
Miracle question after de Shazer:
Imagine a miracle happens overnight and all your problems are solved. What would be the first thing you notice the next morning that this miracle has happened?
How does this feel?
What has changed?
What have I done, or what could I do, in order to achieve that status?

I recommend now drawing a mind map of the findings and clustering them in order to find the important spots that you want to develop further.

Try to find out from the mind map what your most burning question for this moment in your life will be. Set yourself free of expectations about the topic? Regardless of whether it has to do with your current professional, private, or global political priorities. Go for it.

And with that input, now try to make the first version of your minimum viable Mission Vision statement. Again, let yourself be inspired by examples of Mission Vision statements that you derive from playing around with your favorite AI tools. Your first draft of your minimum viable Mission Statement should not be longer than three sentences for the Vision and three sentences for your mission that describes what you want to do or achieve.

If you feel comfortable with that, you are ready prepared now to leave this island and to head towards your waiting ferryman. Say thank you to your imaginary guide, the serendipitous dreamer, and go aboard your ferry.

Tell your imaginary ferryman about your journey and the findings. If you like, you can at this point ask someone who is very familiar and close to you in real life.

It is always a good point to open up discussions with somebody you can trust and are familiar with to open up about your deep inner life.

The Island of "Vision and Alliance"

Imagine the ferryman has set you off and you are welcomed by your next guide and coach,
"The Explorative Seer"
who makes you familiar with the new rules and guidelines
Your task at this island is to refine your vision by your first step of social interactions. Be open to what comes from the feedback of discussing your vision mission statement with others.

The guidelines are very simple:

Keep always on your EXPLORATIVE mindset and stay open for new findings that emerge from the surprising contacts that you learn to know on the island.

There's only one rule: When talking to people in real life, don't open up your inner dreams too early and too extensively. Ask them what they think about your ideas and dreams. Be clear that, for now, it's a vision, and you're uncertain about its feasibility. This opens a dialogue for new perspectives and offers you new contacts and people who might be of interest to you. Remember, you are still in the exploratory phase. Don't make promises you can't keep at this stage. It could hinder you from making the bigger move in the next phase.

The explorative seer, your guide and co-traveler, will ask you questions to help you find your allies. You choose the questions and their order. Remember: you are in safe mode, so you can overcome any barriers that might hinder your thinking. You are safe because your dialogue partners know that you are speaking of visions, not promises or immediate solutions.

Questions of the explorative seer:
- Whom do I already know in my network who could contribute?
- Who are the thought leaders around your vision and the topics?
- How can I find people who have already solved similar questions in other fields or failed and ask them to share their experiences and root causes?
  - If you know them in person, access them directly.
  - If you don't know them, try to explore all the information you can get over existing channels (of course always legally and with respect to one's privacy).

- Again, use all kinds of AI, platforms like LinkedIn, search engines, publications, and so on. Use the findings for improving your insights, and use the new sources as inspiration for deeper insights.
- Try to find out models and predictions for the future relating to your topic.
- Check if the UNSDGs provide some inspiring areas of interaction.
  Choose at least 5 of the 17 UNSDGs in order to open up interaction.

Now it is time to refine your Vision/Mission statement and try to derive something that I like to call as "Impact explanation" statement. This statement will help you in your next step as we define our innovation or change project together with our co-workers.

The most important step is to write down the contribution that your project will have to the four levels of value contribution – remember the four areas of the user, the organization, the ecosystem, and the society. Make your vision now longer and more tangible by developing more and better contributions to the four value levels.

At this point it must not be 100% correct or formulated. It is important that you have a better feeling about the impact and meaningfulness. And of course, a better understanding of the landscape of possible co-innovators.

If you feel comfortable with that, you are ready prepared now to leave this island and to head towards your waiting ferryman. Say thank you to your imaginary guide, the visionary seer, and go aboard your ferry.

Tell your imaginary ferryman about your journey and the findings. If you like, you can speak now very openly within your personal network about your vision and plans.

The Island of "Open Space Actuation"

The ferryman has set you off, and you are welcomed by your next guide and coach,
"The Visionary Leader"
who makes you familiar with the new rules and guidelines.

The task: Your job now is to work on making your vision a reality, and the challenge here is that you must switch between the mindsets "explorative" and "exploitative" effectively. You've got to discuss realization with partners, but you also must stay open to their input. It's a critical phase, and I've seen a lot of the best well-defined innovation projects start to fail here. In this phase you act as a collaborative, visionary, and dynamic innovation leader. You can do it because you are well prepared with insights about value contribution, concerns, and expectations of the affected people. You are the one who sees the unconnected dots in the game, because you have used the benefits of modern AI tools in order to create these insights. And most importantly, you are the master of renewal, the best version of the modern *Homo Innovaticus*—because you have realized that our species only survives because of its ability to adapt to environmental change. And because you are the director of balance between your inner intuition and connectedness to the world on a spiritual level and the indispensable cooperation with reality

The guidelines here are the key:

As this is the most critical phase of our endeavor, enter the island where the four immutable laws of the mind, according to Harrison Owen, are the guiding principle:
- No matter who is present, they are just the right people.
- No matter when we start, it is just the right time.
- No matter what happens, it is the only thing that could happen.
- When it's over, it's over.

That means for you, as you learn from your guide, the visionary leader, you more and more grow into your own version of this leader. Your attitude in this role means that you make the very best of the resources that you have available within your own zone of influence. With the people, the system, the knowledge, and the good and the bad things that surround you. You are happy because you already have your own vision and your insights from the people you learned to know in the course of the second phase of the journey. You heavily use the described communication tool of R-ICE because you are the one who defines the spirit of action and impact. You know that the only right point of time is now. You don't waste time and energy by thinking about why you didn't do that already or why the others did not do it already. Now is the only right time to act. You let yourself be surprised by the impactful power of like-minded helpers. You filter out the ones who will share their vision with you and enable them to melt into one bigger move. You don't let yourself be taken away by events that would have happened anyway, even if you hadn't done anything or been directly responsible for them. The only responsibility you have now is to realize the shared vision. Your responsibility is also to recognize which things need to be let go, discarded, or completely renewed, because you are aware that innovation and exnovation must always be allies. If something is over, it's over.

How to act

The more we come now nearer to bringing our vision into the world, the fewer questions we ask, and the more we go into the realization mode that makes decisions, makes fixed agreements, and starts its leadership by orchestrating the preparation for the launch. You are now coming nearer to the point of no return! This is the point where you are responsible for your actions and promises. Your role now is that of the architect and orchestrator of the realization. So, you prepare by using tools.

Visualization is the key for that. You need to find easy-to-use tools to replace or supplement the key innovation tools that professionals use in this case. Maybe you do not need a business model canvas, an innovation radar, or a financial risk analysis. But in any case, you need a simple roadmap that is showing the path for the realization of the involved people and structures and a simple description of the few (1 up to 4) areas of change.

Now start to prepare those simple drawings. Hand drawings are enough. Your guide is here to support you. A simple version could be:
- Draw a timeline of a minimum of 1 year: if your project is going longer, up to 3 years.
- In the above area, write the milestones that you want to achieve; on the downside, draw the groups of actors resp. involved participants.

This is now your core communication tool. Use it at any time together with your shared and again refined vision and mission tool.

Even if it is a small change for you, maybe others need a picture of what happens.

Now it is up to you, whatever you need for realization. You are the master of this change. You can let yourself be inspired by the innovation radar and by other examples in the book. But again, you keep it simple and understandable for the target groups of communication. Always remember the affected people are the ones that always need information, integration, or motivation to stay on board.

If you feel comfortable with that, you are ready prepared now to leave this island and to head towards your waiting ferryman. Say thank you to your imaginary guide, the visionary leader, and go aboard your ferry.

Tell your imaginary ferryman about your journey and the findings. He is now something like your flight readiness officer and is asking you questions:
- Think about where you are now in the process.
- Did it already start?
- Is everybody on board?
- Think about who needs what information and prepare fine corrections.

The Island of "Orchestrated Change"

The ferryman has set you off. and you are welcomed by your next guide and coach,
"The Dynamic Orchestrator."

Now you have reached the last island of change. This is your destination. Even if the harbor of embarkation is always within reach. As an early version of the *Homo Innovaticus.* Your purpose in life is to stay as long as you can in your current role and place and provide positive contribution. One day you will feel that it is time to start a new adventure. And with the experiences and findings, you will easily find your way when your mission here is completed. But for now, you stay fully concentrated on making your project a successful and impactful one.

The task: Your job now is to orchestrate the deployment and the dynamics of your change project. As you bring with you already the rough milestone plan, communication stuff, and insights, now is the time when your 100% attention and commitment are asked. The two main tasks now are that you, as the architect of the system, take care that the milestones are understood and that you provide now something like a Stage-Gate thinking. Meaning that you draw a simple Stage-Gate process. It may only consist of two or a maximum of five phases. It is up to you if you communicate the picture broadly, because it may not be understood, but for your personal ride, you should have the people in mind that need to be informed and asked when you enter the next milestone. Because it may be that you need their commitment for the next level of realization.

The second task is: You now have a new role. No matter if you are the leader, the inventor, or simply a co-worker in your project. You have now the additional role of the relationship manager. It is important, because remember our examples: Your biggest enemy now may not have a name or is not a real person—it is simply the barriers that are produced by systemic and/or personal issues. And it is the role of the relationship manager to perceive them and to address them.

The rule: Tit for Tat Guidelines for Using Tit for Tat (The Tit for Tat method is described in detail in chapter 18: "The basic core tools of the Homo Innovaticus"):

1. Start with Cooperation:
    Begin always by cooperating in the first interaction. This sets a positive tone and encourages the other party to do the same.
2. Monitor Responses:
    After the initial round, continue to cooperate as long as the other participant also cooperates.
3. Retaliate if Defected:
    If the other party defects (fails to cooperate), promptly mirror their action by defecting in your next move. This reinforces the principle that defection will lead to immediate consequences.
4. Be Forgiving:
    If the opponent returns to cooperation after defecting, respond by cooperating again. This fosters a more collaborative relationship and helps restore trust.
5. Avoid Holding Resentments:
    The strategy should be adaptable. Don't carry complaints against a player who has defected in the past; instead, give them the opportunity to rebuild the cooperative dynamic.

Further notice when applying:
Maintain Clarity: Ensure that your strategy is evident to your opponent. This clarity helps set expectations and encourages cooperation.
–   Adjust to Context: While Tit for Tat can be effective, it's essential to gauge the context and adjust your approach if necessary. Some situations may require a more forgiving or aggressive stance depending on the behavior of the other party.
–   Apply in negotiations, personal relationships, and especially in conflict resolution

The guidelines
You make sure that blueprint comes to life in a way that really hits the mark with the people involved. Since the exploitation mindset is the main way of thinking, you stay alert to unexpected things happening. And don't forget Mike Tyson's famous words: "Everyone's got a plan 'til they get punched in the face." Those moments are inevitable, and when they happen, you should remember our well-explained rule from Harrison Owen's universal law: "No matter what happens, it is the only thing that could happen." That'll make you strong, not losing confidence when the first storm hits your project. It'll help you stay strong and keep your confidence when things get tough.

From now on you always will take care that the involved people have what they need and that they are not held back by barriers that can be averted by bringing the right information. As you always already have blended external requirements with your strengths, you have built a learning ecosystem where creativity and discipline reinforce each other. It is important that you keep this behavior in mind even during active implementation. You just won't need it as often. And you can always return to one of the islands described with a detailed question about a problem that arises to get new input.

You are now at your destination. Welcome to real life!

You're in the middle of the change you've initiated. No matter how long it takes to implement it. Now is the time to celebrate! Take a moment to reflect on your achievements, and then take advantage of the good momentum to maintain relationships and strengthen motivation for further implementation.

When your further input is no longer necessary, in other words, when you see that your continued efforts are not bringing any added value, you'll feel that now it's time to let your things go on their own. Then now is the perfect time to embrace new opportunities. The bow is not made to chase the arrow but to give it energy and direction. Take yourself out and dedicate yourself to your next adventure of change.

I've discovered that those who bring about change and make it possible have completely different characteristics and skills than those who enjoy implementing and stabilizing the new. Each in their own place and at the right time.

Kahlil Gibran's metaphor in his famous book The Prophet always resonated with the guiding picture in me: There is a beautiful and profound passage about the role of parents in the chapter titled "On Children." Gibran uses the metaphor of a bow and arrow to describe the relationship between parents and their children. He explains that parents are like the bow, and children are like the arrows. The bow provides the energy and direction for the arrow, but it does not chase after it once it is released.

It is so apt that I want to quote it here:

Your children are not your children.
They are the sons and daughters of life's longing for itself.
They come through you but not from you,
And though they are with you, yet they belong not to you.

You may give them your love but not your thoughts,
For they have their own thoughts.
You may house their bodies but not their souls,
For their souls reside in the house of tomorrow, which you cannot visit, not even in your dreams.
You may strive to be like them but seek not to make them like you.
For life goes not backward nor tarries with yesterday.
You are the bows from which your children as living arrows are sent forth.
The archer sees the mark upon the path of the infinite, and He bends you with His might that
His arrows may go swift and far
Let your bending in the archer's hand be for gladness;
For even as He loves the arrow that flies, so He loves also the bow that is stable.

Homo Innovaticus is now needed elsewhere; he follows the call of life's longing for itself!

Perhaps even the hour of death will send him young towards new spaces. Life's call at him will never end.

Take care and be well.

End of the journey

Chapter 18
The Basic Core Tools of the *Homo Innovaticus*

We've already talked about this with AI. We use first-time tools that let us make decisions based on their own neuronal processes. It's both wonderful and dangerous.

That's why we're talking about "Future Preparedness in the Age of AI." It needs some extra care.

Here are a few more things to know about the MVIP process.

AI is basically our constant life companion. The new *Homo Innovaticus* will keep us on our toes by helping us think and act in a way that's always changing and adapting.

The MVIP journey is also meant to shield us from in-group bias. First, we find and refine our own vision. We start with our deep inner beliefs and connect to our inherent "tactic" knowledge.

The Hungarian psychologist *Mihaly Csikszentmihalyi* is well known for his systemic model on Social Exchange in Creativity. *He suggests creativity as much as a social and cultural process as it is an individual one. He further states that ideas gain creative value only after they go through a process of social exchange—being communicated, judged, and accepted by others in society.*

This is exactly what we are trying to do in steps 2 and 3 of our MVIP.

Our vision for the future is becoming clearer, and it's all moving into the next phase: engagement. It's really important that we find and bring on people and organizations that share our goals. We bring our collective expertise to the table by working together to explore new ways to move forward. We're all united in our goal to have a positive impact on the planet, and that's a key factor in our decision-making.

The next steps involve taking action—we put our plans into action by working with the best team members and using the most effective methods to achieve our goals. We've got the right mix of intentions, talent, and strategic approaches, so we're all set to deal with whatever the future throws at us. This will only make us more effective.

We need to change the way we work because the world around us is changing. We need to be more flexible, work better together, and think in new ways if we want to solve problems. We can switch to new strategies that help our systems grow and develop. If we realize that our challenges are all connected and we all work together, we can make sure that future generations have a brighter, more sustainable future. It's time to start thinking and acting. We can't afford to take things lightly anymore. Because of the huge impact that our interaction with AI can have, I want to highlight a few important final thoughts and recommendations.

https://doi.org/10.1515/9783111448329-021

Tit for Tat, the Mindset Game Changer

One key finding in the study of human behavioral innovation is undeniable. *"Tit for Tat,"* as well-known as the *Axelrod experiment,* is a great way to think about and deal with difficult situations. It's got to have a prominent place in the book's context. I was immediately impressed by this powerful behavioral finding when I was thinking about how to improve the quality of our innovation processes. These processes had been supported more and more by computer software and access to global knowledge in the early days of the Internet during the 1990s.

The "tit for tat" strategy is one of the most fascinating findings in the field of game theory, particularly in the realm of cooperation and competition. *Robert Axelrod* made it famous in the 1980s, especially through his work on the Iterated Prisoner's Dilemma (IPD), which is a classic example in game theory. The Iterated Prisoner's Dilemma is a game where two players can either work together or betray each other. The results depend on their choices. If they work together, they'll get some decent rewards. If they betray each other, they'll both end up with minimal payoffs. If one person cooperates while the other doesn't, the person who cooperated will lose a lot.

We must say that this game is not a promising example of how to develop trust on a broader level. But what Robert Axelrod found out when, in 1980, he was organizing computer tournaments that were intended to overcome IPD risk was groundbreaking.

Axelrod initially solicited strategies from other game theorists to compete in the first tournament. Each strategy was paired with each other strategy for 200 iterations of a Prisoner's Dilemma game and scored on the total points accumulated through the tournament. The winner was a very simple strategy submitted by Anatol Rapoport called *"tit for tat"* (TFT) that cooperates on the first move and subsequently echoes (reciprocates) what the other player did on the previous move. The results of the first tournament were analyzed and published, and a second tournament was held to see if anyone could find a better strategy. TFT won again. Axelrod analyzed the results and made some interesting discoveries about the nature of cooperation, which he describes in his book *A Passion for Cooperation.*[49]

In both the actual tournaments and various replays, the best-performing strategies were nice. A lot of the competitors tried really hard to gain an advantage over the "nice" (and usually simpler) strategies, but it didn't work out. Trickier strategies fighting for a few points generally didn't do as well as nice strategies working together. TFT (and other "nice" strategies generally) won by getting the other player to cooperate, not by doing better than them. It promoted the mutual interest rather than exploiting the other's weakness.

49 Robert Axelrod, *A Passion for Cooperation: Adventures of a Wide-Ranging Scientist* (Ann Arbor: University of Michigan Press, 2023).

Most of the games that game theory has looked at so far are "zero-sum," meaning the total rewards are fixed and a player can only do well if other players do badly. But real life isn't zero-sum. Our best prospects are usually in cooperative efforts. Actually, TFT can't score higher than its partner. The best it can do is "as good as." But it still won the tournaments by coming in second place pretty often, with all kinds of partners. Axelrod sums it up like this: *"Don't be envious."* Basically, that means don't go for a payoff that's bigger than what the other player's going for. When it comes to TFT, the best approach is to just cooperate. Axelrod calls this *"clarity."* Or, as they say, *"Don't be too clever."*

How can we put TFT into practice? It's a simple but powerful mindset, and the game plan is a piece of cake.

– Start by cooperating, which encourages your opponent to cooperate too.
– Always echoe (reciprocate) what the other player did on the previous move.
– If the other person does something dishonest, just respond with defection. That'll discourage the opponent from taking advantage.
– After a defection, return to cooperation if the opponent cooperates in the next round. You're always cool with things.

It's a breeze to apply, and it always builds trust!

Axelrod's work is impressive. Even in fields like economics, political science, biology, and sociology. It's the best proof that we can work together even when we're competing. It also shows how important it is to give back in social situations. This means that we can work together even when we're just thinking about ourselves. That's why I started my "R-ICE" method that was explained in detail in chapter 12 in the section on "Cracking the Code of Systemic Inertia: How to Lead Through Reciprocity" with the "R" for reciprocity.

You should use the TFT rules in all areas of your life. Make them a cornerstone of your personal value model and behavior. The more you use it, the more you will be seen as a trusted dialogue partner. Use the R-ICE method, especially when preparing for meetings in the context of innovation, where you often won't have a second chance to meet again. If you don't address the topic in the first few sentences, you won't get a second chance. Always remember as a *Homo Innovaticus* you may have insights that your dialogue partner does not have. Be aware of that. And this triggers resistance and, in many cases, even hostility. So it makes sense to invest in the extra round of thinking about interests, concerns and expectations. In some cases, it is only a few minutes writing down the R-ICE statements and formulating your entrance message. We could see it that way: Tit for Tat sets the mood, and R-ICE opens the door!

But not only in the context of innovation can experimenting with R-ICE be good advice:

– Negotiations: Use the method in common business negotiations where ongoing relationships matter.
– Personal Relationships: Apply it in teamwork or family scenarios to encourage mutual support and understanding.

- Conflict Resolution: Use R-ICE in conflicts to foster cooperation while discouraging exploitative behaviors.

Innovation is all about working together with a bunch of different people. It's really important to build a solid foundation of trust, but trust doesn't just happen. It takes time and effort to earn people's trust. R-ICE is always a good resource for that.

Trustworthiness becomes a cornerstone; being seen as a reliable person who values honesty—even when perspectives diverge—can lead to more constructive exchanges. In German, the term *"Wahrhaftigkeit"* captures this idea of authenticity and integrity, which are key to building trust. The way we interact with others in our lives is important. It's mostly shaped by what we were like when we were kids. That affects how likely we are to trust people.

You might not always be honest because you're afraid of how people will react, thinking that showing weakness is a bad thing. TFT can help you deal with these fears.

My professional journey has taught me the indispensable value of embracing the behavioral patterns underscored by the Axelrod Experiment. It's important to develop win-win relationships, and that means being transparent, respectful, and communicative. This approach matches up with Peter Senge's teachings and the *"systems factor"* that underlines the importance of having a big-picture view when dealing with the tricky world of innovation.

AI as a Source of Inspiration, Knowledge, and Networking

Imagine you need advice for a difficult problem and already have an idea of what you want to do, but you don't know what the environment for this change looks like. You need expertise, insights, examples of failed projects, and suggestions for learning examples of what has already been done somewhere in the world.

But until now, it has always been very difficult to gain access to this data. For us, this is a dream come true. A few years ago, without the help of AI, we couldn't have imagined it. It's almost like a genie has come to life, just like in that fun TV show, "I Dream of Jeannie," and has brought together the best and brightest minds in the world to help us figure out the big questions we're facing right now. They are all gathered in front of you, in one room, at the same time. And they are looking at you with their eyes wide open, waiting for your questions. They give us their best answers without hiding anything. And we can open a dialog with them, ask them more questions, and challenge them. The newly produced data, which in many cases are also hallucinations, are valuable inputs that we can merge with our intuitive inner world. To send them into social exchange with real people again and again. And ultimately, to gain new insights that not only help solve problems but also satisfy the moral demands of society. Whatever new topics and areas of knowledge emerge, our helpers can quickly recognize cross-connections, find and summarize facts, and even develop them further. They are patient and quick, and only you decide when the question time is over or even when there is a break.

That is precisely what I feel AI is for us now. The things described will happen right now. All specialists are at your disposal 24/7. We must always remember: The produced results must undergo social exchange and control gates to ensure readiness for public deployment.

Anyway, the first phases described described in the MVIP process are precisely the advantages of modern artificial intelligence platforms and services.

And now we can finally be sure that before you go to market with an innovation, you have already obtained all this knowledge and even built in all this enormous data and application knowledge and the things that improve your findings into your innovation. Without having to take the risk that all these things will only be experienced after the baptism of fire on the market or during implementation.

This is roughly how we can see the revolution of artificial intelligence in the field of innovation and the most important fact is that it puts ourelves into the gatekeeper for the moral aspects that never will be fullfilled by our future AI agents itself.

It is time to place this process at the forefront of the innovation process, rather than relegating it to the sidelines in iterations or even at the culmination of the market, where customers become unwitting test subjects.

As previously mentioned, and as Geoffrey Hinton has stated, we are unaware of the full scope of some AI technologies' outputs. We know from our experience with many AI tools that having two control gates instead of one is better. The first phase enhances creativity and provides an expansive, boundless space for exploration. Gate 1 is the one that controls what we accept in our deepest, innermost thinking and brain. The second phase is where we tap into our intuition and intelligence to refine it for future social interactions with real people. Gate 2 is the control gate. It is where we first share our new beliefs with a broader audience. *Homo Innovaticus* is unwavering in his commitment to truthfulness and to realizing his visions, rather than allowing them to remain as mere dreams. The dilemma is clear: to be innovative, you must dream; to gain trust and power, you must be seen as a realistic visionary. It's not easy.

Homo Innovaticus and the Role of Intuition

We are reaching the end of this book and have not yet discussed the role of our intuition, especially in relation to our *Homo Innovaticus* approach when we venture beyond the familiar.

Results from intuition and non-verbal communication will make a significant contribution to a better understanding of ourselves and our fellow human beings. This will build a bridge to a new form of togetherness.

We can gather deeper insights into human behavior and the narratives that shape our societies through the lens of intuition. *Ortega y Gasset* was right. We are collectively ignorant of our condition. Awareness, prompted by intuition, is the first step toward uncovering deeper truths about us, our societies, and the paths we can forge together.

The first two stages of our MVIP process, serendipity and finding like-minded supporters, benefit tremendously from intuitive insights and encounters with people. Serendipity, often described in the context of accidental discoveries, is enhanced by direct human contact and open nonverbal communication. Intuition often leads us to the people with whom we are connected on a deep, unconscious level. This level is strengthened through emotional resonance and empathic interactions.

You can find like-minded supporters in two ways: by actively seeking out a community or by serendipitously encountering one. When we are on our search for allies, we can sense whether a person understands us on a deeper level without the need for words. This nonverbal exchange can take the form of eye contact, body language, and energy. Intuition gives us limited access to other people's inner worlds and allows us to build deeper relationships based on trust and shared values.

Another aspect is the utopia that we can outline in these reflections. Imagine what we could achieve if we fully explored and integrated these nonverbal connections and intuitive insights into our daily lives. We could unlock a new level of communication that currently seems impossible. Developing models of this kind demands us to think outside the box and find new, innovative ways to interact and cooperate with each other.

I am convinced that consciousness and human experience, as revealed by the latest research in quantum communication, will soon yield groundbreaking findings thanks to interdisciplinary collaboration. It is clear to me that there is an interconnection between people that we do not yet understand when I examine many "mass phenomena" in our time and in history. Depression and fear of the future are on the rise. Despite our advances in medical research, new widespread diseases such as Alzheimer's and dementia are on the rise.

The challenge of the hour is not to dismiss our intuitive abilities as sentimentalism and to rediscover an unblinkered approach, which is particularly strong in young children in terms of intuition, imagination, and wishful thinking. This will help us to act from our own security, free from any dependence on external recognition. Courageously, surprisingly, and with humor, responsibly, and with the help of AI. Embedding the AHA experiences gained in this way with joy and gratitude. This is the mindset in which *Homo Innovaticus* feels comfortable and is in top form. This is also the reason why the first two steps of the proposed process are to savor this free of implementation pressure and external influence. As a protective zone and breeding ground for solutions in the modern world of networking and holism.

The fact that our ability to use our intuition is a key skill for the future and can be trained and honed is described in the very impressive book by intuition researcher *Dr. Regina Obermayr-Breitfuß.*[50]

There are so many weak signals around this topic of nonverbal communication and intuition; they all are showing us that we are only exploiting a fraction of the possibilities that are available to us as human beings.

---

50 Regina Obermayr-Breitfuß, *Intuition: Theorie und praktische Anwendung* (Norderstedt: Books on Demand GmbH, 2005).

Chapter 19
The Ultimate Destination: The Feeling of Connection and Safety

The Rise of the Innovation Steward: A New Role for a New Era

As ever more of us are feeling uncertainty through the increasingly complex social, ecological, and economic challenges, a new kind of professional is emerging—one who acts not unlike a judge in a trial, but whose role is to guide transformation, foster innovation, and align change with the well-being of people, nature, and future generations.

This evolving role—whether described as a change manager, innovation steward, or transformation coach—calls for more than just business acumen. It requires a moral compass, a systems-thinking mindset, and a deep commitment to sustainability. Rather than enforcing rigid laws, this new steward would operate under guiding principles, similar to the UN's Sustainable Development Goals (SDGs) or the Inner Development Goals (IDGs), offering ethical direction and strategic support in times of organizational or societal stagnation.

Imagine a company suffering from "intellectual bankruptcy"—not due to financial loss, but due to a lack of innovation, vision, or ethical direction. Just like a financial liquidator assesses assets and liabilities, this innovation steward would examine three vital forms of capital: human, natural, and social. They would identify cultural blind spots, leadership gaps, or unsustainable practices and recommend concrete actions to reset the system's course.

This model could eventually evolve into a regulatory framework, enabling courts or coalitions to mandate innovation interventions when organizations do more harm than good. A first version of such a thought is already brought to us by the standardized innovation management system of both ISO 56001 and ISO 56002. They are intended to serve as an essential blueprint, offering clarity and consistency and placing the responsibility where it belongs if we speak about organizations, especially in corporate environments: On top management's agenda in to champion the innovation vision and embed it in the organization's strategy and operations.

The brand-new globally recognized standards of ISO 56001 and 56002 don't place innovation straight on the shoulders of top leadership; they place it on three foundational pillars:

- **Culture** —fostering curiosity, learning, and the courage to experiment.
- **Leadership**—modeling vulnerability, open-mindedness, and vision.
- **Strategy**—embedding innovation into the core of an organization's purpose.

https://doi.org/10.1515/9783111448329-022

Together, these pillars form the infrastructure for sustainable innovation—not as a buzzword, but as a living practice.

Beyond individual organizations, this model could shape entire society. Imagine convening future conferences—forums where communities collectively define long-term goals for both economic vitality and social well-being. Drawing inspiration from ancient cultures like the Mayans, we can adopt a mindset of "futuring"—actively shaping the world we want, rather than reacting to the one we fear.

But for this future to be possible, we must shift how we measure success. As long as financial metrics alone dominate our value systems, human, ecological, and social capital will remain undervalued.

We need a fundamental rethinking. We must acknowledge the intuitive, sometimes inexplicable drive within us—that longing for discovery, creation, and deeper meaning. This drive is the essence of life. It's also the essence of innovation.

This is why *Homo Innovaticus*—the forward-thinking, ethically grounded innovator—is more urgent than ever. Not only to spark new ideas, but also to nurture the systems, values, and learning cultures that allow them to thrive.

The future is not a forecast. It's a co-creation.

Let us be bold enough to rethink. Humble enough to learn. And brave enough to lead.

We Can Feel Safe in the Age of AI When Rooted in Human Innovation

As we stand at the threshold of an era defined by artificial intelligence, it is natural to feel a mix of excitement and uncertainty.

Many ask: Can we truly feel safe in a world where machines learn, adapt, and even create? The answer lies not in resisting change, but in understanding its nature—and our role in shaping it.

In such a behavior lies a deep reason to feel safe—on both a psychological and evolutionary level.

Psychologically, AI offers us a powerful new way to access insights easily and at high speed that helps reduce uncertainty. It gives us the ability to capture, synthesize, and apply the lessons of our history and evolution—lessons we once risked overlooking or forgetting. In this way, AI does not just automate processes; it amplifies human learning. With that, it holds the potential to serve as a mirror of our past, to provide an overview map for our present, and with that, not surprisingly, to become something like a compass for our future.

In the context of psychological safety, it is more than important to draw a clear line between what we call "Artificial Intelligence" and the obvious further thought of an "Artificial Innovation." Intelligence, no matter how complex or algorithmically enhanced, may be machine-driven. But innovation—the true leap of imagination, the moral compass guiding change, the courage to envision something better—can never be replicated artificially. Innovation is human. It is born from the friction of lived experience, the embrace of uncertainty, and the spark of purpose.

AI can mimic patterns. It can analyze vast amounts of data and even generate surprisingly creative outputs. But it does not carry responsibility, nor does it feel the pain of injustice or the joy of connection. Innovation, in contrast, is deeply human. It is inseparable from our emotional, moral, and spiritual intelligence. It lives in our relationships, in our cultures, and in our ability to dream across generations.

This is why we can feel safe—not because AI will fix our problems for us, but because we are still the ones holding the pen.

We can feel safe when we use AI as tools to reduce ambiguity and extend our cognitive capacities. When we use it to learn from the past more precisely and prepare for the future more proactively. In this way, AI is a powerful extension of human potential. Yet it is only when we use it with the intention that it truly serves us.

From an innovation perspective, it is crystal clear that we must build systems that integrate technological advancement with human-centered design. In the course of this book, I have tried to provide insights into important systems and mindsets that are helpful, like the chaordic principle, which can show us how to thrive between chaos and order. Or the Inner Development Goals and many other behavioral models and values that offer a roadmap for cultivating the wisdom, compassion, and resilience needed to lead in uncertain times.

Around the world, global initiatives—from UNESCO's AI ethics framework to the rise of collaborative, decentralized systems—are aligning technology with values. This growing consciousness gives us a real chance to not only manage disruption but also to transform it into renewal.

So yes, there are risks. I wanted to show that we are not starting from scratch. We carry with us the accumulated insight of generations, the lessons of history, and the enduring strength of our interconnectedness. With these, we are more than equipped to face what's ahead. The law of "survival of the most adaptive" is still valid. We are the *Homo Innovaticus*. We are designed for dynamic adaptation and our insatiable curiosity is our helper.

AI is not the author of our future. We are.

Let us not retreat into fear. Let us rise with purpose. If we lead with vision and humanity, AI will amplify our best instincts and expand the reach of our shared dreams.

The tools are here. The moment is now. The path forward belongs to all of us.

Words of Thanks

Special thanks to the entrepreneurial dynasty of the Swarovski family that offered me a culture and environment where I could evolve and connect to the world more than an average engineer in Austria could have hoped. A very special thank you goes to my longtime boss and mentor Helmut Swarovski and to Markus Langes-Swarovski and his father Gernot, who always supported me with openness, trust, and free space for intrapreneurship.

I am deeply grateful to all who walked parts of this journey with me. To the mentors who challenged me, the teams who trusted me, the thinkers who inspired me, and especially the next generation—whose courage and creativity will shape the future we all share.

I'm extremely grateful to my wonderful wife, Barbara, for her patience and understanding during the times my thoughts wandered into the world of innovation and change, instead of being fully present in our conversations.

Special thanks go to:

My kids, Patricia and Christoph, who always reminded me of the real important things in life.

My philosopher friend and mentor, Allan Yanik, who helped me so much with his brilliant ideas.

My colleagues, Graham Hench and Wolfgang Kathan, who showed me—a "non-native digital tribe apprentice" —how to adapt to the digital world and the next generation of professionals.

I'm so grateful to my professors Justyna Dabrowska, John Bessant, and Tom Hench. They helped me find my voice, content, and interconnections to the academic world.

To the ambidexterity PhD Gudrun Töpfer, who showed me very openly where I was unclear and too superficial in my writing.

https://doi.org/10.1515/9783111448329-023

Bibliography

Arrien, Angeles. *The Fourfold Way: Walking the Paths of the Warrior*. New York: HarperCollins Publishers, 1993.

Axelrod, Robert. *A Passion for Cooperation: Adventures of a Wide Ranging Scientist*. Ann Arbor: University of Michigan Press, 2023.

Berkes, Howard. "Remembering Roger Boisjoly: He Tried to Stop Shuttle Challenger Launch." NPR, February 6, 2012. https://www.npr.org/sections/thetwo-way/2012/02/06/146490064/remembering-roger-boisjoly-he-tried-to-stop-shuttle-challenger-launch.

Bont, C. de, P. H. den Ouden, R. Schifferstein, F. E. H. M. Smulders, and M van der Voort, eds. *Advanced Design Methods for Successful Innovation*. The Hague: Design United, 2013.

Capodagli, Bill, and Lynn Jackson. *The Disney Way: Harnessing the Management Secrets of Walt Disney in Your Company*. New York: McGraw-Hill, 2007.

Chesbrough, Henry. "Open Innovation in the Age of AI." *Laerbro*, October 12, 2024. https://laerbro.com/insight/2.

Christensen, Clayton M. *The Innovator's Dilemma: When New Technologies Cause Great Firms to Fail*. Boston: Harvard Business Review Press, 1997.

Cooper, Robert G. *Winning at New Products: Creating Value Through Innovation*. 5th ed. New York: Basic Books, 2017.

Dabrowska, Justyna, Henry Lopez-Vega, and Paavo Ritala. "Waking the Sleeping Beauty: Swarovski's Open Innovation Journey." *R&D Management* 49, no. 5 (2019): 775–788. https://doi.org/10.1111/radm.12374.

De Liefde, Willem H. J. *Ubuntu: In der Gemeinschaft Lösungen finden und Entscheidungen treffen*. Munich: Signum Verlag, 2006.

den Ouden, Elke. *Innovation Design – Creating Value for People, Organizations and Society*. London: Springer Verlag, 2012.

Dweck, Carol S. *Mindset: The New Psychology of Success*. New York: Ballantine Books, 2006.

Erler, Hannes. "Why the New Logics of a Connected World Affect Traditional Innovation Structures from the Bottom Up – and the Role of Open Innovation Networks & Ecosystems in Finding Proper Answers." *Journal of Innovation Management* 4, no. 3 (December 19, 2016): 7–11. https://doi.org/10.24840/2183-0606_004.003_0003.

Erler, Hannes, Markus Rieger, and Johann Füller. "Ideenmanagement und Innovation mit Social Networks – Die Swarovski i-flash Community." In *Kommunikation als Erfolgsfaktor im Innovationsmanagement: Strategien im Zeitalter der Open Innovation*, edited by Ansgar Zerfaß and Kathrin Möslein, 159–176. Wiesbaden: Gabler, 2009.

Erler, Hannes, and Doris Wilhelmer. "Ein neues Paradigma – Mit Netzwerken Innovationsprozesse steuern." In *Open Innovation umsetzen – Prozesse, Methoden, Systeme, Kultur*, edited by Serhan Ili, 225–270. Düsseldorf: Verlag Symposion, 2010.

Feynman, Richard P. *Surely You're Joking, Mr. Feynman!*. New York: Bantam Books, 1985.

Goldschmidt, Nils, and Hans G. Nutzinger, eds. *Vom homo oeconomicus zum homo culturalis: Von Handlung und Nutzen in der Ökonomie*. Kulturelle Ökonomik, Band 8. Hans G. Nutzinger, 2009.

Graeber, David, and David Wengrow. *The Dawn of Everything: A New History of Humanity*. New York: Allen Lane, Penguin Random House, 2021.

Hauschildt, Jürgen, and Hans Georg Gemünden, eds. *Promotoren: Champions der Innovation*. Wiesbaden: Gabler Verlag, 1998.

Hessel, Stéphane. *Time for Outrage!*. BrightSummaries.com, 2017.

https://doi.org/10.1515/9783111448329-024

Hinton, Geoffrey. "'Godfather of AI' Geoffrey Hinton: The 60 Minutes Interview." *60 Minutes*. CBS News, November 2023. https://www.youtube.com/watch?v=qrvK_KuIeJk.

Hüther, Gerald. "Wie Lernen gelingt – Gerald Hüther." YouTube video, 52:42. Posted by "AKAD Bildungsgesellschaft," March 6, 2017. Accessed August 10, 2024. https://www.youtube.com/watch?v=gbre5Hh2pvQ.

Innovation Roundtable®. Accessed July 20, 2025. https://innovationroundtable.com/about-us/.

Inner Development Goals. Accessed July 20, 2025. https://innerdevelopmentgoals.org/.

ISPIM – International Society for Professional Innovation Management. Accessed July 20, 2025. https://www.ispim-innovation.com/.

Katzenbach, Jon R., and Douglas A. Smith. *High Performance Teams*. Boston, MA: Harvard Business Review Press, 2016. Originally published 1995.

LinkedIn. "SI Design Network." Accessed February 10, 2025. https://www.linkedin.com/company/si-design-network/posts?lipi=urn%3Ali%3Apage%3Ad_flagship3_company_posts%3Bl3j0Ry5nTm%2BZPrhQ0Ibiaw%3D%3D.

Lingens, Bernhard, Veronika Seeholzer, and Oliver Gassmann. "The Architecture of Innovation: How Firms Configure Different Types of Complementarities in Emerging Ecosystems." *Industry and Innovation* 29, no. 9 (2022): 1108–1139. https://doi.org/10.1080/13662716.2022.2123307.

Mails, Thomas E. *Secret Native American Pathways: A Guide to Inner Peace*. Tulsa, OK: Council Oak Books, 1988.

Marcus, Gary. *Taming Silicon Valley: How We Can Assure That AI Works for Us*. Cambridge, MA: The MIT Press, 2024.

Moore, Geoffrey. *Zone to Win: Organizing to Compete in the Age of Disruption*. New York: Diversion Books, 2015.

Nowotny, Helga. *Insatiable Curiosity: Innovation in a Fragile Future*. Cambridge, MA: MIT Press, 2008.

Obermayr-Breitfuß, Regina. *Intuition: Theorie und praktische Anwendung*. Norderstedt: Books on Demand GmbH, 2005.

Osterwalder, Alexander. "Rebells and Pirates Will Be Hung Up." *Die Presse*, February 28, 2023. https://www.diepresse.com/6252568/achtung-bei-zielvorgaben-rebellen-werden-gehaengt.

Owen, Harrison. *Open Space Technology: A User's Guide*. San Francisco: Berrett-Koehler Publishers, 2008.

Peter Rosegger. *Schönheit der Technik*. Monatsschrift Heimgarten Nr. 3. Graz: Verlag Leykam-Josefsthal, 1909.

Ries, Eric. *The Start-Up Way: How Modern Companies Use Entrepreneurial Management to Transform Culture and Drive Long-Term Growth*. New York: Crown Publishing Group, 2017.

Robson, David. "How Studying Babies' Minds Is Prompting Us to Rethink Consciousness." *New Scientist Weekly*, February 15, 2025.

Rogers, Everett M. *Diffusion of Innovations*. 5th ed. New York: Free Press, 2003.

Senge, Peter. *The TFD Field Book: How to Proceed to Build Learning Organizations*. Crown Currency, 1994.

Stadler, Christian, Julia Hautz, Kurt Matzler, Stephan Friedrich von den Eichen, and Gary Hamel. *Open Strategy: Mastering Disruption from Outside the C-Suite*. Cambridge, MA: The MIT Press, 2021.

Stanford Online. "Design Thinking." Accessed July 19, 2025. https://online.stanford.edu/courses/design-thinking.

United Nations Environment Programme. *Global Foresight Report*. Accessed November 3, 2024. https://www.unep.org/resources/global-foresight-Mreport.

"Value Models for Meaningful Innovations." Accessed December 11, 2024. https://www.tue-lighthouse.nl/Images/Propositions/20161003%20Value%20models.pdf.

Wilhelmer, Doris, Johannes Erler, and Jeff Zimmerman. "Innovation Network – An Integrated Organizational Structure for Organizational and Management Learning." In *Leadership Learning for the Future*, edited by Klaus Scala, Ralph Grossmann, Marlies Lenglacher, and Kurt Mayer. (Publisher not specified), 2013.

Wilhelmer, Doris, Hannes Erler, and D. Holste. "Innovation Network – An Integrated Organizational Setup for Management Learning." Paper presented at *M/O/T 2010 – International Conference on Management Learning*, 2010.

YouTube. "Wird es eine neue 'Spezies Mensch' geben? Die Antwort auf fast Alles." ARTE. Accessed June 12, 2025. https://www.youtube.com/watch?v=-NMrO6biEv8.

Index

action-oriented approaches 57
activity-based working 71
adaptation process 91
advisors 109
African culture
– industrial companies 94
– large group conversations 93–94
– leadership style 95
– organizational skills 95
– sense of awareness 94
– spirituality and leadership 94
– subculture 95
– tribal leader 95
agile management 42–43
Agricultural Revolution 112
AI Advisory Body 141
Amazon 41
ambidexterity
– building 62
– communication flow and transparency 62
– economic success, rules of 75
– genuine innovation 75
– Gordian knot 62
– greenhouse 63
– Horizons Framework 64–66
– innovation 62, 63
– instinctive behaviors 74
– new leadership mindset 74
– organizational/contextual 62
– planet centricity establishment 63–64
– power teams, role of 66–70
– societal and organizational structures 74
ambidexterity trap
– activity-based working 71
– advantage 73
– challenge organizations 70
– cross-functional/hierarchical operations 71
– customer-oriented core project 72
– digital glass process 74
– entrepreneurial culture and awareness 71
– entrepreneurial innovation 70
– exploitation and exploration principles 72
– findings 73
– growth board logic 71
– innovation networks 71
– "metered funding" 72
– network collaborations 71

– personalization and on-demand production 74
– systemic intervention 71
– systemic organizational development process 70
analysis paralysis 186
archetypes 92–93
Argüelles, Jose 105
Arrien, Angeles 87
artificial intelligence (AI) 111, 137, 138, 194
– applications 173
– astronomical research 145
– Big Tech 142
– ChatGPT 142
– daydreaming process 169–172
– educational systems 143
– employees benefit 142
– generative 142, 143
– global collaborations 141
– hallucinations 193
– indigenous cultures 144–145
– innovation processes 144
– knowledge production 142
– Oxford 143
– safety and moral aspects 142
– science *vs.* ethics 144
– serendipitous dreaming approach 169
– synthetic data 146
– trustworthy institutions 141
– United Nations 141
Artificial Neural Networks (ANNs) 155
Aspirations and Key Insights (AKIs) 60, 88
Austrian Institute of Technology (AIT) 32
autonomous teams 68
autopoiesis 125
Axelrod experiment 203
Axelrod, Robert 203

bell curve 13
Berkes, Howard 119
Big Tech 140
biodiversity 105
B Corps 117
Bob Dylan 161
Bolles, David 103
Boulton, Jean 135
Brittle, Anxious, Nonlinear, and Incomprehensible
   (BANI) model 114
broker function 67–68

https://doi.org/10.1515/9783111448329-025

Brown, Tim 38
Buddhist tradition 144
building trust 127
Business Model Canvas method 122, 187

California Institute of the Arts (CalArts) 46
Change by Design (Brown) 38
chaordic model 134
chaordic organization 134
ChatGPT 142
Chesbrough, Henry 154
Christensen, Clayton
– American steel industry 21
– digital photography 23
– disruptive technologies 23
– employee ideas 25–26
– The Innovator's Dilemma 21
– "Jobs to Be Done" theory 23
– market leadership 21
– product development teams 24–25
– shareholder returns 23–24
– sustaining and disruptive technological
    change 21–22
climate change 190–191
Club of Rome 63
cognitive ambidexterity 171
collaborative spirit 127
communication strategy 108
Complexity Science Hub in Vienna 143
Constantinian Turn 166
continuous leadership learning 49
Cooper, Robert G. 45
corporate environments 209
creative destruction 153, 158
creativity 143
cross fertilization 47
Crossing the Chasm 13–14
cultural blind spots 209
cultural evolution 163
cultural recognition 172
customer relationship management (CRM) 27,
    52–53

Dabrowska, Justyna 53
The Dao of Complexity (Boulton) 135
The Dawn of Everything (Graeber and Wengrow) 111
daydreaming 63
de Bont, Cees 124

decentralized leadership 45
decision-making process 118
– AI-powered tools 186
– analysis paralysis 186
– built-in gates 187
– Business Model Canvas 187
– democratized information sharing 184
– dynamic tool 187
– environment changes 188
– impacts 184
– innovation process 185
– innovation RADAR 186, 187
– innovation technology CALENDAR 186, 187
– R-ICE method 187
deep learning
– AI-driven processes 154
– collaboration 159
– Cooper's Stage-Gate principles 158
– creative destruction 153, 158
– CRISPR/Cas9 gene 154–155
– economic integration 153
– entrepreneurial spirit 153
– evolutionary skills 157
– exnovation vs. innovation 157
– game-changing prediction 158
– global scale 153
– human growth 161–162
– ideal environment 159
– Innsbruck experiments 160
– physics education 160
– quantum mechanics and implications 159
– quantum teleportation 160
– risk taking 153
– serendipity 161–162
default mode network (DMN) 170, 171
De Liefde, Willem H. J. 94
den Ouden, P. H. (Elke) 121, 124
design thinking 37–39
Diffusion of Innovations (Rogers) 13
digital photography 23
digital revolution 49
digital transformation 137, 146
Disney, Walt 46–48
disruptive technologies 41, 137
divergent thinking 143
diverse and decentralized organization 48–49
dorsal attention network (DAN) 170
Dresden Codex 104

"dry-training" exercise 172
Dweck, Carol S. 82
dynamic innovation ecosystems 131

e-commerce 137
economic factors 166–167
economic vitality 210
ecosystems 30
entrepreneurial management techniques 40
entrepreneurial spirit 153
Erler, Hannes 49, 58
Erler, Johannes 50
European industrial landscape 16
evidence-based approaches 113
executive control network (ECN) 170
experimental prototype community of tomorrow
      (EPCOT Center) 46
external collaboration 26
external specialists 109

Failure Mode and Effect Analysis (FMEA) 17
financial crisis 51
financial metrics 210
financial risk analysis 198
flexible business models 26
foresighting vs. linear assumptions 110
foster intergenerational synergy 135
4-level value model
– ecosystems 122
– framework 123–124
– organization 121–122
– resilience and motivation 120
– society 123
– user 121
Freezing Point 16
Front End of Innovation (FEI) conference 120–121

gap-oriented behavior 8
Gartner Hype Cycle Curve 37
Gassmann, Oliver 57
global AI condensation 137
global distribution 10
Global Ignorance Test 100
Goldschmidt, Nils 155
Gordian knot 62
Graeber, David 111
greenhouse 63
Growth Boards 40

hallucinations 205
Hamel, Gary 132
Harvard Business Review 142
Hautz, Julia 132
health and environmental problems 109–110
Hessel, Stéphane 165
Hinton, Geoffrey 138
Homo Culturalis 155, 156
Homo Innovaticus 97–98, 156
– adaptive and dynamic social structures 166
– adaptive systems 165
– African culture 190
– AI and serendipity 176, 178–180
– AI hallucinations 193
– basic core tools 202–208
– best-performing strategies 203
– building trust and reliability 175
– climate change 190–191
– collaborative open space 176, 182
– collective expertise 202
– collective knowledge and resources 167
– cultural evolution 163
– decision making (See decision-making processes)
– democratic system 163
– economic factors 166–167
– effective methods 202
– ethos of cooperation 175
– fast-changing environment 175
– framework condition 189–190
– fundamental and long-term prosperity 172–173
– game theory 204
– global structure 165
– holistic human nature 167–169
– Hopi Blue Star Prophecy 190
– human experience 163
– human rights 164, 165
– innovation 205
– innovation management 163
– innovation principles and findings 174
– innovators possess 173
– inspiration, knowledge and networking 205–206
– interconnectedness and interdependence 192
– intuition and serendipity 193–195
– Intuition Method 178
– learning apprentice vs. courageous
      adventurer 191
– minimum viable innovation process (MVIP) 173,
      175, 202

– navigation tool 164
– neuronal processes 202
– open space actuation 197–199
– orchestrate and ride the change 176–177, 183–184
– orchestrated change 199–201
– overview effect 189
– personal value model and behavior 204
– power structures 165
– principles of action 177
– professional environments 175
– promoter model 166
– resource management 190–191
– R-ICE method 204
– role of intuition 206–208
– self-discovery journey 192
– self-fulfilling prophecy 190
– Social Exchange in Creativity 202
– spaceship Earth 189
– spiritual practices 192
– survival and transformation 163
– systemic-related narrow-mindedness 164
– systems factor 205
– thinking model 166
– tit for tat (TFT) 203–205
– value system 166
– virtual gatekeepers 177
– vision and alliance 176, 180–181, 195–197
Homo sapiens 69, 156
Hopi Blue Star Prophecy 190
human-centered approach 38
human-centered design 211
human humanity 156
human innovation 210–211
human rights 164
human skills 140–141
Hüther, Gerald 87

i-LAB experience 45–48
imagination
– ancient civilizations to modern societies 99
– cognitive bias 102
– cognitive psychologist 100
– data-driven world 99
– future generations 101
– generation 99
– human ecology 101
– Indian traditions 99

– innovation and leadership 101
– modern innovation 99
– Netflix 102
– "pink elephant" effect 100
– spiritual prophecy 100
– tools and practices 99
incubation zone 41
indigenous wisdom 91
industrial culture 16
industrial-process driven 20
Industrial Revolution 153
Inner Development Goals (IDGs) 147, 209, 211
"INNO network" approach 51
innovation ecosystems
– business and science 58–60
– close feedback loops 54
– continuous learning 54
– development phases 53
– effective collaboration 54
– employee cultural dialogue 44
– high-performance product development organization 44
– leadership and management style 60
– vs. natural 56–58
– organizational model 54
– transitional period 53
innovation journey
– global collaboration and sustainable development 9–10
– industrial structures 9
– international and inter-organizational networks 9
– methods 9
– national economies 9
– Stage-Gate® Tool 10
innovation management system 209
innovation network
– diverse and decentralized organization 48–49
– soft governance model 49–52
innovation radar 198
Innovation Roundtable 158
innovation theater 31–32
The Innovator's Dilemma (Christensen) 21
Innsbruck experiments 160
"integration of everything" 192
intellectual bankruptcy 209
intelligent navigation 135
Interests, Concerns, and Expectations (ICE) 127

international and inter-organizational networks 9
International Science Council 109
intricate networks 56
intuition 206–208
Iterated Prisoner's Dilemma (IPD) 203

"Jobs to Be Done" theory 23

Katzenbach, Jon R. 66
knowledge sharing 26

large organizations 40–41
Law of Two Feet 35
leadership gaps/unsustainable practices 209
leadership learning 92–93
Leading Product Development Executive
    Program 118
lean startup methodology 39–40
learning algorithms 139
learning opportunities 68–69
Lingens, Bernhard 57
Lopez-Vega, Henry 53

machine learning 29
Massamba Thioye 147
Mahatma Gandhi 174
Mails, Davis E. 106
Mails, Thomas E. 106
Marcus, Gary 140
Matzler, Kurt 132
Mayan culture
– calendars 103–104
– hierophany 104
– prophecies 104–106
– senses of time 103–104
– Spanish and native populations 102
The Mayan Factor (Argüelles) 105
medicine-wheel approach 93
Megatrend Theory 108
mental-spiritual dimension 85
Microsoft 23, 42
Minimum viable innovation process (MVIP) 173,
    174, 175, 179
Minimum Viable Product (MVP) 39
Moore, Geoffry 41–42, 64
multilevel value
– BANI model 114

– behavior and decision-making 113
– Challenger Commission 120
– creation 116–117
– decision-making process 118
– economic self-interest 113
– ethical and moral decision-making 114
– forward-thinking organizations 115–116
– 4-level value model (See 4-level value model)
– global crises 113
– "humane" intelligence 114
– innovation management 114–115
– organizational culture 118
– U.S. government 118
– value-driven innovation development 115
– values 113–114
– Volatile, Uncertain, Complex, Ambiguous
    (VUCA) 113, 114

navigation tool 146–148
Netflix 102
networking principles 49–52
neural networks 111, 138–139
Newness Matrix 24
nightmare competitor challenges 132
non-verbal communication 206–208
Nutzinger, Hans G. 155

Objectives and Key Results (OKRs) 60, 87
open innovation model
– cutting-edge tools 28–29
– data and platforms 27
– democratization 27
– digital revolution 26–27
– implementation 28
– industry innovation culture 27
– intrapreneurship programs 30
– machine learning 29
– network period 52–53
– operating model 31
– partnership projects 30
– platform-based businesses 30
– social process 27
– theater 31–32
Open Space Technology
– business fields 32
– company-wide innovation 34
– organizing conferences 33

– participants 34
– people, diverse group of 33
– product group 34
– rules 34–37
organizational frameworks 49
organizational interventions 13
Organizations in Movement 125
Osterwalder, Alexander 60, 88, 187

A Passion for Cooperation (Axelrod) 203
performance zone 41
platform-based businesses 30
point of no return (PONR) 16, 60
poly-crisis 57, 109
power teams
– agility and adaptability 68
– collective aspiration 69
– effective teams 67
– experiencing and learning journeys 70
– functional expertise 67
– goals and purpose 67
– Homo sapiens 69
– i-Lab team 69
– integrative innovation network 67–68
– leadership roles 70
– learning opportunities 68–69
– new leadership styles 69
– phases 67
– pioneering experience 66
– places of togetherness 70
– product development 66
– psychological and motivational measures 66
– self-directed 68
– types 67, 68
problem-solving abilities 143
product zone 41
promoters
– artificial intelligence 5–6
– barriers to "ability" 6
– gap-oriented behavior 8
– innovation research 7
– lack of "willingness" 6
– model 5
– power 6, 8
– process 7
– psychological safety 5
– relationship 7

– restrictors/opponents 7
– specialist 7
psychological safety 79, 210

quantum teleportation 160

Reciprocity, Interests, Concerns, Expectations (R-ICE) method 128, 129, 187
regional and stakeholder consultations 109
relationship-oriented approach 126
resilience 79
resource management 190–191
Responsible, Accessible, Supporting, Creating, and Informed (RASCI) 18
Ries, Eric 71
risk taking 153
Ritala, Paavo 53
Rogers, Everett M., Dr. 13
Rosegger, Peter 155

Schifferstein, Rick 124
The Sciences of the Artificial (Simon) 38
Secret Native American Pathways (Mails) 106
Seeholzer, Veronika 57
self-awareness 88, 148
self-control 148
self-discovery journey 192
self-empowerment 123
self-fulfilling prophecy 190
self-organization 45, 91
self-regulated organization 125
Senge, Peter 68
Simon, Herbert 38
Smith, Douglas A. 66
Smulders, F. E. H. M. 124
social diffusion 14
social environments 15
social exchange 205–206
Social Exchange in Creativity 202
social interaction models 85, 111, 122
social leadership models 146–147
social psychology 126–127
social skills 48
social well-being 210
Society for American Archeology 103
sociocultural ecosystems
– artificial intelligence 82

– climate and political crises 81
– fixed and growth mindsets 83
– framework conditions 81
– human qualities 84
– innovation 81
– integrative innovation process 84
– "non-technocratic" factors 81
– Open Space methods 82
– power of mindset 83
– principles 84
– stability and psychological safety 82
– thoughts and feelings 83
sociocultural patterns 13
spaceship Earth 189
spiritual dimension
– adventures and transformative challenges 85
– artificial intelligence 88
– embodied knowledge 88
– ethics and economics 89
– generative AI 88
– innovation network 89–90
– integrative and systemic-oriented leadership 87
– mental-spiritual dimension 85
– recognition 87–88
– religion and secularity 85–87
– self-awareness 88
– social interaction 85
– storytelling 85
spiritual practices 192
Stadler, Christian 132
Stage-Gate process 199
– balancing creativity and mass production 18–19
– domestication of creativity 16–18
– firms 20
– Gasthaus Schwan 11
– global distribution 10, 11
– from grown to formable structure 15–16
– Hundredth Monkey Phenomenon 11–14
– ideal innovation process 19
– industrial-process driven 20
– innovation management 10
– physical products 20
– product development performance 10–11
– self-generation 20
– technology diffusion 11–14
– variation 19

Stage-Gate® Tool 10
Star Trek 63
The Startup Way (Ries) 71
storytelling 85
strong reasoning/evidence 129
sustainability and progress 110–112
sustainability challenges 57
Sustainable Development Goals (SDGs) 110, 123, 209
sustainable innovation 210
Swarovski Spirit 50
system-aware approach 126
systemic inertia 129
systemic thinking
– balancing chaos and order 134–136
– bias 128–131
– global thinking 128–131
– human element 132–134
– living systems 126
– *Organizations in Movement* 125
– principle 126
– reciprocity 126–128
– resistance 126
– role models 132–134
– survival instinct 128–131
– systems theory 126
– top-down planning 131–132
systems factor 205
systems theory 126
systems-thinking mindset 209

technology-driven projects 108
telecommunications 137
Total Quality Management (TQM) 16
transformation zone 41
transformative mentor 191
tribal power source 106–107
tribal wisdom 93
– biological processes 96
– cultural differences 96
– innovation 96
– leadership program 96
– learning organizations 97–98

UN Environment Program 109
UN General Assembly Resolution 141

UN Human Charter 115
United Nations Framework Convention for Climate Change (UNFCCC) 147
United Nations Sustainable Development Goals (UNSDGs) 167
UN's Office of Information and Communications Technology (OICT) 141

value-driven innovation development 115
value system 166
van der Voort, M 124

virtual gatekeepers 177
Volatile, Uncertain, Complex, Ambiguous (VUCA) 113, 114, 151–152
von den Eichen, Stephan Friedrich 132

Want, Find, Get, Manage (WFGM) model 28
Wengrow, David 111
Wilhelmer, Doris 49, 50

Zimmerman, Jeff 50
Zone to Win (Moore) 41–42, 64

www.ingramcontent.com/pod-product-compliance
Lightning Source LLC
Chambersburg PA
CBHW061810210326

41599CB00034B/6947